Banditry in West Java 1869–1942

Financial support for this study was provided by the Netherlands Organisation for Scientific Research (NWO).

Banditry in West Java 1869–1942

Margreet van Till

Translated by David McKay & Beverley Jackson

NUS PRESS
SINGAPORE

First published in Dutch by Aksant Publishers in Amsterdam.

NUS Press
National University of Singapore
AS3-01-02, 3 Arts Link
Singapore 117569

Fax: (65) 6774-0652
E-mail: nusbooks@nus.edu.sg
Website: http://www.nus.edu.sg/nuspress

ISBN 978-9971-69-502-6 (Paper)

National Library Board, Singapore Cataloguing-in-Publication Data

Till, Margreet van.
Banditry in West Java, 1869–1942 / Margreet van Till; translated by David McKay & Beverley Jackson. – Singapore: NUS Press, c2011.
p. cm.
Includes bibliographical references and index.
ISBN-13: 978-9971-69-502-6 (pbk.)

1. Brigands and robbers – Indonesia – Jakarta – History. 2. Outlaws – Indonesia – Jakarta – History. 3. Brigands and robbers in literature. 4. Brigands and robbers – In motion pictures. 5. Jakarta (Indonesia) – History. I. McKay, David, 1973– II. Jackson, Beverley. III. Title.

HV6453
364.10660959822 – dc22 OCN649903242

Typeset by: International Typesetters Pte Ltd
Printed by: Vinlin Press Sdn. Bhd.

Contents

List of illustrations and maps ix

Introduction **1**

Batavia and the Ommelanden, 1869–1942 2

Inclusion in the world-system 4

The discourse of modernization and banditry 8

Robbers and *jagos* 10

THE SETTING

1 **Batavia and the Ommelanden** **19**

A celebration and an insurrection 19

Batavia 22

The Ommelanden 24

Policies towards banditry in the preceding period 27

The economy of the Ommelanden 30

The press, 1870–1915 36

THE BANDITS

2 **The Economics of Banditry** **47**

Robbery and economic cycles 47

Crime pays 51

Occupational hazards: Arrests and convictions 55

Occupational hazards: Prison 59

3 **The Organizational Structure of Criminal Gangs** **63**

Indigenous entrepreneurs, the mafia, and robbery as a business 63

The organization of a robbery 66

Robbery and other forms of crime 72

Robbers and the public authorities 72

Jagos and robbers 75

4 **Firearms** **79**
The possession of firearms 79
The provenance of firearms 81
Firearms and rebellions 83
Firearms and bandits 85
The effectiveness of firearms 88

5 ***Jagos, jimats,* and *dukuns*** **92**
Jagoism 92
Mysticism 95
Pencak silat: Indigenous martial art 98
Subversion, inversion, and tactics 100

THE CITY-DWELLERS

6 **Progress and Degeneration** **107**
Progress versus degeneration 107
Sex in the Ommelanden 113
Case study: Si Kesen 116

7 **From Bandit Novels to Detective Stories** **120**
The modern age 120
Impenetrable wilderness 123
Identity 126
Commissioner Hinne: An Indo detective 129
The Indo detective's greatest triumph 133

8 **The Bandit Si Pitung and Popular History** **136**
The colonial sources 137
Si Pitung for Dutch readers 141
Oral tradition 142
Pramoedya Ananta Toer 145
Pitung in popular history … 147
… and in Hobsbawm 148

THE STATE

9 The Fight Against Crime **155**
Rampok in the press: Gentis and Gantang 156
Bandits and government revisited: The *demang* of Bekasi 160
Focus on private estates 164
The police until 1908 167
The slow pace of reform 171
Rampok in the Great Depression 177
1937 178
From *rampok* to *bersiap* 181
Robbers and people's militias 183

Concluding Remarks **186**
The variegated world of Indonesian crime 186
Bandits and the authorities 188
Banditry and the economy 190

Appendices **192**
Appendix I: The organization of security 192
Appendix II: Robberies between 1890 and 1920 193
Appendix III: The calculation and planning of robberies 194
Appendix IV: Robberies in four peak years 196

Notes 212
Abbreviations 242
Glossary 244
Bibliography 251
Index of personal names 276
Index of place names 280

List of illustrations and maps

The western residencies on Java, based on the political and administrative organization in 1900.	3
Batavia and environs. Koninklijke Vereeniging Java Motor Club (Royal Java Motor Club Association), List of names (alphabetical by residency) of the enterprises, rental properties and private estates mentioned on the map of Java and Madoera, 1926.	39
Djaisin, Rais, and Ateh. They were the robbers of the jeweller Steuerwald.	54
The notorious robber-chief Lias, the other gang members, a policeman and his wife who caught the robbers.	56
Pa-I, a gang-member who was active around Cibarusa in 1936–7.	58
Tongtong, a wood-block on which warning signals could be made.	87
Wayang golek puppet representing Si Pitung as a typical 'jago'.	94
Mantri police class, probably 1928.	127
A.W.V. Hinne (1852–1915), who served as a police officer in Batavia from 1887 until 1911.	130
Wayang golek puppet representing 'Schout' Hinne.	132
Investigators in training, probably 1928.	135
The house of Hadji Sapiudin, currently the Pitung Museum in Marunda.	138

A scene from one of the Si Pitung movies from the beginning of the seventies. 149

The country estate of Tjimanggis (Cimanggis), as it looked during the 1990s. 167

Guardhouse at the entrance of a kampong. 170

Street scene, Tjikini. 172

Police station, Batavia, probably 1928. 174

Police barracks, Meester Cornelis, probably 1928. 175

Rural police ready to go on patrol, probably 1928. 176

Gang member, just arrested, who had been participating in the wave of crime in 1937 in Cibarusa. 179

Gang members. 179

Mohammed Hassan, who participated in many arrests of bandits. 182

Pa-I. The text with this photo read: The magic circle of crime has been broken. With his pulses in chains Paih is being photographed, with Satian joining enthusiastically. 184

Radjamoekah 1 194

Radjamoekah 2 196

Introduction

> For instance, last night at 9 p.m. another *rampok* was committed within the city limits. The victim was a Chinese shopkeeper in the Chinese camp near the bridge at Kampong Melajoe. Six *rampokkers* forced their way into his house and stole 160 guilders' worth of jewellery and 140 guilders' worth of other goods. As they retreated with their loot, they fired their revolvers to keep pursuers at a distance.[1]

This article comes from the *Bataviaasch Nieuwsblad*, one of the most influential newspapers in Batavia, the capital of the Dutch East Indies. The leafy lanes of the city — which was also known as the *Koningin van het Oosten* (Queen of the East) — were shady and inviting by day but looked very different by night. The threat of the dark world that surrounded the European colonists is expressed in the novels *The Hidden Force* by Louis Couperus and *Country of Origin* by Edgar du Perron. The bands of robbers active around Batavia in the early twentieth century provided a solid basis for such fears.

These robbers — or bandits; in this book, the two terms are used interchangeably — soon inspired all sorts of tales, some of which grew into legends. And they aroused not only fear, but also outrage. How could such things take place so close to the centre of colonial authority? Given the number of robberies, the fear and outrage appear to have been justified. At the height of this wave of banditry, or *rampok*[2] — defined for the purposes of this book as theft involving violence or the threat of violence, perpetrated by more than one person[3] — there were two or three incidents a week. Who were the bandits, and why did they keep cropping up in Batavia's rural surroundings, the Ommelanden? The robbers captured the imagination of their contemporaries and won themselves a place in popular history. Since the publication of Eric Hobsbawm's *Bandits* in 1969, scholars have also taken an interest in the relationship between banditry and state formation.

The people of Batavia regarded the Ommelanden as a backward area, the antithesis of civilization. Nevertheless, starting around 1900, the Ommelanden became a focal point of numerous forms of modern development, such as agricultural production for the world market, infrastructural expansion, and the transition from feudalism to a modern property system. The question is whether the problem of banditry promoted the expansion of state authority into areas that had previously been seen as frontier, areas where the state's growing influence led to friction.

Batavia and the Ommelanden, 1869–1942

Batavia and the Ommelanden underwent modernization earlier than the remainder of the Malay Archipelago.[4] The colonial capital was a melting pot in which all groups had economic opportunities and access to the burgeoning mass media. A highly diverse urban middle class took shape, which included Europeans, Chinese, indigenous people, and Eurasians (people of mixed European and Asian descent, also known as Indos).

The emerging local press provided a forum in which Batavians could vent their frustrations about unsafe conditions in the Ommelanden around their city. This had an impact on the development of the state apparatus, an impact that was felt not just in the centre of the colony, but throughout the archipelago. Yet even though other parts of the colony (such as the Vorstenlanden of Central Java) were also plagued by bandits, Batavia was the only place where a variety of news outlets fuelled lively debate about the banditry issue. It was the place where the image of the bandit was formed and, in a sense, set in opposition to the image of modernity. The influence of this imagery is still visible in our present-day thinking about crime in the Dutch East Indies. This study thus addresses the relationship between popular images and historical reality.

The Ommelanden around Batavia were unusual in several respects. For one, the area was subject to a special legal regime, one special feature of which was that Europeans were permitted to own large tracts of land.

Illus. 1 The western residencies on Java, based on the political and administrative organization in 1900. (Collection of the Royal Netherlands Geographical Society)

In contrast with the rest of Java, the Ommelanden thus became home to many private estates. Accordingly, the relationship between the European elite and the indigenous inhabitants there was unlike that in other parts of Java. The special situation in the Ommelanden, which gave the area a 'colonial' character, is discussed at length in Chapter 1.

The geographical scope of this study is the Residence of Batavia around 1900, which included such places as Buitenzorg, Tangerang, and Bekasi. The southern part of this area was later designated as a separate residence, called Buitenzorg.

The study focuses on a period beginning in 1870, when major technological advances and the abolition of the forced cultivation system (*Cultuurstelsel*) led to rapid modernization in the Dutch East Indies, particularly in and around the capital of Batavia. From this centre outward, the colonial state reinvented itself, setting off social changes in the process. From 1870 onward, Batavia was the epicentre from which waves of modernization spread to other parts of the archipelago.

My exact start date is 1869, the year the Suez Canal opened and the Dutch East Indies could suddenly be reached from Europe more quickly and easily. This ultimately altered the size and makeup of the colony's population, as well as its economy and social structure. The year 1869 was also the 250th anniversary of the founding of Batavia. I open the book with the festivities marking this anniversary, which were marred by a local uprising. A surviving account describes in detail how this uprising was experienced by the European population, with their fear of violent acts by indigenous people.[5] The celebration and the uprising introduce a number of themes that arise repeatedly in the course of the book.

The end of the period investigated is 1942, when the process of modernization was disrupted by the Japanese invasion (in the context of the Second World War). The decade that followed 1942 was a turbulent time for the region and its society, marked by the end of colonialism and the emergence of a new nation.

Inclusion in the world-system

The banditry in the Ommelanden seems at first glance to fit the theory advanced by Thomas W. Gallant in his 1997 essay 'Brigandage, Piracy, Capitalism, and State-Formation: Transnational Crime from a Historical World-System Perspective'.[6] Gallant describes banditry as part of the process of state formation during the transition from a traditional to a capitalist economy. In this respect, he differs from Eric Hobsbawm, who sees bandits primarily as representatives of the traditional social order. Gallant's article is couched in rather general terms — the claim that banditry is associated with state formation is open to any number of interpretations — but it is interesting to see what role indigenous banditry played in the frontier region known as the Ommelanden.

Gallant and others claim — drawing on the theory of the modern world-system proposed by Immanuel Wallerstein in the 1970s — that there is a clear connection between the activity of banditry and the economic structure of the area in question.[7] One way in which Gallant uses Wallerstein's model is to shed light on the phenomenon of the bandit as a 'military entrepreneur'.

According to Wallerstein, the expansion of the European economy after the Middle Ages brought about a cohesive, global economic system for the first time in history. But different continents occupied different positions in that system. Roughly speaking, the theory distinguishes between three different positions. First, there were the countries at the core of the system; in other words, Western Europe. This region was the centre of economic development and made other parts of the world dependent on it. The rest of the world, surrounding this core, could be divided into two layers. The outermost layer was the periphery, and in the middle was the semi-periphery, which was like the periphery in some ways and the core in others.[8] Every non-European region influenced by developments in modern Europe had a place in either the periphery or the semi-periphery. The position of a region in this system was not permanently fixed, but could change over time under the influence of local economic developments and tendencies in relation to Europe.

Peripheral regions are typically conceived as being dominated by a class of rich landowners, with a very large group of poor farmers who are tied to the land that they work. Because the domestic market is small and foreign imports are limited, it is impossible to build up domestic industries. The cities therefore remain small and less powerful than the rural landowners. The power of local traders also remains limited, because international trade is controlled by foreign interests. In the semi-periphery, regions have similar characteristics, but the beginnings of industrial development are visible, there is a group of local traders, and the cities are growing in importance relative to the rural landowners.[9]

In the late nineteenth century, the Ommelanden belonged to the semi-periphery. Throughout the seventeenth, eighteenth, and early nineteenth centuries, the region had been cut off from the coastal city of Batavia by legislation (travel documents that were mandatory for anyone leaving the city) and poor infrastructure. After 1850, however, more and more estates in the Ommelanden began trying to produce crops for the world market. The roads between Batavia and the Sundanese hinterland ran through the Ommelanden, turning them into a frontier area.

In practice, it appears that banditry can take place in both the periphery and the semi-periphery. Drawing on writings about banditry from all over the world, Gallant provides examples that support his theory. First, there are categories of bandits that sometimes provide their services to large agricultural companies or rural estates. This includes the dacoits in India,[10] and the phenomenon has also existed in Latin America.[11] This form of banditry arose in places and periods with a weak central state. The only way for landowners to protect their property was by employing private security services, which recruited their staff from the pool of men who otherwise relied on banditry to support themselves.

The rise of large estates that acted as states within the state, as well as the rise in banditry, prompted the government to expand into areas where central state authority had previously been weak. And because banditry was a threat to public safety, it led to the penetration of law enforcers into areas that until then had been beyond the reach of colonial development. Another illustration of how the rise of banditry led to state expansion is given by the Greek historian John S. Koliopolous, in his account of bandits' struggle for a new, liberated Greek state in the nineteenth century.[12]

In his political and economic analysis of Sicilian society, Anton Blok modifies Hobsbawm's thesis in a significant way. Hobsbawm saw bandits primarily as fighters for the impoverished masses, striking out at the elite and the state. Blok's doctoral thesis *The Mafia of a Sicilian Village (1860–1960): An Anthropological Study of Political Middlemen* (1972) sketches the connection between the Mafia and the process of state formation in Sicily. As an agent of violence, the Mafia played an important social role, generally by protecting landowners, since central government could not guarantee public order and security in Sicily. His conclusion, based in part on research in Sicily and elsewhere in southern Italy, was that Hobsbawm's description of the social bandit was a poor fit for quite a few categories of robbers, such as urban robbers and *mafiosi*.

The generalization that threats public safety could lead state law enforcement officers to penetrate into areas that were previously beyond the reach of state authority also applied in European colonies. Nathan Brown describes measures for preventing and fighting banditry in late nineteenth-century Egypt during the British protectorate.[13] There had always been robberies, but in the 1890s, the Egyptian faction in the colonial administration emphasized this type of crime in order to bring about the establishment of a local Egyptian government apparatus. Their hope was that this apparatus could serve to counterbalance British authority. Brown's article deals with the relationship between banditry and the growth of government, a theme that is central to my own research, because the key questions for me are to what extent banditry in and around Batavia contributed to the expansion of modern state authority into what had been frontier areas until then, and to what extent this expansion was successful.

That brings us to an element that is missing from Gallant's survey of the scholarly literature. Although he brings up the propaganda value of government measures to combat banditry, he barely mentions the bandit's role as a 'primitive' response to the development of a modern outlook among city-dwellers. These city-dwellers, in turn, were crucial agents of further state development. Because urbanites saw bandits as their opposites, their literary works, newspaper serials, and films promulgated an image of bandits that still threatens to overshadow the historical bandit.

A world-systems perspective on banditry also raises the question of its economic significance. This issue has not yet been explored in the scholarly literature. It is clear that in agrarian societies, near urban centres and the above-mentioned rural estates, bandits brought recently stolen money into circulation. They also frequently attacked vehicles transporting export products from the rural estates to the coast.[14] In this inquiry, I will therefore also examine the economic aspects of indigenous banditry. How did bandits fit into local economic developments? How much revenue did their activities bring in? How, and how much, did they contribute to the local economy?

Alongside these explanations of banditry through the lens of a single theory based on large historical forces, this study will also devote attention to the specific circumstances in which banditry took place. This is because the banditry in question was a highly distinctive form of violence with a range of social effects, not all of which can be inferred from any one general theory of violence. For instance, the impact of violence (the 'scars') has a profound influence on how 'the Other' is construed within a society, and on the attitude taken toward 'outsiders' or 'enemies'.[15] While making use of general theories, it is essential to remain aware of the specific circumstances in Batavia and the Ommelanden between 1869 and 1942.

The discourse of modernization and banditry

> When people from other regions read that a robbery or *ketjoe* has been committed somewhere,[16] or that a European of some note has been the victim of a theft, the report is usually a simple statement of fact, but in Batavia it is accompanied by wide-ranging commentary, which either has the malicious aim of putting the European administration in a bad light, or is motivated by a cowardly heart that makes every native look like a Gantang [the name of a notorious bandit in the news in 1903, MvT].[17]

These are the words of Charles René Bakhuizen van den Brink, the Resident of Batavia, in a letter written in 1904 to the director of the colony's internal administration.[18]

Nevertheless, the people of Batavia a century ago had good reason to complain about the threats to public safety in their city. In some years, there were as many as 190 robberies. There was also — the resident was right about this — a degree of paranoia about both robbers and public servants. This paranoia led people to overestimate the political and social significance of bandits in the society of the Dutch East Indies. Present-day debate is still muddied by early twentieth-century assumptions about bandits, combined with a rather sloppy definition (or no definition at all) of the varieties of illegal activity in the former colony.

'The City-Dwellers' (Chapters 6, 7, and 8) is the section of this book that most explicitly analyzes the influential discourse which politicized and romanticized banditry. In the colony of the Dutch East Indies, after the abolition of the forced cultivation system in 1870, a period of accelerated modernization began, gathering pace after 1890. The economy was liberalized, new technologies strengthened both internal connections and ties to the rest of the world, the European population expanded swiftly, and the colonial administration's view of its own responsibilities was redefined in its 'Ethical Policy' (*Ethische Politiek*). In short, the state apparatus in the Dutch East Indies was in development and 'modernizing' at a rapid pace. Waves of territorial expansion and reform followed in ever quicker succession, continuing until 1942, when the Japanese invasion brought an end, in practical terms, to the colonial period.

The beginnings of these changes were most visible at the centre of the colony, in the capital city of Batavia, where Dutch modernity was on display in its full glory, with the support of a large group of Dutch Batavians. This was a direct consequence of Western modernization, one of the achievements of which was better global transport connections. In 1869 this led to the opening of the Suez Canal, which reduced the distance of the shipping route between the Netherlands and the Malay Archipelago by more than half. Ships also became faster and more comfortable, so that a trip from the Netherlands to the East became a less daunting prospect. In particular, the number of Dutch women travelling to the colony increased tremendously. Batavia became a city with a strong European bourgeoisie, and this social and ethnic class quickly gained in importance.

A European and a Malay press also developed, both influenced by notions of modernization. One result was that, in the late nineteenth century, there was a growing tendency to see the Ommelanden around Batavia as a violent, uncivilized region. The Ommelanden had once figured in newspaper articles and literature as a 'feudal idyll', and over the past centuries endemic violence had not prevented wealthy members of the Batavian bourgeoisie from building and living in country houses there. But its image had become tarnished, and it was now seen as a place of *burchtheren*, embattled feudal lords in their strongholds, surrounded by bandits, violence, and mud. In the popular myths of the time, the city and the Ommelanden were more and more likely to be opposed to one another. The discourse within which the bandits operated was constructed in part by the fears of the city-dwellers, which were both reported and fuelled by the press. It is therefore not enough to describe the landscape in which the crimes took place in dry, factual terms, through figures and tables; a description of the rhetoric of insecurity is also essential.

When we look at the discourse underlying press coverage of *rampokkers* in the Dutch East Indies, it becomes apparent that the state was taken to be responsible for the safety of all its subjects, whether European or indigenous. Journalists asked why the police in the Dutch East Indies were so much less effective than those in other European colonies. The poor performance of the Batavian police was viewed as one of the factors giving *rampokkers* such a free hand. To solve the problem of banditry, two measures were proposed. The first was to modernize the police force, and the second was to open up the Ommelanden to modernization by buying up the estates and civilizing the local people. It made no difference whether an author was progressive or conservative; almost everyone took part in a discourse in which violent and sexually degenerate bandits were set against the ramshackle backdrop of the Ommelanden. This book will show to what extent that discourse has retained its hold on us and been incorporated uncritically into modern discussions of banditry. Under these circumstances, it is not easy to determine what role bandits played in the economy and social structures of the Ommelanden, since the absence of first-person accounts makes us almost entirely dependent on reports in the colonial press.[19]

Although Dutch, Chinese, and indigenous Batavians saw the countryside around the city as backward and medieval, in the mirror of history we can see this region as a semi-peripheral area around a centre where diverse processes of modernization and state formation were taking place. In this sense, the Ommelanden were under pressure and can be regarded as a frontier region.

This explains the intensity of public interest in banditry, which was not in itself a new phenomenon. Bandits had plagued the Ommelanden for centuries, but press coverage and improved infrastructure brought them to the attention of the Batavian public for the first time. It was easy to draw connections between banditry and all sorts of problems confronting the colonial authorities and the city's Chinese, European, and indigenous people. Banditry was seen as a consequence of the estate system of land ownership in the Ommelanden, which impoverished the indigenous population.

Robbers and *jagos*

Rampok is a Malay word adopted into Dutch, which refers to violent robbery committed by groups. Incidents of *rampok* took place throughout the Dutch East Indies, usually under cover of night. Throughout the colonial period, this crime was endemic on the island of Java. During the early colonial and pre-colonial periods, bands of *rampokkers* tended to have more than ten members. It was often difficult to distinguish 'ordinary' robbery from looting in the context of armed conflict, or from insurrection. In both pre-colonial and colonial times, the state had little authority at local level,[20] and there were plenty of opportunities for bands of men to engage in looting. In nineteenth-century Batavia, this situation changed: robberies tended to be committed by smaller groups. This is the fundamental difference between *rampok* in the Ommelanden and *ketjoe* in the Vorstenlanden, which was perpetrated by much larger gangs.

Between 1870 and 1942, there were some years with an unusually high number of robberies. For instance, in the capital city of Batavia, which was the colony's largest urban agglomeration by far, there were more than 160 incidents of *rampok* annually in the years around 1920 — in other words, one robbery every two or three days. This type of crime generated considerable fear among the public.[21]

The original meaning of the work *rampok* had been a sport in which a number of men with lances surrounded a tiger, which tried to escape. It always ended with the tiger leaping onto the lances. In other words, the literal meaning of *rampok* is an attack by many people armed with lances. At the Javanese courts, this sport was a ritual part of certain festivities.[22]

In the jargon of the Dutch colonial administration, there are several near-synonyms for *rampok*, such as *kampak* and *ketjoe*. Like the incidents of *rampok* around Batavia, the *ketjoe* robberies in the Vorstenlanden of Surakarta and Yogyakarta were regarded as a serious threat to public safety. *Ketjoe* was a topic of great interest among specialists in Javanese culture who produced numerous analyses that found their way into the professional literature for colonial officials.[23] Their descriptions of *ketjoe* reveal that it was seen as a vestige of the wars between villages in the precolonial Javanese kingdoms. This hypothesis was thought to explain the overt and large-scale character of the robberies, which did strongly resemble wartime looting.

That brings us to the special character of robbery as a variety of crime. In sociological terms, robbery has certain unusual features. Robbers are considered to be people who band together in an organized fashion and position themselves outside society, or are so positioned by others. They provide for themselves by threatening working people with violence. The significant features of robbery are not only its violent nature — which challenges the state's monopoly on the use of force — but also the number of participants. The earliest European legislation refers to a group of six men or fewer as thieves, a group of 7 to 35 as a gang, and a group of 36 or more as an army. The Batavian public and the colonial authorities had a similar outlook, living in fear that gangs of robbers would grow into armies which would storm the city of Batavia.

In the didactic novels of Peter Hansen, a Dutch businessman living in Java around 1900 who used the pen name Boeka, the scenes of rural Javanese life include a number of robberies. Boeka argued that the high incidence of this type of crime — which often took the form of cattle theft — was due to shortcomings of the colonial administration, particularly its lack of expertise about the Javanese world, along with the difficulty of determining which indigenous chiefs could be trusted. In this respect, his views differed from those of Eduard Douwes Dekker, who wrote under the name of Multatuli and regarded all indigenous officials as fundamentally 'bad' or at any rate unreliable. In one of Boeka's books a *bupati* (the indigenous head of a regency) says that the indigenous population is best protected against crime in the parts of Java where indigenous leaders are still in full control. Strikingly, he adds that law enforcement is also relatively effective in frontier areas. Such areas were under the direct control of the colony's military authorities. The *bupati* explains that the rest of the population, governed by means of indirect rule, suffers a host of injustices.[24] In this passage, Boeka is making a significant reference to a threat to public safety highlighted by many later studies of crime in the Malay Archipelago: the intermediaries between the indigenous population and the European colonists on whom the colonial authorities relied.

These intermediaries are also one of the main topics of Henk Schulte Nordholt's article 'De jago in de schaduw' ('The *jago* in the shadow'), published in 1983, which describes Java's precolonial states as 'contest states', a term borrowed from Michael Adas.[25] The implication is that states were in constant competition for trade, labour, and arable land. When central rulers accumulated too much power, lower-level elites rose up in opposition. Villages also competed for essential resources such as water and agricultural land, and in the heat of battle they did not shrink from destroying each other's crops and other possessions. This occurred mainly when central authority was weak or entirely absent. In such situations of widespread insecurity, patron-client relationships are all the more important. Farmers, who are vulnerable by definition because they cannot easily move elsewhere, looked to powerful individuals, or strongmen, in their communities to provide security. The more power these strongmen could show that they had, the more support they won among local farmers.

Henk Schulte Nordholt calls these strongmen *jagos*, borrowing the term from colonial commentators such as Boeka and C.A.A. Amand, a private tobacco grower who brought the phenomenon to the attention of the colonial authorities in 1877.[26] *Jago* literally means fighting cock. Schulte Nordholt goes on to claim that during the period of Dutch colonial rule in the Malay Archipelago, the central authorities (like their precolonial predecessors) were incapable of extending their influence all the way down to the local level. For instance, they lacked the money and manpower to maintain public order so that the forced cultivation system

(1830–70) could function properly. At no point in the nineteenth century was there a well-organized police force that could operate effectively at village level. According to the same colonial sources, any village chief who sought to maintain public order and meet his economic obligations to the administration was well advised to have a *jago* on his territory, who would act as a kind of local police officer. One disadvantage of this tactic was that in order to make a comfortable living *jagos* needed to keep robbing other villages. They worked with other *jagos* to commit these robberies, and sometimes even made deals with them. According to sceptical colonial observers, this made the Javanese countryside unsafe.

To this day, little is known about the pool of candidates for the position of *jago*. Some authors have discussed their training programme, however.[27] A *jago* underwent a lengthy period of instruction under a guru who taught him martial arts and the secrets of the profession. He then completed his training with a period of asceticism, and by travelling and meeting other members of the *jago* order.

It is reasonable to ask at this point what *ketjoe* and Javanese *jagos* have to do with Batavian *rampok*. The issue is clouded by the meaning of the term *jago*, a meaning which is rather broad and has changed over time. The above description relates to the *jago* as an agent of violence in the time of the forced cultivation system and during the period that followed. But in the course of the twentieth century, the meaning of the term *jago* grew ever broader, and it has come to refer mainly to masculinity or machismo, sometimes but not always with violent connations.

To avoid confusion about the meaning of the term *jago*, I have chosen to use the term in two well-defined ways. First, I use it for the *jago* as described by Schulte Nordholt: an agent of violence in rural areas of nineteenth-century Java. In the remainder of this study, I use the term 'rural *jago*' in this sense. Second, I use the term *jago* to refer to a Javanese macho. The advantages and disadvantages of this approach are discussed in Chapter 5.

In and around Batavia, there were other words for people who had fallen into a life of crime, such as *preman* (from the Dutch *vrijman*, 'free man', meaning one who was not a slave), *jagoan* (quasi-*jago*), and *buaya* (crocodile). In the nineteenth and early twentieth centuries, the term *barisan preman* ('force of free men') was used to refer to Batavia's European citizen militias — the counterparts of the respectable groups of armed civilians who acted as city guards in the Netherlands, a model transplanted to the Dutch East Indies with varying success.[28] The word *preman* was also used for the security forces of the private rural estates around the capital. In the early twentieth century, the word *buaya* (crocodile) came into use as a synonym for 'robber'.[29] It was normally applied to pubescent Indo boys. Both terms, *preman* and *buaya*, therefore suggest a Eurasian, mixed-race identity.

To move closer to a typology of criminals as seen by their contemporaries, the nineteenth- and twentieth-century inhabitants of Batavia, we might consider a statement made in 1903 by an inhabitant of Meester Cornelis, then a satellite town on the southeastern edge of the city:

> The people of the *kampong* are first plundered by the *rampokkers*, of which there are plenty. Next, they are 'squeezed' by the village chief. After that, the landlord's *preman* extorts money from them. Then they still have to pay taxes to the tax authorities, they are tapped by religious leaders, and finally the *jago* stops by.[30]

Here, a distinction is clearly being made between the *rampokker*, the *preman*, and the *jago*. In contrast, Henk Schulte Nordholt's above-mentioned article 'De jago in de schaduw' emphasizes the dual role of *jago*-bandits.[31] While they may have had such a dual role in Central Java in the nineteenth century, when we turn to the Ommelanden a different way of thinking seems more promising. I believe that the *rampokkers* did not live independently of one another in different villages (as suggested by the idea of the rural *jago*) but together, in settlements at some distance from areas controlled by the authorities, just beyond the frontier.

In order to clearly state the central theme of this study, it is advisable, at least in theory, to draw a distinction between bandits and providers of protection, such as the above-mentioned rural *jagos*. In recent work, Diego Gambetta has drawn an illuminating distinction between the Mafia and robbers or bandits, arguing that they do entirely different things.[32] The Mafia trades in protection, while bandits make a living through the use of armed force. In their books, Florike Egmond and Anton Blok have described 'pure' bandits. The robbers that terrorized the Dutch countryside in the eighteenth and nineteenth centuries were not in any sense intermediaries between the state and the population, nor did they play a role in maintaining public order. On the contrary, their social origins and 'unclean occupations' (such as flayer and butcher) placed them outside society. As robbers, they emphasized the fact of their social exclusion in all sorts of ways.

The parallel existence of robbers and the Mafia is described in Gavin Maxwell's *God Protect Me From My Friends* (1956). The book recounts the life of the well-known Sicilian bandit Giuliano Salvatore, who had to not only watch out for the regular police force but also avoid treading on the Mafia's toes. On the face of it, rural *jagos* most closely resembled *mafiosi*, while Batavian *rampokkers* were robbers and bandits. There may have been some overlap between the two 'occupational groups', but there is no reason to suppose that there must have been. It appears as if the rural *jago* described by Henk Schulte Nordholt had a clear dual role or, if you prefer, an intermediary function. But *rampokkers*, or robbers, lived outside the system.

THE SETTING

CHAPTER 1

Batavia and the Ommelanden

A celebration and an insurrection

In the spring of 1869, Batavia was preparing to celebrate its 250th anniversary.[1] The 'Coen festival' — named after Jan Pieterszoon Coen, the city's founder — was to take place from 25 to 28 May and would include a flower parade, a pleasure garden, and fireworks, culminating in a grand masked ball in the Harmonie, the town's largest European club. During the festival, the foundation stone was to be laid for a statue of Coen. As so often on such occasions, there were spoilsports, who refused to participate in the celebrations. The monument to Coen drew particular ire. One protester objected to the proposed location of the monument near the government buildings in the new district of Weltevreden. He suggested that a more appropriate place for Coen's statue would be the square by the old town hall, 'where one can still hear the cries of pain uttered by poor Mr Cortenhoeff, who was executed there while the girl he loved, twelve-year-old Sara Specks, was flogged, both by direct order of Mr Coen'.[2]

Nevertheless, the majority of the population was looking forward to the event with great excitement. It provided them with an excellent reason to order all sorts of luxury goods from Europe. Not only the ladies but also the gentlemen of the town talked of almost nothing but what they would wear to the masked ball. The *modistes* (seamstress) were busy conferring with customers about their costumes, and had to import all sorts of materials from Europe.

That same year in Bekasi, a village twenty kilometres to the east of Batavia, a man named Nata was negotiating with the authorities about his alleged hereditary rights to the estate of Tambun. Many claims of this kind had been made in the past, not by old Javanese families, but by ordinary locals who claimed that the Dutch East India Company (VOC) had made them certain promises. In the seventeenth and eighteenth centuries, the VOC had given this land *in possessie* to locals who were converting the wilderness around Batavia into rice fields. This legal construct amounted to a long-term, inheritable lease, often with an official deed of transfer. But starting in the late seventeenth century, the VOC had given away the same land to Europeans, but this time *in donatie*, a subtle legal distinction which meant that in practice the Europeans became the owners. The locals were outraged.[3]

While the colonial authorities were investigating Nata's claim, he purportedly engaged in such egregious misconduct that he was imprisoned in Meester Cornelis, a village about halfway between Batavia and Bekasi. Soon afterwards, he was deemed to be insane and transferred to a hospital in Batavia. In the meantime, however, his friends had banded together. They headed for Meester Cornelis, where they believed Nata was still being held, with the goal of liberating him.

The authorities flew into a panic. In 1869, the infrastructure connecting Batavia to the surrounding Ommelanden was still very poor; for instance, there was no telephone line between Batavia and Bekasi. Law and order were enforced by a single European sheriff (*schout*), and a few local policemen armed with sabres. When news of the uprising reached the authorities, Assistant Resident E.R.J.C. de Kuijper decided to leave Meester Cornelis for Bekasi at once, along with a number of deputies. When they arrived in Bekasi, the sheriff told them it would be imprudent to engage the insurgents without military assistance. The Assistant Resident, however, felt it was his duty to deal with any problems on his own, and he believed his dignity and status would be enough to subdue the group. A *jaksa* (indigenous public prosecutor) offered to speak to the rebels and resolve the conflict by diplomatic means, but de Kuijper rejected this proposal.

With the *jaksa*, the sheriff, and a few local policemen in his train, he advanced on the group. They had only six firearms between them. There were a full 170 insurgents, and though not one of them had a gun, they were armed with machetes and pickaxes. The Assistant Resident ordered them to lay down their weapons, and when they refused, de Kuijper fired on the mob. The *jaksa* and the sheriff followed suit. Several insurgents were killed, and the others exploded with rage, trying to lay their hands on the Assistant Resident and his deputies, who had just enough time to flee into a dilapidated building at the side of the road. It was not long, however, before the infuriated mob had forced its way in. All the officials were killed, except for the *jaksa*, who managed to reach Batavia and describe what had happened.

A company of soldiers, armed with breechloaders, were immediately dispatched to Bekasi. As they made their way to the rebel village, they were followed by the Batavian authorities, headed by the resident and including a number of policemen. Halfway there, they ran into the cart that was taking the body of Assistant Resident de Kuijper to Batavia. Later that day, they reached Bekasi and surrounded the insurgents, who soon surrendered.

Though order had been restored, the European families who had fled Bekasi during the uprising began spreading the story in all its gory detail. Unsurprisingly, the townspeople were agitated by the news, and even more so when they saw the bodies of the Assistant Resident, sheriff, and policemen, who lay in state at the Assistant Resident's home in Meester Cornelis. In the weeks that followed, Batavia was abuzz with rumours about both real and imaginary insurrections in the city's outskirts. Eventually, the story circulated that as soon as the anniversary celebrations reached their climax, the local people would attack the Europeans and kill them all. A military officer named Perelaer later recalled that:

> when Batavia and its suburbs were swarming with cavalry piquets clutching their carbines; when the rumour spread that the ceremonial troops at the festivities were armed with live ammunition, and that the caissons of the field batteries responsible for the festive cannon fire were well-stocked with cartridges and prepared to sow death and destruction, then every heart was stricken with fear, and the festival was a pitiful debacle.[4]

The Chinese inhabitants of central Batavia, whose weapons had been confiscated by the authorities, had concerns of their own. Was this a reprise of 1741, when revolts in and around the town, combined with the disarmament of the Chinese community, had led to the slaughter of thousands of Chinese Batavians by their European neighbours?

Servants warned their employers not to go to the festival without a weapon, and likewise:

> to reassure the young ladies, many a gallant had to promise them not to attend the celebration unarmed; and various persons later swore that many a costume had concealed a revolver in its folds and that, if all the guests at the ball in the Harmonie had had occasion to draw their weapons, daggers would even have appeared in the hands of several young ladies.[5]

When the governor-general delivered his address at the Coen monument, he seemed distinctly ill at ease. Despite all this, the event went off according to plan, and the public drowned its fears in clamorous hero worship:

> Impassioned, overjoyed, they cry again: 'Come see! Come see!'
> 'A flag, a fleet in sight! 'Tis Coen! He's come to set us free!'
> . . . .
> Do not their words still fortify our hearts and fill our ears
> As if one day had passed and not two hundred fifty years?[6]

Batavia

The previous section is based on a factual, if somewhat sardonic, account by G.H. Pannekoek, one of the few such accounts to dwell at any length on the colonists' fear that the locals might turn violent. This fear does crop up repeatedly in literary sources, however, most famously in *The Hidden Force* by Louis Couperus, which explores the mysterious menace of the Javanese world. After writing this novel, Couperus published personal recollections in newspapers and magazines describing his own fear of the local population during his childhood in Java. 'De vloekzang' (The song of curses), by Sicco Roorda van Eysinga, describes what would happen to the Europeans if the islanders ever seized power.[7] Closer to Batavia, the fear of nightfall is a recurring theme in Edgar du Perron's *Country of Origin*, a description of his childhood in the Ommelanden.[8]

Europeans made up a small minority of the colony's population; in the eighteenth and early nineteenth centuries, Batavia had mainly been a Chinese town. The Chinese lived in the old or 'lower' town, which was where most trading took place. Ever since the foundation of Batavia, the Chinese had been welcome guests, helping to keep the city's economy afloat. In the period covered by this book, the Chinese made up about 15 per cent of the population of Batavia and its environs; this was about twice the percentage of Europeans (7 per cent).

During the nineteenth century, the administrative centre of the Dutch East Indies shifted southwards, to the new district of Weltevreden, and clusters of European homes sprang up here. Koningsplein, now Taman Merdeka, was in this part of town, and the well-known shopping areas of Noordwijk and Pasar Baru were close by. Another part of Batavia was the port area of Tanjung Priok, about ten kilometres further east. This area had a spacious, rural feel, and merged quite gradually into the private estates that surrounded the town. To the south, Buitenzorg (now Bogor) and Mount Salak, a volcano, formed the southern border of Batavia's outlying districts, the Ommelanden. To the west of Batavia was the Chinese town of Tangerang.

The Europeans and Eurasians in this district led monotonous lives. The men went to work in the lower town, and soon after returning home in the evening, they were off to the club. Events like the celebration of Batavia's 250th anniversary were welcome diversions.

The areas between Batavia's European residential districts were occupied by Indonesian settlements known as *kampongs*, which were home to a wide variety of ethnic groups that had settled there over the years. These included the Mardijkers — the descendants of Portuguese slaves from the period before Dutch rule — as well as the Balinese, Buginese, and Ambonese, whose ancestors had arrived in Batavia as slaves and soldiers in the seventeenth and eighteenth centuries. There were also many Indians, who had their roots in the VOC posts in South Asia, and large Arab and Chinese communities. The kampongs had originally been divided along ethnic lines, but soon became quite mixed.[9] Until well into the twentieth century, though these colonial kampongs were in the city, they were relatively isolated from the urban (and later modern) world around them. In Kebun Kacang, for instance — just a stone's throw from Koningsplein — the entire period prior to the Japanese occupation was known until recently as *zaman normal*,[10] a period of calm with little government interference in everyday life.

Urban culture included numerous varieties of Indonesian theatre and music, but for the purpose of this book, it is more important to note that in the nineteenth century many ethnic groups had fairly long memories. This is clearly illustrated by their differing interpretations of the events surrounding the city's 250th anniversary. Dutch nationals of mixed descent linked these events to the story of Kortenhoeff and the injustice done to their Eurasian ancestors. The Chinese were reminded of the events of 1741. And Nata, the Indonesian, could still recall several grounds on which he had a right to the estate. All this suggests that the fear of bandits can in part be traced back to the experiences of the Batavian population with bandit and rebel leaders in the Ommelanden over the previous two centuries.

The city of Batavia tended to look to the sea, which connected it to other cities in Java and the Outer Islands. It was not until the late nineteenth century that the interior became more accessible. That was when railways were introduced, for instance; the first one was built in the residency of Batavia in 1871. According to a report on the first trip in the *Java-bode* newspaper, it was as if the train were 'slicing through a virgin forest, where only the voice of nature could be heard'.[11] The growth of Batavia as a European city led to greater self-confidence and the ability to face the Ommelanden unflinchingly.

It was this combination of growing confidence and lingering fear that set the tone for the discourse on twentieth-century banditry.

The Ommelanden

In the sixteenth century, the Ommelanden (literally 'the Environs' or 'the Outlying Districts') were a fairly unattractive landscape for human habitation, consisting chiefly of low-lying swamps. To make matters worse, the area was depopulated in the early seventeenth century by the VOC's wars with the Javanese empire of Mataram, the kingdom of Pajajaran in the Preanger highlands,[12] and the sultanate of Banten (the rival city-state on the northern coast, known in the colonial period as Bantam). After 1620, the area around Batavia was resettled, this time by Javanese immigrants. The land there came under cultivation, an effort coordinated and promoted by Jan Pieterszoon Coen, who hoped that a coordinated programme of European settlement would create an agricultural belt around Batavia and protect the city from invasion. This type of cultivation extended as far as Buitenzorg, where Chinese settlers played a major role by building sugar mills. In the eighteenth century, the region was still plagued by bandits and violent thugs. The VOC attempted to make the region somewhat safer by sending a modest number of judicial and law enforcement officers (*heemraden* and *landdrosten*).

In the early nineteenth century, dire financial straits forced Governor-General H.W. Daendels to sell many more large parcels of land to private parties. By 1916, Batavia was surrounded by 800,000 *bouw* of farmland,[13] extending from Tangerang to Indramayu and from Menteng to Mount Salak. In metric units, it was approximately 100 kilometres from west to east and 50 kilometres from north to south. There were about 250 private estates, more than half of which were in Chinese hands. Most of the others were owned by Europeans, and a few dozen by Arabs. For a detailed list of the private agricultural estates and the crops grown there, the reader is referred to the map and list at the end of this chapter.

In 1903, the private estates in the residency of Batavia had a population of about 1,556,000.[14] These nineteenth-century estates can best be compared to large modern-day haciendas in Latin America. Some of them produced goods for the market — generally rice, but sometimes rubber, fruit, or vegetables as well. Local peasants had to relinquish up to one-fifth of their crops to the landowner, for whom they were also required to perform forced labour. These serfs were not generally natives of the Ommelanden, but came from central and eastern Java, the city of Batavia, and many other regions. Many had previously served in wandering bands of mercenaries, a fact that was later repeated *ad nauseam* to emphasize the 'criminal personality' of the Ommelanders. Likewise, Du Perron's *Country of Origin* does not describe the Javanese as docile in character. On the contrary, according to Du Perron, the Batavians respected a *jago* (whatever his ethnic origins might be). In his typically open-hearted style, Du Perron often refers to the people of Batavia as possessing a kind of forthright honesty.[15]

The landowners in the Ommelanden had let some properties for large sums of money to lessees, mostly Chinese, who wanted to set up *pasar*s (markets), *warung*s (shops), and, inevitably, opium dens there. New residential clusters formed around these markets and were named after them, such as Pasar Minggu, Pasar Tanah Abang, and Pasar Senen.[16] Even today, there are districts of Jakarta named after these *pasar*s. To reshape Indonesia's collective memory after independence, the new authorities changed many street names. Koningsplein became Lapangan Medan Merdeka, Van Heutz Boulevard became Jalan Teuku Umar (*jalan* means 'road') and Oranje Boulevard became Jalan Diponegoro.[17] However, quite a few suburbs and other districts of Jakarta kept the names of colonial estates and *pasars*, such as Menteng, Lebak Bulus, Kebayoran, and Kuningan. This is curious when we recall that these estates were particularly strongly associated with colonial violence.

Landowners were expected to provide for their own security. Appendix I shows the structures that existed to ensure public safety and security in colonial Batavia and the Ommelanden. The landowners appointed village heads and *mandoer*s (overseers) to maintain order. The system for maintaining order on their private estates differed in several important respects from that elsewhere in Java, where the organization of the police was closely interwoven with that of the colonial administration. Both the administration and the police had two parallel structures: a European one, known as the internal administration (*binnenlands bestuur*), and an Indonesian one. The European administration worked alongside the Indonesian one in a system of indirect rule. The internal administration was headed by residents, with Assistant Residents and *controleurs* working under them; these officials were responsible for residencies, districts, and subdistricts, respectively. The Indonesian administration was headed by regents, with district heads (*wedana*s, called *demang*s in the Ommelanden) and subdistrict heads (assistant *wedana*s, or assistant *demang*s in the Ommelanden) working under them. Further down the Indonesian hierarchy were the local administrators, village chiefs and *desa* heads. Both the European and Indonesian administrations had police officers at their disposal. The core of the security system was the *desa* police, led by the *desa* head.[18]

Indirect rule did not extend to the Ommelanden, where the landowners selected village heads and police chiefs. These candidates were then officially appointed by the colonial authorities, who could theoretically dismiss them for poor performance, but very rarely did. The powerful influence of the landowners led to rumours that they were setting villains to catch villains, and the impressive physical strength of many security officers was certainly of some importance. A passage from Du Perron's novel illustrates how late nineteenth-century landowners (specifically, the author's father) tended to deal with security issues.

> My father was warned that one of the *djuragans* had connections with the bandits. He lined up the tenants of the Chinese for a roll call to get to know them better. He came to the name of Ali Biman, a stocky Malay, who got up from his crouching position, walked over, and stood very close to my father, who was still sitting with the roll at his desk. The man stretched, looked down at him, and said with the contemptuous voice of a Javanese who feels he has the advantage, emphasizing each word, 'I am Ali Biman.'

Right away, however, the elder Du Perron faced up to Ali Biman, and emerged from this test of wills as the victor.

> Later, it turned out that he was really involved in robberies. My father told him in advance that he would hold him responsible for every

> robbery that occurred on his estate. 'I'm not a policeman and have nothing to do with other estates, but if something happens here I know where to find you, Ali Biman.' Nothing happened....[19]

In other words, Du Perron was the boss of his own estate. He was a man of the old school, and descended from the established Eurasian elite. Around the same time, the estate of Janglapa had a very different power structure. A man named Kaslan had settled there, using the aristocratic title of *Raden* and claiming that his mother had been of high rank. He had returned to Janglapa after serving a three-year term of forced labour, and over the next ten years, he had built up so much authority that the new lessee consulted him on everything. Even the local *camat* (subdistrict head) admitted that Kaslan was the real boss. In fact, Kaslan not only ran the estate, but was also suspected (like a true *jago*) of collusion in robberies on other estates, of cattle theft, and of trafficking in amulets.[20]

The central colonial authorities had almost no influence over the landowners or those who lived on their estates. Because the landowners had full legal control over these estates, the authorities had very little ground for intervening when things went wrong. Often, the administration did not even bother to report on the situation in the Ommelanden. This may have been in part because landowners were uncooperative, but it is also because colonial authorities simply accepted that the Ommelanden were outside their jurisdiction. In the administration's lengthy reports about 'pauperism', the economy, and the police, the Ommelanden were often left out.

Policies towards banditry in the preceding period

The history of Java includes no small number of bandits. Like pretenders to the thrones of sultanates, or other dissatisfied vassals, they tried their luck in the political arena,[21] which was much less institutionalized than in Western states. There was not much of a clear hierarchy within the ruling elite. In comparison to bureaucratic Western states, the state organizations on Java were loosely organized units, which have been termed arena states. They could absorb foreign elements — such as rebels, bandits, and even the VOC — with relative ease.[22]

It was in this political environment that Surapati (?–1704) made a name for himself.[23] Surapati's career demonstrates that in the early colonial period even the lowest robber chief could become king. He started out as a slave in a mixed-race colonial household in Batavia, but is said to have become dissatisfied with his position when he realized that his owner was only a Mardijker, the descendant of a slave. Furthermore, Surapati's owner had given him the most simple jobs to do. There were also rumours, however, that Surapati had been sent to prison because of a love affair with his boss's daughter. But Untung (the 'Happy One'), as he was called in those days, escaped to the Ommelanden, the no man's land around the capital.

There he swiftly became the leader of a group of escaped slaves. Untung and his men roamed the environs of the city, until they were hired by the VOC and he took the title of Lieutenant Surapati. It wasn't long, however, before he became dissatisfied again and deserted. He took with him not only a few of his followers, but also a knowledge of European military tactics. Surapati headed east to Kartasura, which was the Javanese court of the *sunan*, the sultan of the great kingdom of Mataram.

In those days, the *sunan*'s relations with the VOC were tense; among other things, he claimed to be unable to repay a VOC loan. Believing he might be able to use Surapati against the Dutch, the *sunan* invited him to stay at his palace. The VOC took this as a sign of hostility, and the Dutch sent a military expedition to Kartasura. But their soldiers were lured into a trap by the *sunan* and Surapati, and not one of them survived.

For safety's sake, Surapati fled further east, where he acquired more personal power at the expense of his nominal superior, the *sunan* of Mataram. He started to act like a sultan, and adopted all the trappings of the office: a harem, *pusaka* (regalia), and a *kraton* (palace). He managed to maintain this position until 1704, when he died in combat with VOC troops. Two of his sons were imprisoned then too, but enough members of the Surapati family remained at large to continue making a mark in the years that followed. They clearly did not harbour a grudge against the VOC; the two sons who were captured in the battle of 1704 even resurfaced in 1721 as officers in the VOC army in Ceylon.[24]

The VOC made long and determined attempts to put Surapati out of commission, probably because of the fear that his military skills inspired. In other, not infrequent cases, both greater and lesser bandits were simply ignored by the VOC, and the disturbances they caused were often smoothed over by diplomatic means.

One hundred years later, Surapati's career served as a model for another, lesser-known strongman: Mas Djakaria (1772–1827). Djakaria is mentioned in Sartono Kartodirdjo's book *The Peasants' Revolt of Banten in 1888* (1965).[25] This Indonesian historian described Djakaria as a typical member of the 'out-elite'. Djakaria's ancestors had, in particular, resisted the authority of the sultans of Banten. After the abolition of the Banten sultanate in the early nineteenth century, the position of the out-elite also changed. They tried to turn the new situation to their benefit, but this drew the attention of the colonial government in Batavia.[26]

Djakaria's contemporaries considered him a bandit,[27] according to Sartono Kartodirdjo, who came to this conclusion after studying source materials, such as the memoirs of colonial officials, written at least 20 years after the events in which Djakaria figured. Yet if we read newspapers and government documents from Djakaria's own day, it becomes clear that his contemporaries saw him as more than just a bandit. He is described as a dangerous and respected actor in the political arena. Official documents do not call Djakaria a bandit, but a rebel (*muiteling*), an insurgent (*oproerling*), and a militia member (*partijganger*).[28]

Given the power vacuum that colonial authorities allowed to exist in the Ommelanden, the best way to deal with ambitious local leaders was to incorporate them into the administrative system. The alternative was to crush them by military means if their following grew too large. Each decade of the nineteenth century saw a major uprising in which, though the rebels did not march on Batavia, they did enter surrounding villages such as Cilegong, Bekasi, and Tangerang, sending the Chinese, European, and Eurasian villagers fleeing to the capital.

Mas Djakaria seems to have been the last rebel leader with such lofty political and military ambitions. The absence of major revolts near Batavia in later years may indicate that Dutch colonial authority was growing stronger. Over the nineteenth and twentieth centuries there were quite a few lesser uprisings, some quickly forgotten, while others were commemorated at length. The revolt in Tambun described at the start of this chapter belongs to the second category. Another well-known uprising took place in 1886 on the estate of Ciomas, which bordered on Buitenzorg. Attempts to rationalize and intensify the estate's operations — in essence, an extension of the forced cultivation system (*Cultuurstelsel*) with no respect for the old privileges of lower-level chiefs — led to a rebellion. Several hundred people took part in this uprising, protesting the landowner's demands. After an incident in which some were injured, the conflict escalated. The local authorities called for military assistance, which arrived by the recently constructed railway. The uprising was swiftly crushed. The insurgents escaped to the opposite side of a ravine and refused to give up their weapons. They were visible along the edge of the ravine, and the soldiers fired on them. About 40 people were killed.[29] This incident caused such a stir that it was analyzed in pamphlets and newspaper articles for decades afterwards, in both the colony and the mother country, and was even debated in the lower house of the Dutch parliament.

In the period that followed, there were still occasional fatalities during rebellions in the Ommelanden, though in the 50 years from 1880 to 1930, the total number was probably not much more than one hundred. The suggestion that the colonial authorities were pursuing a deliberate policy of oppression probably gives them too much credit. In truth, both the landowners and the colonial authorities were largely powerless and out of the picture.

In the meantime, the estates had become more businesslike. The old landed Indo aristocracy gradually made way for Chinese estate owners. Large enterprises also came into the picture, with management boards in the Netherlands running private estates in the Ommelanden. The role of the colonial authorities thus remained limited. When disturbances broke out, the authorities were quick to panic. Often the few colonial officials on the scene were so outnumbered that they agreed to negotiate in order to save their own skins, after which the crowd returned home.[30]

As for the ambitious bandits, after 1850 their role in politically and ideologically motivated rebellions was negligible. Instead, the instigators of these later rebellions tended to be religious leaders, *dalang*s (wayang performers and experts on Javanese culture), or the farmers themselves. At least, this is the conclusion suggested by colonial authorities' background investigations of the rebels, which were often very thorough.[31] Kartodirdjo, in his book *The Peasants' Revolt of Banten in 1888*, likewise reports that after 1890 a new type of bandit appeared, not motivated by politics or ideology. The journalist Karel Zaalberg wrote in his memoirs that in the final decade of the nineteenth century, the latest trend among criminals was *rampok*,[32] which is precisely the subject of this study.

The economy of the Ommelanden

Rough sketches of the economy of the Dutch East Indies generally devote little attention to the activities of the indigenous population, except in agriculture. Such sketches tend to portray the Europeans as the administrators and the owners of the large companies, the Chinese as the intermediate, mercantile class, and the Javanese as farmers and labourers.

The economy of the Ommelanden was dominated by private estates (which were also found in other parts of Java, such as the north coast, around the towns of Pekalongan, Semarang, Surabaya, and Pasaruan). As mentioned earlier in this chapter, Governor-General Jan Pieterszoon Coen had been the driving force behind the system of private estates around the capital. At first, the leading argument for these estates had been that they protected the city, but later, the government had sold land to private parties mainly in order to fill its coffers. Many of these private estates were vast properties, tens of thousands of hectares in area. In the days of the VOC, the landowners were almost always high-ranking Company employees, who saw their land as an investment. Their positions in the VOC made it easy for them to obtain the credit that was needed to buy land. When they left Batavia (to go elsewhere in the archipelago or to the Netherlands), they generally resold the land to another Company employee. In the eighteenth century, almost all the estates in the Ommelanden were in the hands of a small number of Company officials, and little economic activity took place there.

This situation changed dramatically in the nineteenth century. After the VOC went bankrupt, a period of British dominance followed, which was marked by profound changes. Many prominent officials were discharged from active duty, but the international political situation did not permit them to return to the Netherlands. They had little choice but to concentrate on their own properties in the Ommelanden. These estates were no longer bought and sold freely, as they had been, but remained in the family. A caste of landowners formed, who passed down their property by inheritance. The estates had become more than just a temporary investment; for the new lords of the countryside, they were a world unto themselves. Because land was sold on a large scale in the British period, the number of estates around Batavia swiftly grew.

This transition to a new style of estate management went together with new government policies that cleared the way for private enterprise. For the first time in the Dutch East Indies, it became possible to gain wealth and status independently of the colonial authorities, through private trade and land ownership.[33] The estates began producing export crops. As the century went on, the gradual reorientation of the Ommelanden towards the world market unleashed an economic revolution. Though the landlords continued to put on displays of wealth, feeling this was necessary to maintain their status and authority among the indigenous population, they had in fact become industrial farmers whose aim was to extract the greatest possible profit from their land and from the people who worked it — who, by that time, were very numerous indeed. A 1742 census had found fewer than 5,000 indigenous people in the wide area surrounding Batavia and Buitenzorg, but in the nineteenth century that number grew to many tens of thousands.[34]

This was the century in which the environs of Batavia were incorporated into the modern economy — or, in terms of Wallerstein's modern world system, became part of the periphery of the modern Western economy. The population grew as a result of both rising birth rates and the immigration of indigenous people from elsewhere in the Dutch East Indies, particularly other parts of Java. The dispossession of small farmers to make room for large private estates, a phenomenon which according to Thomas W. Gallant invariably occurs at this stage of modernization,[35] barely took place in the Ommelanden, or in any case was not the predominant tendency. Nevertheless, in the course of the nineteenth century, a growing number of Indonesians — tens of thousands in all — came to inhabit the estates in the Ommelanden. Advocates of private estates pointed out that many immigrants had come specifically to work on those estates, and that there was no genuinely local population with rights that it could assert.[36]

The colonial authorities soon grew uneasy about the growing influence of 'private parties' over such large groups of Indonesians. As early as 1823, Governor-General Van der Cappelen compared the landlords to parasites, who had 'forced their way between Javanese society and the administration to enrich themselves at the expense of the general population and the Dutch treasury'.[37] The colonial government felt that it should control the economic exploitation of the land and its inhabitants. The introduction of the forced cultivation system (*Cultuurstelsel*) in 1830 was the most direct manifestation of that ambition, though in that system private entrepreneurs still played an important role.

In the 1830s, the authorities took other measures that affected private landlords, especially in the Ommelanden. Until then, these landlords had held unrestricted authority over the indigenous inhabitants of their estates. Only on rare occasions were there written agreements between the estate owner and the locals. In the early decades of the nineteenth century, the colonial authorities intervened in the affairs of the estates several times to prevent serious abuses, such as the gross mistreatment of the local population. For instance, they set a maximum on the fees that landlords could charge the locals. In 1836, general regulations were adopted on the relationship between the authorities, private estate owners, and the inhabitants of the estates; they applied to Javanese farms west of the Cimanuk River, the approximate border between West and Central Java. This area to the west of the Cimanuk included the Batavian Ommelanden in their entirety. There were fewer restrictions on private estates in Central and East Java, where the 'brief regulations' in force did not impose any restrictions on the relationship between the landlord and the locals. Landlords in that area therefore had a great deal more liberty to do as they saw fit. The private estates elsewhere in the archipelago tended to be smaller in size and less economically significant; in essence, they were small plots of land governed by the usual rules of property law.[38]

The general regulations of 1836 remained in force, with slight amendment now and then, until 1912, when they were replaced by new regulations (which showed many similarities to the old ones).[39] Under these new regulations, landlords had full ownership of their land. The private estates were described as being occupied by 'the Native population and equivalent groups' (meaning indigenous, Chinese, and Arab inhabitants; in the Ommelanden, most areas were inhabited entirely by indigenous people). Landlords cultivated the land at their 'own risk and expense'. In legal terms, the landlord allocated the land to the people living there under a ground lease. In return, they had to pay fees to the landlord. Landlords' powers with respect to the inhabitants of his land were restricted by the general regulations of 1836. They could not evict tenants from their estates against their will, but conversely, individuals could not take up residence on an estate without the landlord's consent. This ground-lease system did not cover the entirety of the estate. The exceptions were areas developed or cultivated by the owner at his own risk and expense, certain built-up areas, wastelands, and forests not yet subject to regular management.

The general regulations detailed precisely what charges the inhabitants could be required to pay. There were several: first of all, the *tjoeké* or tithe that farmers had to pay to the landowner, traditionally one-tenth of their annual produce. The regulations set a maximum of 20 per cent, but allowed the landlord and the farmers to make 'voluntary' arrangements about this ('in friendly consultation'), possibly for a multi-year period. The maximum share of fishermen's catch was also 20 per cent. Tenants also paid rent for their land and gardens and, finally, contributed their corvée or forced labour. A landlord could order any male tenant aged 16 to 50 to work for him up to one day or night a week, in return for a reasonable wage. The regulations also permitted the tenant to send a replacement, or to buy off the corvée under certain specified conditions. Charges other than the ones listed here were prohibited.

The general regulations included detailed provisions on the landlord, the inhabitants of the estate, and the colonial authorities. For instance, the landlord was responsible for appointing village chiefs and 'general chiefs', who generally had police powers.

The landlords maintained a distinctive lifestyle. While in the early years they tended to be 'great lords', true aristocrats in their own domains, this situation changed in the course of the nineteenth century.[40] To produce crops for the world market, they had to become much more economically active. While they went on living large — often to the point of incurring large debts — their motive was presumably to impress the local population, including their corvée labourers. Without pomp and circumstance, they could not maintain their authority on their own properties. It is difficult to overstate the luxury with which some landlords surrounded themselves. The renowned estate owner known as Majoor Jantje ('Major Johnny'), who held sway over Citrap House in the mid-nineteenth century, threw parties almost daily, which generally involved European, Chinese, and Indonesian orchestras, a gala dinner, fancy-dress festivities, and a ball to round off the evening. Some 25 'obliging slave girls' served the single men.[41] The ladies of Batavia did not display much stronger moral fibre, as a mid-nineteenth-century letter reports: 'They do nothing there, and spend the evenings dancing, speaking of nothing but fine clothes, balls, love affairs, and handsome men.'[42]

As noted, however, landlords worked harder and harder as the nineteenth century went on. They understood the local language and culture (because this was the only efficient way of gaining access to the local labour pool), and so they often gained recognition as experts on their own territories. To remain competitive, their businesses had to keep up with the latest innovations, and so it was often the landlords who introduced new techniques to their estates.[43]

Insight into these developments can be gained from the article 'Haciendas and Plantations in Middle America and the Antilles' by Eric Wolf and Sidney Mintz,[44] which describes the differences between the hacienda system and the plantation system. The dichotomy described by Wolf and Mintz can be applied to the Ommelanden in the nineteenth century; the hacienda is exemplified by older estates such as Majoor Jantje's, and the plantation by the sprawling PT Pamuka estates, for instance. Hacienda estates mainly served the regional market; in the Ommelanden, that meant Batavia. Partly because there had been relatively little opportunity for investment in earlier years, the crops that they produced were quite varied and included rice, vegetables, and grass for the town's coach horses. These traditional estates were usually run by the family that owned the land, and the locals were tied to the estate by more than just the wages they received for their work. For instance, some of them held leases for parcels of land, and a web of mutual obligations, both written and unwritten, tied the landlord and tenants together.

Modern plantations, in contrast, served the world market and tended towards monoculture. The labourers preferred simply to receive wages, and the landowners did their best to break free of customary law. The rise of the banking system made large investments possible. While hacienda owners focused on immediate consumption and prestige, the plantations were oriented towards accumulation of wealth. Much of the social unrest around Batavia and the sometimes harsh criticism of private estates are easier to understand if one keeps this dichotomy in mind. The haciendas and plantations sometimes existed side by side in the Ommelanden, and in other cases one succeeded the other; specifically, a hacienda was replaced by a plantation. The opinions of landlords, labourers, the authorities, and the public about social conditions on these estates are easier to understand if one is aware of which context each commentator (consciously or unconsciously) has in mind: the hacienda or the plantation.

A commission appointed in 1903 to study Java's economic troubles was pessimistic about the prospects for the Javanese in trade and industry. Unfortunately, the commission did not discuss the private estates in its published reports, though Buitenzorg and Krawang received a little attention.[45]

The Ommelanden differed from the rest of the Javanese countryside in that there were many more *bujangs*, workers (often young men) without permanent ties. It was also easier to find a new job in the Ommelanden, because the commercial centre of Batavia and the port of Tanjung Priok were both nearby. In the vast rice fields of Tangerang, there were many Chinese rice-husking mills. The region was also home to many little workshops that made roof tiles and pottery. Finally, there were a few cottage industries, mainly producing textiles and hats. Tangerang hats were a fairly significant export item. The residency of Batavia boasted about 5,000 shops in total. About four per cent of the indigenous population was involved in trade and industry, and so despite the relative poverty of the Ommelanden there were quite a few wealthy indigenous households. One might think of Javanese farmers as dirt poor, but the proceeds of individual robberies in the Ommelanden were often quite considerable.[46]

The press, 1870–1915

Compared to the small number of sources discussing banditry in the colony's administrative and legal archives, the abundance of information on this subject in the Batavian newspapers is very striking. It sometimes seems almost as if the debate on the causes of robbery, and the response to it, was initiated by the newspapers. Who made up the public whose opinion was being shaped, and who were the cultural actors who served as opinion leaders? In other words, who were the readers of Batavia's newspapers, and who were the journalists?

Until 1850, the colonial authorities had almost total control of the press. As part of a more liberal policy introduced in the mid-nineteenth century, laws and regulations on the press became more permissive. This led to the emergence of newspapers, which provided their readers with independent news and opinion. From 1870 onwards newspapers flourished, because the telegraph, shipping, and the railways had greatly improved communications — both within the colony, and with Europe. The result was a colonial press with a distinctly local character. Since censorship had not been abolished entirely, journalists were constantly at loggerheads with the authorities. Many a newspaper found itself in hot water because its publishing licence had been temporarily revoked or one of its editors had died of a tropical disease.

Another typical feature of Batavia's newspapers was the so-called 'tropical style', an emotional, assertive way of writing. The close contact between rival newspapers and their readers could lead to lifelong feuds between editors, who joined forces only to battle their common enemy: the government and its laws.

Sometimes the sweltering heat was given as an excuse for journalists' 'irresponsible' outpourings. A more probable explanation is the political frustration of both journalists and their readers. For lack of other outlets for criticism, the papers were used to vent feelings of dissatisfaction.[47]

By the late nineteenth century, however, newspapers were also commercial enterprises. The editor P.A. Daum turned the *Bataviaasch Nieuwsblad*, established in 1885, into an authoritative and widely-read daily. Daum developed a formula for his paper that proved quite successful. The *Bataviaasch Nieuwsblad* was made affordable by aiming at the large Indo community in the capital. Leading articles and serialized novels forged a bond between the newspaper and its readers. The number of subscribers rose to 5,000 around 1900, at a time when Batavia's total population was just under 150,000.[48] The *Bataviaasch Nieuwsblad* became a model for other papers.

Between about 1890 and 1910, many new Malay-language papers came onto the market, but most of them folded after just a few years. Colonial historians have identified sloppy management as the main cause of their economic failure, along with an inability to make subscribers and advertisers pay.[49] Perhaps these less successful newspapers found it difficult — just as we do — to figure out why someone might subscribe to a Malay paper rather than a Dutch-language one like the *Bataviaasch Nieuwsblad* or *Java-bode*. There were, of course, readers who preferred Malay — more specifically, the pidgin Malay used at the *pasar*, also known as Betawi Malay. Yet readers started protesting as soon as editors shifted to the more sophisticated classical variant. Malay newspapers found their readers among Eurasians who preferred the Malay language, Indonesian merchants and shopkeepers, and the *peranakan* (Chinese families that had lived in Batavia for generations). All these groups needed a newspaper for business reasons. Newspapers provided information such as market prices and shipping schedules.

The advertisements in Malay papers open a window onto the lives of their readers. For instance, the goods advertised include European and local medicines, Swiss watches, Danish butter, French perfume, strong drink, and passage to Jeddah for the pilgrimage to Mecca.[50] The advertisements in the *Bataviaasch Nieuwsblad* were not very different, though they more often peddled automobiles, property, and typically Dutch products. The readers of the *Java-bode* were more interested in pianos, *haute couture* (top fashion), still more expensive imports, and copies of government publications.

The average Malay-language newspaper had an official circulation of about 900.[51] We can safely assume, however, that the actual number of readers was much larger, because so many copies were shared or even read aloud to illiterate fellow Batavians. Newspapers such as *Pemberita Betawi* must therefore have been more influential and widely distributed than one might expect given the number of subscribers. It should be added that this is true not only of Malay-language papers, but also of Dutch-language ones.

We still have no clear picture of the typical reader of the *Bataviaasch Nieuwsblad* and the main Malay-language papers, such as *Pemberita*

Betawi, *Hindia Olanda*, and *Bintang Betawi*. Moreover, the editors, publishers, and journalists came from many different walks of life. From the early 1880s to some time in the 1890s, the Eurasian journalists were the most conspicuous group, perhaps because they were the most proficient in written Malay. After 1890, Chinese journalists and publishers gained new prominence, and Chinese publishers often replaced European ones.

Ahmat Adam has described the relationship between the development of the vernacular press and the growing political consciousness of the Chinese and indigenous segments of the population. Despite the demonstrable existence of such a relationship, at the close of the nineteenth century the Malay press kept a fairly low political profile. Eurasian, Dutch, and Chinese reporters worked side by side with indigenous journalists like Tirtoadisoerjo, who later became active as Indonesian nationalists.[52]

Malay newspapers supplied their readers not only with advertising, and local and international news, but also with leading articles, which often dealt with local affairs. At that point, they did not have well-defined political ambitions. The historical events discussed in these papers include the poor economic situation in the Ommelanden and the massacre of 1741 in Batavia. Emulating the successful *Bataviaasch Nieuwsblad*, Malay papers began producing their own serialized novels. These were often translations of classic novels, but they also included narratives set in Batavia and written by the journalists themselves, which were very popular.

In Chapter 6 and Appendix VI, I discuss a few of these serials, such as the Kesen serial, originally based on a news item about a bandit who had overplayed his hand and been put out of commission by his partners in crime and the authorities. In the serial, however, the main character, Si Kesen, was transformed into a thoroughgoing villain. There were thus three versions of Kesen's story: a report by the Assistant Resident of Tangerang, an article about his crimes in the Dutch-language *Bataviaasch Nieuwsblad*, and a serialized novel in the Malay-language *Pemberita Betawi*. By comparing these sources, we can see how the newspapers altered and retold the bandit's story, adapting the narrative in the official report in accordance with ideas about the social environment in Batavia and the Ommelanden. In the Malay press, Kesen's story is full of moral lessons emphasizing the friction between the *jago* bandit and his modern-day environment.

This shows that the role of the colonial press in creating legends about bandits should not be underestimated.

Illus. 2 Map of Batavia and environs. Koninklijke Vereeniging Java Motor Club (Royal Java Motor Club Association), List of names (alphabetical by residency) of the enterprises, rental properties, and private estates appearing on the map of Java and Madoera, 1926. (Collection, KITLV)

Key for the residencies of Batavia and Buitenzorg (according to the original text, in the old spelling):

Residency of Batavia

Number on the map	Name of enterprise/estate	Product(s)
1	Serpong Lengkong (government-run)	rubber
Private estates		
I	Karangserang Dalem & Tjileuleus	paddy, etc.
II	Gandoe	paddy, etc.
III	Tjilongok	paddy, etc.
IV	Radjak	paddy, etc.
V	Ketapang (Mauk) & Tegal Koening	paddy, etc.
VI	Karangserang Laut (Rawah Kidang)	paddy, etc.
VII	Kramat & Pakoeadji	paddy, etc.
VIII	Sepattan	paddy, etc.
IX	Selapandjang-west	paddy, etc.
X	Kedawoeng-west	paddy, etc.
XI	Tegal Angoes	paddy, etc.
XII	Pekadjangan	paddy, etc.
XIII	Pangkalan	paddy, etc.
XIV	Teloeknaga	paddy, etc.
XV	Bodjong Renged	paddy, etc.
XVI	Selapandjang-oost	paddy, etc.
XVII	Kedawoeng-oost	paddy, etc.
XVIII	Kamal	paddy, etc.
XIX	Pasar Poetih	firewood
XX	Slingerland	firewood
XXI	Tjengkareng	paddy, etc.
XXII	Burgvliet	paddy, etc.
XXIII	Batoetjeper	paddy, etc.
XXIV	Paroengkoeda	paddy, etc.
XXV	Rawah Boeaja	paddy, etc.
XXVI	Tanah Kodja	paddy, etc.
XXVII	Poris	paddy, etc.
XXVIII	Amstelveen	paddy, etc.
XXIX	Tjikokol	paddy, etc.

Number on the map	Name of enterprise/estate	Product(s)
XXX	Gondrong (Tjipondo)	paddy, etc.
XXXI	Panoengangan	paddy, etc.
XXXII	Bergzicht	paddy, etc.
XXXIII	Priang	paddy, etc.
XXXIV	Tjihoeni	paddy, etc.
XXXV	Lengkong-west	paddy, etc.
XXXVI	Lebak Boeloes & Simplicitas	paddy, etc.
XXXVII	Pondok Laboe	paddy, etc.
XXXVIII	Tigaraksa	paddy, etc.
XXXIX	Tjikajoe	paddy, etc.
XL	Antjol Pasir	paddy, etc.
XLI	Ragoenan	paddy, etc.
XLII	Tandjoeng-west	paddy, coconut, etc.
XLIII	Tandjoeng-oost	paddy, coconut, etc.
XLIV	Hermendal	paddy, coconut, etc.
XLV	Tjililitan	paddy, coconut, etc.
XLVI	Pondok Gedé	paddy, coconut, etc.
XLVII	Pondok Klapa	paddy, coconut, etc.
XLVIII	Tjakoeng	paddy, coconut, etc.
XLIX	Telok Poetjoeng	paddy, coconut, etc.
L	Karangtjongok	paddy, coconut, etc.
LI	Bekasi-oost	paddy, coconut, etc.
LII	Pisangan	paddy, coconut, etc.
LIII	Gaboes	paddy, coconut, etc.
LIV	Babelan	paddy, coconut, etc.
LV	Soengei Bintaro	paddy, coconut, etc.
LVI	Pondok Songa Parakan	paddy, coconut, etc.
LVII	Karatan	paddy, coconut, etc.
LVIII	Pondok Doewa paddy, coconut, etc.	
LIX	Soengei Njamoek	paddy, coconut, etc.
LX	Oedjoeng Krawang	paddy, coconut, etc.
LXI	Tjabang Boengin & Kampoeng Boegis	paddy, coconut, etc.
LXII	Pebajoeran	paddy, coconut, etc.
LXIII	Tamboen	paddy, coconut, etc.
LXIV	Gedoeng Gedeh	paddy, coconut, etc.
LXV	Soeradita	rubber & tea
LXVI	Antjol Victoria	rubber, paddy, etc.
LXVII	Poeloe Daon	paddy, etc.

(*cont'd overleaf*)

Residency of Buitenzorg

Number on the map	Name of enterprise/estate	Product(s)
Enterprises		
1	Paroengpandjang	rubber
2	Tjimoelang	rubber & tea
3	Tjiomas	tea
4	Pasir Angin	tea
5	Pasir Geulis	tea
6	Pasir Karet	tea
7	Podok Gedeh Landen	tea, cinchona bark, rubber
8	Koeripan	rubber
Private estates		
I	Djanglapa & Tjikopo Majak	paddy, tea, etc.
II	Trogong	rubber
III	Tjiloleang	rubber
IV	Goenoeng Sindoer (Djampang-ilir)	rubber & tea
V	Djanglapa	rubber
VI	Roempin	rubber
VII	Djasinga	rubber & tea
VIII	Bolang	rubber & tea
IX	Nanggoeng (Nirmala)	rubber & tea
X	Tjampea, Tjiboenboelan & Sadeng	tea, etc.
XI	Tjibodas	tea & rubber
XII	Dermaga	rubber, etc.
XIII	Tjileboet	rubber
XIV	Bodjong Gedeh	rubber
XV	Tjitajam	paddy
XVI	Depok	paddy
XVII	Mampang	paddy
XVIII	Sawangan	paddy
XIX	Pondok Tjabe	paddy
XX	Tjinere	paddy
XXI	Pondok Tjina	paddy
XXII	Tjimanggis	paddy
XXIII	Tjilodong	paddy
XXIV	Tjilingsi	paddy
XXV	Tjibaroesa	paddy

Number on the map	Name of enterprise/estate	Product(s)
XXVI	Klapanoenggal	birds' nests
XXVII	Tjipaminkis	paddy & tea
XXVIII	Noord Tjiliwoeng	tea
XXIX	Tjiliwoeng	tea & cinchona bark
XXX	Goenoeng Mas	tea
XXXI	Tjisaroea-zuid	tea
XXXII	Tjikopo	tea, cinchona bark & paddy
XXXIII	Tjisaroea-noord	tea

THE BANDITS

CHAPTER 2

The Economics of Banditry

Pondering the prominent social status of certain known robbers in Javanese *desas*, the former Resident G.L. Gonggrijp remarked in 1911: 'I have been thinking that we might convert all Java's villeins into villains. Then they would all, perhaps, become prosperous.'[1] In his regular column of 'letters' to the daily newspaper *Bataviaasch Handelsblad*, 'Brieven van *Opheffer*', Gonggrijp outlined his views regarding the everyday lives of the Javanese and the attempts of officials infused with a sense of high moral purpose to 'elevate' [*opheffen*] them. The irony of the above quotation reflects the scepticism with which he viewed such attempts. They nonetheless encapsulate the thrust of this chapter: in the late nineteenth and early twentieth centuries, plain robbery — though obviously a criminal activity and part of an informal economy — was one of the few lucrative sources of income in the Javanese countryside.

Robbery and economic cycles

To clarify the financial incentives for taking up robbery as a livelihood, the following pages will examine the correlation between the economic cycle and the frequency of robberies. Since colonial statistics will be an important source, it is fair to start by questioning the value of crime figures gathered by colonial officials. Some studies, such as Robert Sindall's *Street Violence in the Nineteenth Century* and Stanley Cohen's *Folk Devils and Moral Panics*, draw attention to the unreliability of crime statistics. They hold that the figures reveal more about city-dwellers' fear of social change than about the true state of affairs in relation to crime.

Undoubtedly the urban population and the government sometimes saw things that were not there. But in Batavia in any case, the opposite is also true: attention was finally drawn to a problem that had existed for hundreds of years, one that had caused, and was still causing, real suffering to a large part of the Indonesian population. It would therefore be wrong to dismiss the reaction to robberies as 'moral panic'. As far as the high incidence of robberies known as *rampok* in the crime statistics is concerned: according to the *Welvaartsrapporten* (colonial reports that focused on the problem of poverty), lower-ranking administrative officials tended not to report crime, which implies that the true figures must have been higher still.[2]

Several elements of colonial statistics require clarification. First, there is *rampok*, a term frequently encountered in colonial officialese. It derives from Javanese usage, in which it refers to a crime in which four or five men robbed a house at night. Administrative officials distinguished between various types of robbery, such as tunnelling under the wall of a house for the purpose of robbing it, robbery with violence, and robberies carried out by gangs. Large-scale robberies described as *ketjoe*, most notably in the Principalities area of Java, sometimes involved as many as ten perpetrators. In addition, *rampok* and *ketjoe* were distinguished from robbery without the use of violence, such as burglary, pickpocketing, shoplifting, and cattle theft, another prominent form of crime in the Javanese countryside.[3]

When considering standards of living in the rural districts surrounding Batavia (the *Ommelanden*), we should pause to consider the best criterion for measuring them. One useful criterion is the price of rice. It should be noted, however, that since Batavia was close to the supply routes, it was relatively immune to the effects of a failed harvest. We can probably state, with minor reservations, that the area around Batavia did not witness any 'subsistence crises' after 1850. Still, fluctuations in market conditions influenced living standards, and the region would certainly have been affected by job losses and rising prices.

In his article 'From Subsistence Crises to Business Cycle Depressions', Peter Boomgaard describes a long succession of crises in Java.[4] The early 1880s was a time of scarcity, caused by a series of failed harvests and rising rice prices. Ten years later (1890–92) came another poor rice harvest, accompanied by numerous outbreaks of disease. The 1880s are known as the Great Depression, which afflicted a range of crops in the Indonesian archipelago, most notably sugar. The year 1892 is associated with the famous robber Si Pitung, but few other gangs appear in the records at that time. Ten years on, around 1903, Java in particular was hit by a succession of poor harvests. The year 1903 witnessed an enormous increase in the number of robberies in the area surrounding Batavia. During the final years of the First World War, Java suffered a double blow: not only were the rice harvests poor, but rice imports were also held up because of the war. The island also suffered, along with much of the world, from the devastating effects of Spanish flu. Organized robberies in the Indonesian archipelago peaked in 1920. Finally, in the 1930s the Javanese countryside suffered from the consequences of the worldwide economic crisis.

Taking a broad look at the period from 1880 to 1930, we find that the peaks in robbers' activities corresponded roughly to economic slumps, although there were also exceptions. The years 1907/8 witnessed a large number of robberies, but there was no particular problem with the economy at that time that might have acted as a trigger. The converse is also found, in that the malaise of the 1930s was not accompanied by any noteworthy increase in the number of robberies.

According to the colonial statistics, *rampok* was fairly uncommon in the Batavia region before the 1880s. If this form of crime was indeed rare in the mid-nineteenth century, there cannot have been any relationship between economic malaise and the *rampok* 'business' in that period, since the 1830s in particular were a time of great poverty in the Javanese countryside as a result of failed harvests and the forced cultivation system (*Cultuurstelsel*). In fact the number of robberies increased while the Dutch East Indies was enjoying a period of relative prosperity. Starting in 1905, the Javanese population acquired a measure of social security. Pierre van der Eng claims that between 1902 and 1940, agricultural production in Java gradually grew to keep pace with population growth.[5] This meant that the calorie intake of an average member of the Javanese population in that period fluctuated around the critical limit of 1,900 per day. Rice production then decreased dramatically with the Second World War and the postwar period, and did not reach an adequate subsistence level again until the late 1960s. This suggests that robbery was not inspired solely by dire poverty.[6] The Karawang region, which was particularly prosperous as the 'rice barn' of the Dutch East Indies, was also notorious for its *rampok* activities.[7]

Banditry as described in this book — that is, banditry with few if any political motives, lightning actions with the use of revolvers — was related to the economy of money and luxury goods. After all, cash and jewellery were ideal as quick booty. We may posit a relationship between the increase in robberies and the rise of a relatively 'affluent' section of the population who took part in the money economy and owned portable luxury goods.

It is also useful to look at possible links between the robbers' activities and other social trends. The bar diagram in Appendix II shows that the robbers became more active between 1890 and 1920, precisely at a time of reorganizations in the police force. These reorganizations, which involved a shift from an enforcement apparatus managed by the internal administration to a professional police force, started around 1900 and were completed in 1925. In this specific period, there were years in which the robbers were extremely active. Still, the reorganizations proved their worth: once the Dutch East Indies finally had its own professional police force, the heyday of Indonesian banditry was over. The relationship between these two developments is discussed in Chapter 9, which deals with the organized police and its efforts to combat the robbers.

The activities of the robbers after 1890 can also be linked to the modernization of firearms, especially the growing popularity of the revolver (see Chapter 4). Another technological advance may also have played a role. Street lighting became more common after 1870, reducing the difference between the light and dark hours of the day. The clear onset of darkness was universally regarded as a boundary indicating the domain of crime, and this boundary therefore shifted under the influence of the new technology.

If we view the robbers' actions in the wider context of global economic trends, as in Thomas Gallant's article on banditry, piracy and state formation (see the introduction), it is striking that in one respect in any case, the robbers did not behave as this article would lead one to expect.[8] This economic phase of the Dutch East Indies, which can certainly be classified as a period of early modernization, witnessed mass exports of produce from inland estates to overseas markets. One might have assumed that robbers would focus on this freight traffic, taking advantage of good returns with relatively little risk. These export products covered long journeys across Java from the production centres in the interior to the coastal ports, providing ideal opportunities for attack. But I have not been able to find any banditry in this area, nor have I discovered any indirect allusions to it. It seems that local gangs were scarcely aware of these modern products and their transportation. Goods were sometimes stolen from warehouses, but the perpetrators were usually company employees.

We can only guess at the reasons for the criminals' lack of interest in export products. Perhaps these products were too bulky to allow for a swift escape. Another possibility is that the market was controlled too strictly for trade in illicitly-obtained merchandise to go unnoticed. Money transports too were left in peace, partly no doubt because they were heavily guarded. Finally, all these targets would have required daytime operations, which was a major disadvantage.

In general, the robbers' tactics and objectives did not change noticeably in the period under review. In this era of incipient modernization, they continued to focus on the same targets as before, namely — broadly speaking — on their prosperous neighbours. It will become apparent in the following chapters that although the colony's economy underwent substantial modernization in this period, much of indigenous society — the world in which the bandits too were raised — was untouched by these changes. Consequently, my study only partly confirms the link between banditry and economic modernization that is posited by Gallant.

Crime pays

Each successive crime wave was accompanied by a media hype, and the *rampok* operations of 1918 were no exception. The press coverage of these crimes differed in one key respect from that of previous decades: by then, the average European journalist considered himself better-informed on the subject. An age had dawned of full-length reports on the East Indies, with journalists going off to research topics themselves instead of copying articles from the East Indies press. Leading articles with titles such as 'A view of Batavia's lower town', 'Trips to the opium den' and 'What did we see in Meester Cornelis?' became common.

An article in the *Java-bode* entitled 'A remarkable case of *rampok*'[9] reported a robbery targeting a house in Klenteng. The crime itself was not in fact particularly remarkable, in that it displayed all the characteristics of a normal robbery in the colony. The only conspicuous anomaly was the number of deaths. Thieves broke into the home of the victims, an affluent Chinese family, at 2 a.m. One of the ten gang members hacked a hole in the roof through which he gained entry, subsequently opening the door for his accomplices. In the ensuing clash, several of the occupants were wounded and two were shot dead. The gang blocked the road during the robbery, shouting the warning cry: 'Dear Chinese residents, stay inside your homes or you will be shot.' In spite of this warning, those attacked were not content to stand by and watch. The two family members who were killed, for instance, were shot when they openly confronted the bandits. Generally speaking, bandits tended to use their revolvers to fire warning shots or to threaten anyone who resisted. Murder and ill-treatment were rare.

Although the brigands in Klenteng were masked, an eye-witness was able to describe some of them. The descriptions contain several standard elements — the eye-witness may have had recourse to clichés in the absence of any real clues as to the robbers' appearance. They were described as tall and/or heavily built, one had a light-brown skin colour, and one had the inevitable handlebar moustache. The booty amounted to 2,000 guilders, an enormous sum of money for this period. The police not only arrived on the scene too late, but actually went to the wrong house.

Another source of information on crime — aside from reports written by the colony's journalists of trips to robbed kampongs — was the coverage of the subsequent trials. These trials were described at length in the newspapers, the aim being not just to present news, but also to identify social abuses or shortcomings on the part of the government. This was partly because it was not easy to criticize the government directly, and this method provided a good way of providing criticism implicitly.[10]

One of the newspapers contains an account of the trial of some members of a gang from Tangerang that had carried out a robbery in Anyer-Kidul on the west coast of Java, 150 km from the capital.[11] Most of the public that filled the courtroom (like the victim) were ethnic Chinese. This account gives an impression of the preparations for a *rampok* raid. Masi, one of the gang leaders, was a merchant from Tangerang who made occasional business trips to Anyer. The account relates that while he was there, he and one Sabam had initially made plans to rob a wealthy *haji*. Then, concluding that this plan was too risky, they decided instead to rob a Chinese man named Oeij Tjioe Sion who lived on Grote Postweg. Opinions were sounded at a party given by the local *mandoer* (foreman) at Cipondok in Tangerang, and the majority approved the new plan. Another seven or eight members were recruited, and the gang set off.

Their first mistake was that after arriving in the area they waited several days to strike, enabling inhabitants of the surrounding villages to identify them afterwards. When the victim Oeij returned from Batavia with 7,000 guilders he had earned there, the gang decided that the time was ripe. The villagers were startled by the sound of shots, and when the master of the house emerged from his front door, he was immediately shot. The thieves grabbed his keys and ransacked his house. A Chinese servant was attacked with a machete and an Indonesian servant was shot. When the robbers found the money they made off with it, stopping briefly to rob the shop next-door. Laden with booty (their second mistake) they were readily identified in the surrounding area within a few days and gradually rounded up — not, it should be said, without putting up a show of resistance. At length they all stood awaiting judgment in court. They acted the part of swaggering, hardened criminals, listening to the sentence 'with grinning faces and without a trace of remorse'. When led away, 'they kept their smiling faces'.

The first thing that strikes one in such descriptions is that for perpetrators who evaded arrest, robberies were extremely lucrative. The spoils often amounted to very large sums of money. The following table of robberies carried out in the Batavia area in the years 1919 and 1920, giving the amount stolen, derives from reports in the *Bataviaasch Nieuwsblad.*

Date [dd-mm-yyyy]	Place	Sum/goods stolen
24-1-1919	Pabayuran	6,000–7,000 guilders in cash and goods worth another 6,000–7,000 guilders
28-4-1919	Meester Cornelis	8,000 guilders
19-4-1920	Gabus, Bekasi	500 guilders in cash plus 700 in goods
8-7-1920	Paal Merah	4,000 guilders plus gold and jewellery
16-9-1920	Jembatan	900 guilders' worth of goods
13-11-1920	Gang Baru	1,300 guilders
16-11-1920	Gedong Panjang	1,000 guilders
13-12-1920	Kali Pasir	1,850 guilders

One of the biggest *rampok* incidents took place at Steuerwald jewellers in 1922, when one Hadji Rais made off with the staggering sum of 40,000 guilders.[12] Hadji Rais was arrested *en route* to Singapore, but escaped from prison soon afterwards.[13]

When the commissioner of Batavia, A.W.V. Hinne, uncovered a large network of receivers while investigating a famous case of robbery with murder

Illus. 3 Djaisin, Rais, and Ateh. They were the robbers of the jeweller Steuerwald. (*De Zweep*, 1922)

(of a woman named Fatima) in 1908, he also found a huge stash of stolen property. All the city-dwellers who had been robbed in the previous two years were invited to the police station to see whether any of the jewellery — valued in total at 80,000 guilders — belonged to them.[14]

Other studies of banditry also draw attention to the personal financial incentives for choosing this occupation, in contrast to Hobsbawm's emphasis on robbery as a form of social protest. *Bandidos*, a survey of Latin American banditry edited by Richard W. Slatta, claims that rural communities generally preferred to express their protests in ways other than through 'social' banditry.[15] Nathan Brown is equally dismissive of the idea of social banditry in his study of Egyptian banditry.[16] One final author who should be mentioned here is Anton Blok, whose criticism of Hobsbawm has already been discussed in the introduction.[17]

In highlighting the importance of brigands' social and political motives, many studies gloss over the actual profits to be made by pursuing a life of crime. Anton Blok and Florike Egmond do include appendices with their findings on the size of the booty seized by gangs. Although the robberies they describe occurred less frequently in the Netherlands than in the Dutch East Indies, here too the profits were very large, amounting to hundreds or even thousands of guilders at a time. Some eighteenth- and nineteenth-century bandits were indeed quite prosperous, but their wealth was not easy to trace, since they tended to convert their money into non-durable luxury goods.

Successful Indonesian bandits led comfortable lives in the vicinity of Batavia, just out of reach of colonial society. One such place was the kampong of Gabus Dukuh, whose village headman ('R') owned a great many rice fields, buffalo (ploughing cattle) and numerous houses. He also had deposits of some 56,000 guilders in bank accounts in Batavia.[18]

Occupational hazards: Arrests and convictions

The moment of arrest was frequently the first time a bandit emerged from the anonymity of the kampong. It would also shatter any myths that had grown up around him. The arrest would be followed by a trial of strength: while the authorities did their best to undermine the prisoner's charisma, the bandit would put up a show of swagger to sustain his image. When police officers insulted Si Pitung after he had been shot, he replied by singing a merry little song. Even when the court pronounced sentence, often imposing several years of forced labour, the men in the dock generally reacted with laughter, which the Europeans construed as a show of utter contempt for the legal process.[19]

The arrests were almost always made by junior local administrative officials, aided by the local police, and tended to be extremely violent. Meek surrender was not an option, and the authorities tackled their task with grim determination. This explains the Indonesian police's reputation for bravery; it was said that 'Orientals' believed fatalistically that they would not go before their time and therefore had little fear of death.[20] The sizeable bounty on the brigands' heads probably served as an added incentive. An arrest might easily yield up to 1,000 guilders.[21]

Some people urged that arrests be attended by a European official to prevent the violence escalating.[22] At the apprehension of the brigand Lias, the resulting clash had degenerated into a wild shooting-match, with local policemen even shooting their own fellow-officers who were lying in ambush some distance away. During the subsequent arrest, the local district police chief kicked Lias in the head. Many bandits died during arrest, something the police did little to prevent. The indifference concerning police violence even found its way into official documents, with the head of the district criminal investigation bureau, Scheepmaker, using *neerleggen* ['to cut down'] as a synonym for 'arrest':

> Thus bringing in (or cutting down) the *rampok* miscreant Oesoep and the escaped Arsad, who were already condemned to death, may well be the only way of preventing any recurrence of the previous state.[23]

Many well-known brigands were killed in gun battles with the police. Of the generation that was active around 1918, Lias (bounty 1,000 guilders [*f*]), Ambot (*f*800), Briti, Hadji Anwar, Toit (*f*1,000), Sabindjak (*f*1,500) and Nawi were all killed during arrest. Oesoep, a notorious bandit who will be discussed later in this chapter, was a friend of Lias' who was active in the same period, and who turned up again in the mid-1920s after a number of escapes.[24]

It seems that victims of robbery seldom settled their own accounts with the perpetrators. Kees van Dijk and Freek Colombijn recently wrote about the lynching of criminals around 1999 in the essay collection *Roots of Violence in Indonesia*.[25]

Both explain this phenomenon by noting that outsiders are viewed in Indonesia as threats to the community, and both refer to the historical roots of lynching. In my own studies of colonial newspapers, however, I have found very few cases of criminals being ill-treated or killed by members of the community.

Illus. 4 The big picture on the left shows the notorious robber-chief Lias, the three smaller portraits next to it show the other gang members. The pictures on the right show a policeman and his wife who caught the robbers. However, the gang escaped from prison only a month after the arrest. (*Nederlandsch-Indische Politiegids*, November 1917)

There was certainly plenty of public interest in the fate of brigands following their arrest. The subsequent trials frequently became major spectacles, attracting hundreds, sometimes thousands, of spectators. In 1937 the trial of the brigand Pa-I, who had been active in Batavia in the preceding few years, was watched by a crowd of 1,000 — 'even though the rice in the paddies had to be cut that day',[26] as one journalist remarked. There is an account of the complete humiliation of the bandit Pa-I, under the heading 'The great *Stamboel* at Cileungsi: two hours' *maloe* [embarrassed – MvT] worse than eight years inside':

> 'Go ahead, act it out then', the presiding judge encouraged a witness who had offered to demonstrate the way in which Pa-I had tried to cut his throat to get hold of his 75 cents, all the money he had. The witness was directed to play the part of Pa-I, with Pa-I taking the part of the victim. The witness hesitated for so long that the public started calling him a coward and stamping their feet in indignation. Finally the witness gingerly placed his fingers around Pa-I's throat gently, prompting loud cries of 'harder'! The presiding judge smiled all the while, commenting: 'Well well Pa-I, this is certainly your unlucky day, dear me!'[27]

The hapless Pa-I also had to endure other taunts from the judge: 'Well well, so this is the great Pa-I. I must say I had imagined that you would look very different.'[28] The entire trial was conducted like this, so that the defence counsel was eventually prompted to ask for a more lenient sentence since Pa-I had suffered such wholesale humiliation.

One could not find a better example of what Anton Blok calls 'theatrical reproduction' in his *De Bokkerijders*. Blok describes the attempted re-enactment of crimes in public hearings, noting that symbolic and theatrical elements were added to reinforce the ritualistic nature of the punishment and the message it conveyed, making it a better deterrent.[29] In the twentieth century, public trials were no longer followed by public corporal punishment in the Dutch East Indies, as they once had been, unless one were to regard a chain-gang in this light.

For all the playful humiliation meted out to Pa-I, trials frequently escalated into ruthless clashes. The bandits would seize any opportunity to intimidate witnesses, even during the trial. During one trial in 1920, an offender shouted to his wife from the dock — who had recognized a garment her husband had worn as one lost at the scene of the crime — that he would take his revenge for her testimony. In the same trial, one of the bandits went right up to a witness, stared at him, 'eyes ablaze', and said, 'Don't stand here telling lies, tell the truth!' Witnesses were clearly in a difficult predicament, eager to avoid a possible charge of perjury but cowed by the bandits' threats. Many steered a middle course, neither lying nor giving conclusive evidence.[30] The risk of criminals escaping from prison and coming to take their revenge could certainly not be discounted, given the percentage of escapes and the poor organization of the prison system.

Death sentences were carried out quite frequently, although this practice diminished in the twentieth century and was reserved for bandits who had killed someone in the course of a robbery. In 1893 the death sentences handed down for the well-known bandits Pitung, Dji-ih and their gang members were commuted into long terms of imprisonment, since the offence of which they had been found guilty (the robbery of Hadji Sapioen) had not been accompanied by any bloodshed.[31] Such criminals would generally receive sentences of 10 to 15 years' forced labour.[32] But in one of the few robberies targeting a European — Mr Van der Capelle, in 1903 — the perpetrators were put to death, even though no one had been killed or suffered serious injury.[33]

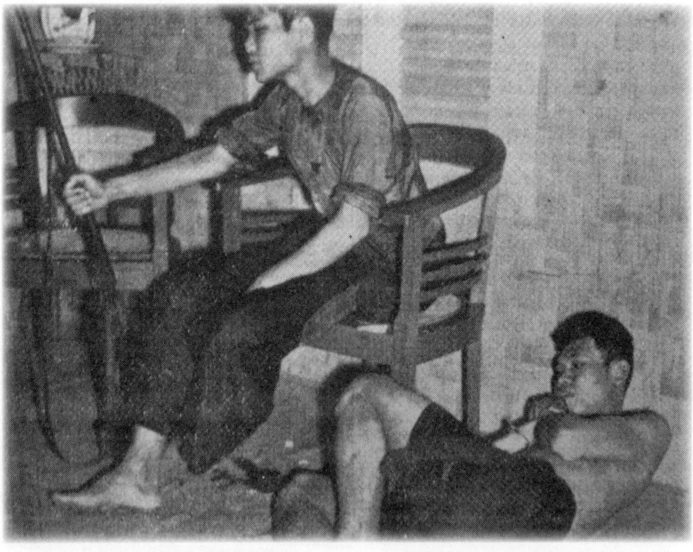

Illus. 5 Pa-I (lying down), a gang-member who was active around Cibarusa in 1936–7. (*Nieuws van den Dag voor Nederlandsch-Indië*, 5 April 1937)

Occupational hazards: Prison

Prisons in the Dutch East Indies did not function in the same way as those in Europe. While the latter emphasized the inculcation of discipline, rehabilitating criminals through work and removing them from pernicious surroundings, this scarcely applied in the colonies. It was believed that 'Orientals' were not capable of change or improvement. Peter Zinoman's book *The Colonial Bastille* describes the corruption and rife that held sway in Vietnamese prisons under French rule.[34] A.N.M. Bruinink-Dalang's study *Het penitentiair stelsel in Nederlandsch-Indië van 1905 tot 1940* suggests that the Dutch colonists took a more ambitious approach in setting up their own prison system. From 1905 onwards, the colony's judicial circles contained some at least who favoured convicts being assigned useful work in prison, a form of probation and aftercare, and differentiating between types of criminals. Still, Bruinink-Dalang concedes that plans to improve prison conditions often foundered for lack of resources and that some prisoners were thought to be beyond redemption.[35]

Many of the robbers probably belonged to the latter group. In addition, work was very important in the colonial system, so it would have been strange to exempt precisely those who had been found guilty of a crime. Many high-profile bandits who were believed to pose a high security risk were sentenced to forced labour again and again. Of the notorious robber Gantang, described at length in another part of this book, it was said that it was a waste to have such a strong man idling in a cell when he might be so productive in a chain gang.[36]

Because of the extreme heat, it was uncommon for prisoners to be locked into cells in the Dutch East Indies. The large prison in Glodok, Batavia, was known for its very informal regime. Shopkeepers threw food over the walls for the inmates, and guards and prisoners were on quite friendly terms.[37] One poem or *rancak* relating the experience of an 'ordinary Indonesian' sent to a colonial prison focuses largely on the difficulty of getting used to different mealtimes, the rules about visits, homesickness, and quarrels about cigarettes.[38] For this category of offenders — who had been sent to prison for fighting or breaches of employment contracts — prison will not have been so very different from their ordinary everyday lives, which were also dominated by coercion and poverty.[39]

Bruinink-Darlang's study of the penal system in the Dutch East Indies includes a description of prison conditions. Unfortunately, it is based primarily on government reports and tells us little (nor indeed does it claim to do so) about prisoners' conduct. For instance, her study does not tell us about the risks run by wealthy Indonesians — including robbers — of being terrorized by the staff. The guards at the Cipinang prison in Batavia made these wealthy detainees work hard and ill-treated them until the detainees' relatives sent an appropriate bribe. Glodok had its own variation on this theme. The prisoners who failed to pay were sent to the Outer Islands, which often meant a doubling of their sentence. Those who did pay were given light work to do in the prison.[40]

The percentage of escapes was extremely high, partly because prisoners were not held in isolation. Here is a description published in the *Nederlandsch-Indische Politiegids* of the cell from which the bandit Lias had escaped.

> I call it a cell, but the space in which they were confined does not merit this name, as we shall see. The room is quite spacious, 4.5 metres high and furnished with long wooden beds; the ceiling is made primarily of planks, the rest consisting of pine timbers; immediately above this is the roof. A room of this kind has to accommodate twelve prisoners, who do not therefore have to be acrobats to escape from it. One of the timbers had been sawn through, a few roof tiles had been displaced, and two large knives were found in the attic, one of which had been fashioned into a saw.[41]

According to the official statistics, 168 detainees escaped from the prison on Java in 1925 while another 554 escaped from forced labour outside the premises. Cipinang penal institution near Meester Cornelis, with 3,000 inmates, witnessed an average of one escape every day.[42] There were calls for Javanese criminals to be transferred to prisons elsewhere, to reduce the risk of their receiving help from sympathetic locals.[43] But the number of escapes was also high outside Java, especially among those doing forced labour. A notable example is Ombilin coalmine at Sawah Lunto on Sumatra, a place as notorious for the number of escapes as for its appalling working conditions.[44] Guarding all the mine's many exits was simply not feasible.

We can trace the prison careers of some of Batavia's most notorious bandits in the Ombilin mine.[45] The most important one, perhaps was Oesoep, a gang leader in Batavia around 1920, who was feared even more, perhaps, than Pitung or Gantang. Oesoep was arrested several times and sent to Glodok and the Ombilin mine at Sawah Lunto, but managed to escape every time, apparently with the aid of his large network of acquaintances and business associates. He had built up this network with his distinctive, gentlemanly demeanour. A fluent speaker of Dutch, Malay and Arabic, he possessed many friends not only in Batavia, but also far further afield, which simplified his escapes. After his escape from Sawah Lunto he returned to the city, where he took charge of a gang of brigands in Pasar Baru, Kali Pasir, Matraman and Menteng. Another example is the bandit Djabar, sentenced to ten years in Sawah Lunto. He too escaped and returned to Batavia, where he resumed his former activities together with accomplices in Meester Cornelis.

The presence of a large contingent of prisoners in Ombilin placed its stamp on the rest of the workforce, which consisted of contract workers and free employees. Relations between these groups were generally tense, with rivals jostling for possession of scarce resources such as food, cigarettes, money and sex (with men as well as women) and trying to secure the lightest form of work in the mine. Contact between the two groups generally ended in violent clashes, with the convicts frequently assailing their opponents with knives or other sharp objects. It was not uncommon for such incidents to end in murder. Fellow-prisoners reported that men such as Oesoep and Djabar scarcely worried about such matters, or about the punishments they might incur, since they possessed *ilmu kebal*, a form of supernatural invulnerability. Contract workers had to choose between running away or adapting to the harsh criminal milieu. The records show that contract employees who worked in the Ombilin mine for extended periods of time ended up committing violent crimes themselves. The law of the jungle prevailed. The most powerful villains stole food from others, or from the distribution point, to supplement their meagre prison rations, as a result of which some fellow-prisoners might be left with nothing to eat at all.[46]

From documentary sources on prison reform in the Dutch East Indies (*Verslagen van de Hervormingen van het Gevangeniswezen in Nederlandsch-Indië*; published for several years from 1921 onwards) we can derive statistics on numbers of escaped forced labourers as well as contract labourers and free employees who absconded from a variety of places, including the Ombilin mine at Sawah Lunto. On average, several men escaped every day, though most were tracked down in the vicinity and returned to the place of work. The growing numbers not only of escapees but also of those who were brought back in a specific period led the authorities to conclude that agreements had been made between prisoners and guards. Since the latter were given a bonus for each returned prisoner, the money could be divided up and make a useful source of income for guards and prisoners alike.[47]

These conditions meant that numerous bandits spent varying periods of time in different prisons. This must have been a matter of concern for spies and prosecution witnesses, who could never feel safe from reprisals. All in all, before 1920 bandits ran little risk of being caught at all. The risk of prosecution resulting in a conviction was smaller still, given the abundance of procedural errors. Finally, the proportion of escapes was very high. All these factors impeded efforts to combat *rampok* and undermined the respect in which the colonial authorities were held.

Even so, the bandits' subjective perception was that robbery was fraught with grave risks, judging by the voice of a 'brigand' in the following (freely translated) verse fragment:

> Well choosing the *jago*'s path is not the wisest way.
> A few thousand *rupiah* will not get you through the day.
> The soldiers and the Company, officials are your foes.
> Simple souls like us can't win, look at clever Pitung's woes.
>
> Let's forget the *jago*'s way and choose the peasant's life.
> A *jago* will soon find the whole Company gives him strife.
> We'll stay our grimy selves, we'll not change, I'll be bound,
> Content with what we have, and our families safe and sound.[48]

CHAPTER 3

The Organizational Structure of Criminal Gangs

This chapter will examine the factors that helped to make robbery a lucrative occupation. The individualism of indigenous entrepreneurs, which has been identified as a major stumbling-block in building up a successful business, proved less of an obstacle when it came to the business of robbery. The lack of organizational structure in robbers' gangs, while limiting the profitability of their activities, also had certain advantages. Viewing robbery from the perspective of a business enterprise can shed new light on the robbers' motives and their role in society.

Indigenous entrepreneurs, the mafia, and robbery as a business

Indigenous entrepreneurship fared poorly in the colonial period. Indigenous businessmen could scarcely compete with the thriving commercial operations run by the Chinese minority. Colonial commentators blamed their lack of success on factors ranging from the climate (even though the heat was felt by everyone) to the islanders' happy-go-lucky attitude and their lack of zest for saving money. In retrospect, several authors, including Christine Dobbin and Clifford Geertz, cite commercial jealousy and individualism as factors that prejudiced working relationships and mutual trust.[1] To this might be added Francis Fukuyama's theory that cultural and social criteria such as the presence or absence of trust in business associates have an impact on economic activity.[2]

An added factor is that in any society, there is probably less mutual trust among criminals than in the population at large. High levels of mutual suspicion are often the Achilles' heel of criminal organizations. While the success of an operation could yield large profits, its failure could have huge consequences and even cost someone his life. Criminal organizations — like the regular commercial sector — have a variety of mechanisms for forging bonds of trust. Cohesive factors include membership of the same extended family, shared ethnic origins, and a range of common rituals. The 'success story' of the Italian mafia, for instance, is one in which mutual trust is sustained by the family and a related, specific system of shared values. Among Jewish gangs, shared ethnic origins forged bonds of solidarity.[3]

The dacoits and thugs of India likewise illustrate the importance of clans as the cohesive factor. Thugs in particular (bandits who strangled their victims before robbing them), knew the family backgrounds of all gang members to several generations. Such family ties, along with various rituals and a strict vow of secrecy, acted for a long time as a powerful shield against the outside world. Yet it appears that this strong social cohesion actually made it easier for the authorities of British India to combat these Indian gangs once they had penetrated a group. For in the mid-nineteenth century it became possible to completely eradicate the criminal activities of the dacoits and thugs by a combination of law enforcement and providing alternative ways of making a living. Javanese criminals did not use many of the above ways of cementing internal ties.[4]

Although the nuclear family was an important organizational unity in the Javanese countryside, criminals frequently maintained close ties with a large extended family, including concubines and mistresses. According to D.H. Meijer, concubines served to widen and consolidate territorial influence. The bandit would set up social networks around each of these women, who sometimes lived tens of miles apart.[5] On the other hand, the sons and daughters who were born from these relationships did not inherit their father's business.

The colonial literature always emphasizes the loose relationships that existed in these circles, and indeed my study of the sources has not yielded a single case of enduring cooperation between two bandits. In Chapter 9, I shall discuss the fierce struggle that erupted between gang leaders when external factors placed their operations under strain.

Unlike the Indian dacoits, robbers in the Dutch East Indies did not come from a single ethnic group. Although certain kampongs in the vicinity of Batavia had a reputation for breeding bandits, many robbers came from elsewhere. Certain cohesive elements may have included teacher-pupil ties (for instance in the martial arts) and the guild-like cooperation that existed among *jagos*. This latter point, however, relies heavily on the nineteenth-century tales of *jagos* in the Javanese countryside as related by Amand, for instance, and it may not have applied to the Batavian bandits of the twentieth century.[6]

Meijer (1949) has described the quicksand on which indigenous gang members built their careers. He focuses primarily on gangs of fish-thieves and the extortioners who operated around coconut plantations. According to Meijer, magic and mythologization were of little consequence as cohesive factors in Javanese gangs. Time and again the gang leader would have to prove himself, and his arrest was taken as a sign that his powers had deserted him. He would therefore immediately be succeeded by one of his rivals. Meijer describes this pattern as generating an atmosphere of unremitting competition among criminals.[7]

In these conflicts, treachery between teacher and pupil or among robbers is a recurrent theme of bandit literature in the Dutch East Indies.[8] Although there seem to have been few conflicts between bandits in the period 1870–1930, full-scale 'gang wars' erupted in the 1930s.[9] On the other hand, memoires and newspaper accounts contain reports of robbers who adhered to the *mores* of the criminal world by refusing to say a word to the police about their accomplices, even when badly wounded.[10] 'Grassing' was punished here as ruthlessly as it was elsewhere. Those who refused to talk could rest assured that their families would be well cared for.

While the relatively high indigenous level of mutual suspicion in the society of the Dutch East Indies might have provided a good breeding-ground for the mafia, here too, individualism was an obstacle. I should add that I am using Gambetta's definition of the term 'mafia' here, as an industry that sells private protection.[11] In other words, the mafia is distinct from gangs of bandits, who steal people's property by force or intimidation, in that it deals in protection rather than violence. The two forms of crime may coexist, as in Sicily, in which case the mafia protects its clients from the thieves. Still, the thieves are sometimes obliged to seek protection from the same mafia, given that thieves, who cannot appeal to the police or other authorities responsible for keeping order, are more in need of such protection than anyone else.[12] This means that mafia can inject a sustained atmosphere of fear into society, generating a vicious circle of mutual suspicion.

Whether this description of mafia-like structures applied to the nineteenth-century Ommelanden, as the *Bataviaasch Nieuwsblad* and *Locomotief* both claimed, is however open to question.[13] There is an illuminating account by an inhabitant of those regions in a Malay newspaper. He relates that the people of the kampong had been visited successively by *rampok* gangs, the village chief, the *preman* of the local overlord, a tax official, religious leaders and finally the *jago*.[14] All these visitors were essentially vying with one another to provide protection in return for money (except for the *rampok* gang, who took money without providing anything in return). The great diversity of formal and informal protectors suggests that Indonesia did not possess a mafia, in the sense of a single dominant network. It seems likely that the indigenous community in the Ommelanden was so unstable that it could not support a thriving mafia.[15]

This instability had the effect of creating more scope for bandits. *Rampok* thrived in such conditions. In contrast to the mafia, the drugs trade and prostitution, the bandits' business operations were scarcely undermined by extreme individualism. By their very nature, robberies called for incidental, flexible forms of cooperation that could be adjusted to suit the circumstances. So the bandits of the Ommelanden operated in cooperative frameworks that were constantly fluctuating. They did not have to relinquish their independence, collaborating only when the occasion arose. Whenever possible, bandits preferred to work in complete autonomy, on their own conditions.[16]

The organization of a robbery

According to the descriptions in daily newspapers, gangs of robbers usually operated with two or three leaders, who gathered a rather loose collection of others around them. They were therefore more like networks than gangs. It seems that robbers often met on some festive occasion. The robbery in Anyer, which yielded pickings of 4,000 guilders, was planned at a party given by a *mandoer* or foreman in Tangerang. The raucous revelry was a good cover for the conspiratorial plans of a group of men who were probably of dubious reputation. Performances of Eurasian and indigenous theatre were also a magnet for bandits. The words *stamboel* and *wayang* crop up with great regularity in witness statements. *Stamboel* performances were surrounded by diverse forms of entertainment that provided opportunities for lavish spending sprees.[17] Much later, cinemas too would be incorporated into the bandits' lives. Robbers were so familiar with the repertoire of variety shows that on one occasion a gang set off towards a robbery loudly singing *krontjong* songs.[18]

Robberies were organized by a hard core of only three or four men, with others being recruited later. The same structure applied to *ketjoe* gangs: groups of ten to fifteen men who would ransack a whole group of houses at a time in the Principalities area of Java.[19]

Rampok gangs generally consisted of about five men, three or four of whom were armed with revolvers. The robbers had to seek prior 'permission' for the robbery from the leading *jago* in the district of the robbery. At least, such was the claim of Chief Detective Buwalda during a case against Sapri, Liham, Djoemaan, Saaba Entjak (who was still at large),[20] Moesanip and Djelane, who were all charged with robbing a Japanese shop in Kramat. In this incident, three Japanese men who had pursued the robbers had been shot. Buwalda had subsequently rounded up the 'usual suspects' from the neighbourhood as well as the *jago* Djelane, who he believed must have known what was going on. In fact witnesses claimed to have seen Djelane near the shop during the robbery, and some even stated that he had fired at the Japanese pursuers. Other witnesses contradicted this testimony, however. The statement made by a European woman, Georgine Freys, settled the matter. She gave Djelane an alibi, telling the court that on the night of the robbery he had been at her home; they had together tended the sick daughter of the *babu*, who was Djelane's friend.

Reading the records of the trial, one has the constant impression that Djelane was bound to emerge unscathed. At every stage, he seemed to proceed just a little more shrewdly than the rest of the gang. Not only did he provide himself with a 'European alibi', but he even married the *babu*'s daughter, freeing her from the obligation to testify. While other gang members threatened the witnesses with 'glittering eyes', Djelane continued to draw the witnesses' attention to inconsistencies in their testimony and to point out procedural errors to the judge. Unsurprisingly then, two of the robbers were convicted — one to life imprisonment and the other to 15 years. The others, including Djelane, were acquitted.[21]

This account reveals an important difference between bandits and *jagos*. The latter's involvement in robberies was more oblique. Rooted in their local community, they could rely on the support of influential people in their surroundings. This did not apply to bandits. Anton Blok gives the following account of the difference between a *mafioso* (whose position is somewhat comparable to that of the *jago*) and a bandit:

> The latter has to hide from the law since he does not have his cards in good order. The former, in his role of accomplice (*manutengolo*) has his cards *in regola*: no evidence can or will be produced against him.[22]

In general, the majority of crime took place in harvest time,[23] when people tended to have more money at home. Newspaper reports about *rampok*, however, are found primarily in the dark rain season from October to February; the bandits took advantage of the fact that the roads were wet and often barely passable. Ramadan was another period that saw a rise in all kinds of crime. It was a time when some people felt a need for extra spending money while others had a lot of ready cash in their homes. If Ramadan coincided with the rain season, we see a sharp peak in *rampok* incidents. Interestingly, the reports also show that robberies frequently occurred in 'clusters'. This creates the impression that certain nights were particularly favourable for *rampok*. Alternatively, such clusters may simply reflect an editorial decision to devote more space to the rise in crime. In any case, the bandits appear to have had a preference for weekend nights,[24] possibly because shopkeepers would have more money to steal, since their customers would just have used their weekly wages to pay off any outstanding debts.

Appendix IV enumerates the cases of *rampok* in the peak years of 1902, 1907, 1908 and 1920, based on reports in the *Bataviaasch Nieuwsblad.* The use of this newspaper is not without certain objections. First, an ordinary robbery with spoils amounting to 25 guilders and in which the victim offered no resistance, perpetrated in some remote region of the Ommelanden, was no longer considered news at all:

> It may be regarded as a curious phenomenon that an offence of this kind, a robbery in the vicinity of Buitenzorg, the seat of the Governor-General, one in which a true battle erupted between the auxiliary police and the brigands, the gang leader was fatally wounded and a native official suffered minor injuries, was reported in the newspapers merely in a plain, brief little report under the heading 'miscellaneous news'. Nor is it at all exceptional for reports of this kind to be communicated in the same indifferent fashion, in other newspapers too. The impartial reader therefore receives the impression, if only through the way in which the diverse incidents of this kind are reported, that a certain fatigue has set in regarding the fight to suppress these abuses, which could quite easily be stamped out. That

> the press, knowing that it is of little consequence, does not even make a particular effort to stay informed about the robberies, which are so frequent in the area.[25]

Apparently, then, the newspapers only reported robberies that were remarkable in some way. For instance, in 1902 the *Bataviaasch Nieuwsblad* only reported 18 robberies out of the 144 recorded in colonial statistics. In the year 1920, 28 of the 157 were reported.

Sometimes a case of *rampok* was reported because it had been accompanied by an excessive use of force, leaving people dead or injured. Cases in which Europeans were among the victims or bandits were also bound to be given press coverage. Another factor was the distance to the main office of the *Bataviaasch Nieuwsblad.* News of incidents that had taken place in remote parts of the Ommelanden, even extremely violent robberies involving large sums of money, sometimes did not reach the paper for a long time, if at all. A selection of those that did find their way into the newspapers is included in Appendix IV. These cautionary remarks should be taken into account in any attempt to derive any statistical conclusions from the reports.

According to the newspaper accounts, most bandits came from Meester Cornelis (known today as Kramat Jati), Kebayoran (nowadays an affluent neighbourhood), Bekasi and Tangerang. The latter, it may be added, are crime-ridden districts to this day. In colonial times, the people of Meester Cornelis had the most unsavoury reputation.[26]

Another dominant theme in newspaper reports was the belief that robbers were concentrated in a number of notorious kampongs and strongholds. This belief frequently led journalists to use strong language regarding the fight against *rampok*, proposing the 'extermination ... of the dens of thieves'[27] or a manhunt followed by a siege.[28]

From his research on Philippine gangs, Greg Bankoff concludes that banditry only flourishes in certain specific geographical conditions. In the provinces of Cavite and Camarines Sur, in the south of the island of Luzon, he claims that banditry was embedded in the landscape, a landscape consisting of forests, deep rivers and volcanic mountains, which he believes has a strong influence on human behaviour.[29] The bandits of the Malay Archipelago may have profited from the landscape in a similar way, although it has to be said that completely different natural surroundings do not appear to have prevented them from pursuing their chosen occupation. The woods near Batavia provided hiding-places,[30] but kampongs in the vast coastal rice-fields also served as brigand bases — the flatness of the land had the advantage of making it possible to see law enforcement officers coming from miles away.[31]

In response to questions from their superiors about the many cases of *rampok* in and around Batavia, the Assistant Residents of Meester Cornelis, Tangerang and Buitenzorg submitted a report on this problem in their districts in 1904.[32] This yielded documents that, if few in number, are of great significance for this book, since they contradict many of the stories that appeared in the press. One difference, for instance, is that while the press tended to posit that much crime could be traced to a single master bandit, the reports suggest that numerous men in the Ommelanden were involved in robbery in varying degrees as a supplementary source of income. One subject about which the reports and newspaper accounts concur is the use of firearms. The report on Buitenzorg states that firearms played a role in 11 out of 33 cases of *rampok* there. Other weapons used included machetes or *goloks*. The guns were sometimes fired, but in none of the cases in these reports was any victim actually hit. The robbers themselves were shot in three cases, however — by fellow gang members!

The ill-gotten gains ranged from a mere pittance to large sums of money. In Buitenzorg, 7 of the 33 cases involved more than 200 guilders, the highest sum being 4,000 guilders. In four cases, the sum was between 100 and 200 guilders, leaving 17 in which the amount stolen was less than 100 guilders. In Meester Cornelis the money seized was considerably less. In 10 out of 44 cases, the robbers left with less than 10 guilders. But in this district, robbers were 'people for whom it is a sport to go out robbing and stealing', according to Assistant Resident J.R. Couperus of Meester Cornelis, a cousin of the famous novelist Louis Couperus.[33]

When the addresses of the robbers are compared to those of the victims, it is striking to see that many robbers lived within ten kilometres' radius from their victims' homes.[34] In fact, those robbed would frequently assert that they were 'acquainted' with the perpetrators. Other sources — newspapers for instance — reveal that the criminals were also similar to their victims in terms of social origin. For instance, indigenous bandits often robbed victims of the same ethnic origin. When the victims were Chinese, there were frequently Chinese robbers among the gang. In the few cases targeting Europeans, a European bandit was almost always involved. This suggests that the percentage of European and Chinese robbers may well have corresponded roughly to the percentage they made up of the population as a whole.

The Assistant Residents' reports also reveal the large number of people who were involved in robberies. None of the 44 robberies in Meester Cornelis or the 33 in Buitenzorg involved the same perpetrators. This means that, based on an average of five criminals for each incident, the combined total of 77 robberies in these two locations in 1903 were committed by 385 men (and a single woman). It is therefore improbable that they were masterminded by a single gang leader, as some newspaper accounts suggested. In any case, it is clear that the Batavian robbers' world consisted of both 'small' and 'large' bandits.

According to the government reports, most of the perpetrators were registered as farmers. Other sources reveal that many of them were middle-aged. Newspaper reports frequently omitted to mention the criminals' age, but one account gives the ages of the gang members involved in a robbery near Buitenzorg in 1902 as 35, 35, 32, 50, 44 and 30.[35] Records of appeals for clemency similarly show that the bandits were aged between 30 and 55. Pitung's comrade-in-arms, Dji-ih, was 35 years of age.[36] So the relatively serious cases of *rampok*, the ones that were reported in the newspapers or that led to stiff sentences, tended to involve middle-aged men.[37] When one bears in mind the life expectancy that applied at the time, robbers who were in their fifties, in any case, can be said to have reached quite a ripe old age. This means that the bandits who operated in the Batavia region were in a different phase of life than similar criminals operating in other parts of the world. We may recall Hobsbawm's emphasis on the link between banditry and adolescence.[38]

The Assistant Residents' reports further note that many of the victims of these crimes were farmers, while a substantial number were merchants of some kind, and women too were frequent targets. We also read that the police frequently sought to recover stolen property, with some degree of success, from the robbers' female accomplices. The fact that capital was found in the possession of women cannot be detached from the position of women in Batavian society.[39] Movable and immovable property was sometimes entrusted to women because men — especially robbers — tended to lead more peripatetic lives.

We have already seen that the newspaper image of robbers differed significantly from the picture that emerges from the reports. While the press continued to assume that robberies could be traced to a single master criminal, the government reports document the existence of horizontal networks. The officials of the internal administration department presented *rampok* as a universal fact of life in the region, and saw every inhabitant of the Ommelanden as a potential brigand. The fact that perpetrators and victims did not generally live very far apart confirms that the causes of *rampok* should be sought quite literally close to home. Newspaper reports frequently note that the victims had recognized the perpetrators as acquaintances.[40] This contradicts the picture of a charismatic, itinerant captain of crime.

Robbery and other forms of crime

Robbers who operated on a relatively large scale also frequently indulged in extortion, demanding money from wealthy inhabitants of the Ommelanden in return for a pledge not to rob them. Needless to say, payment would not keep other gangs at bay. The dividing-line between *jago* and bandit is diffuse here, and the brigands' *modus operandi* appears to be different from that of the mafia.

Bandits were seldom involved in other kinds of crime: pickpocketing and non-violent burglary, for instance, evidently called for a different range of skills. The only exception was highway robbery and 'mugging', which took place along market roads and sometimes in the city of Batavia. Even so, these latter types of crime differed in that they were never carried out by more than two perpetrators and seldom involved firearms. On the other hand, the use of various kinds of knives meant that these attacks were in fact more violent than the robbery of homes at night.

On Java, cattle theft was a major cause of concern in the nineteenth and later twentieth century. It seems that the bandits of Batavia did not take part in this activity, however. The rise of private estates precluded the existence of small farmers with one draught animal, with the result that there was no quarry for cattle thieves.[41] It may be noted that this corresponds to the findings for the same period in the British colony of Ceylon (now Sri Lanka), where the introduction of a plantation economy eradicated cattle theft around 1900.[42]

Robbers and the public authorities

That the robbers maintained close ties with local administrative officials was an open secret. In his satirical columns *Brieven van Opheffer* the former Resident Gonggrijp presents a fictional resident who checks two of his police officers after sending them off to work in the surrounding villages:

> There were some great villains there. I instructed my chief officer to watch the movements of one Kario, a notorious rogue from the *desa* of Padang, and the regular officer to do the same with Pawirono, a fancy customer from the *desa* of Pengkol: 'You will watch all their movements on the sly; I want to know exactly what they get up to, mind! I have every confidence in your sharp nose as detectives. You have watched over me for so long now, it's time for you to watch over a real scoundrel.' The detectives went on their way. For some time I heard nothing from them. One fine moonlit night a certain unease took possession of me, so I called for my sturdy steed Piet to be saddled and set off towards the *desa* of Padang. The sweet tones of the gamelan reached my ears from some distance away, and they proved to emanate from the house of Kario, the villain, who was hosting a large wedding party. The watchful eye of my chief officer was evidently not posing much of a problem there. Charming little bride; but who the devil is the bridegroom sitting over there? No less a person than my very own chief officer! I cannot see his expression, since he is bent over so deeply, but … who are those other two who are also bent over? They are the assistant *wedono* Padoeka and the *mantri* police officer Doro. To keep close guard and to be sure that Kario was not out of his sight for a minute, my chief officer had simply moved in with Kario, who, being a great villain, was a prosperous man; their friendship had become so cordial that he had been promoted to son-in-law. When such a prominent villain throws a wedding feast, the deputy district chief and the *mantri* cannot decline to attend. Kario was generally courteous enough to take a small share of the loot to the assistant *wedono*; the money came from the public coffers, and the *mantri* police thought this a delightful way to proceed. They were almost always able to solve the case, since Kario usually took part in the robberies and was really a fine fellow; he did not like to embarrass the police, and was actually happy to help. My chief officer declared that the whole thing was his own clever plan.[43]

There are certainly documented cases of lower-ranking administrative officials assisting the 'leading' robbers who were active around 1920 — much to the indignation of European and Eurasian journalists. In the case of the robbery in Anyer, for instance, the gang was assembled at a party thrown by the *mandoer*. We have already seen that parties were not just occasions for innocent revelry; they were frequently used to plan robberies. So it is not strange that the administrative authorities often banned parties in problem districts.

The robbers sometimes actually borrowed the revolvers they used during their *rampok* escapades from lower administrative officials, or asked an official to take care of them afterwards in case their homes were searched. The gang leader Oesoep was a house guest of the neighbourhood officer of Menteng for several days prior to his arrest in 1920.[44] When these whereabouts became known and the neighbourhood officer heard that Oesoep was going to be arrested, he sent word that the robber had already left. On other occasions, robbers would leave their ill-gotten gains with the authorities for safe keeping. The house of the headman of a known bandit's village was found to be overflowing with jewellery and wrist-watches after a robbery targeting the jeweller Steuerwald.[45]

Most robbers operated outside the official system, but the largest ones frequently maintained ties with the authorities. Indeed, it seems that the larger a criminal's sphere of operations, the more deeply entrenched he was in the colonial administration. The criminal referred to above as R possessed a substantial network. His agent or *prokureur-bamboe* was the brother of a police officer in the district in which he was active, Babalam. During the investigation of several cattle thefts in this area in which R was implicated, the case files were mysteriously consumed by white ants. The local deputy administrative official was the agent's son-in-law, and it was he who sabotaged the investigation by the military police and criminal investigation department in Bekasi by submitting a succession of complaints about the police's actions. The agent's family network also included the indigenous chief public prosecutor in Batavia.[46]

A wealthy criminal in the Dutch East Indies had just as much need of a good lawyer as his later counterpart in New York. This was the task of the agent or *prokureur-bamboe*, roughly equivalent to the Italian *consigliere*. Although this agent's work receives little attention in the literature, it was frequently of great importance to the judicial process.

But a robber of R's rank would generally also require assistance in higher places; R was assisted by a well-known European firm of lawyers in Batavia, a firm that was at one point accused of attempting to bribe officials. The bandit's final indispensable aid was a private executioner. There was no need for R to leave his home to avenge himself on defaulting debtors or those who had thwarted him in some way: for the sum of 200 guilders, his hit-man would shoot and kill the person concerned. Actions of this kind provided protection from spies or attacks by fellow bandits.

Journalists always wrote in tones of indignation about the ties that existed between lower-ranking administrative officials and bandits, and reported on them at length. It is not easy to establish how extensive these ties were. It must be borne in mind that the lowest rank of officials consisted of men such as untrained neighbourhood officers, who received little or no remuneration and were recruited directly from village communities. The lack of pay combined with their strong local ties made them vulnerable to corruption. Meanwhile, it was primarily the middle ranks of policemen and administrative officials, including the *camats*, *demangs* and assistant *demangs*, who were deployed to combat the robbers. It was they who made arrests, in circumstances that frequently claimed casualties. In situations of this kind, the internal struggle was frequently very fierce.

Jagos and robbers

Given the central role assigned to the *jago* in almost all literature on crime in the Dutch East Indies and even in present-day Indonesia, it makes sense to review this subject in the historiography and to clarify the relations that existed between bandits and *jagos*. The Dutch historian Kees van Dijk published an article in 2003, 'Magic and Violence', enumerating the many different ways in which the role of the *jago* has been viewed down to the present day. He starts off with more than ten literal meanings derived from various dictionaries, including 'champion', 'villain', 'charismatic leader', 'forefighter', 'leader', 'favourite', 'chief' and 'ringleader'.[47]

Clearly, the term *jago* has been construed in diverse, possibly overlapping, ways in different periods. Van Dijk has traced such differences in the scholarly literature on violence in the archipelago, generally in relation to Java as a whole but with frequent reference to the city of Batavia/Jakarta. Generally speaking, we find both negative and positive connotations. Van Dijk notes that *jagos* are frequently seen in negative terms, as villains who imperilled their own communities — powerful personalities who used force for the benefit of the colonial powers and the related local elite. According to this view they were instruments in the service of the public authorities, who were allowed a certain discretionary latitude since the process of state formation was not yet complete.

A more positive connotation, one possibly favoured by non-historians, is that of the *jago* as the protector of his own community, a man who used his influence not to compel his community to bow to officialdom, but to defend the oppressed, a charismatic leader who played a role in the fight against colonialism and the traditional authorities who collaborated with the colonials. In this interpretation, the *jago* was a patriotic champion of the people who played a major role in the later struggle for Indonesia's independence.

Seeking to identify the sources for these interpretations, van Dijk has traced their usage back in time in the academic literature. The more positive view, which defines the *jago* as the adversary of colonialism and other forms of injustice and hence as the staunch champion of the people, is discussed at length in Rudolph Mrázek's study of the Indonesian soldiers who fought in 1945–65.[48] Mrázek builds on Benedict Anderson's approach to the *jago* in the 1960s. In Anderson's view, the *jago*'s authority derived from a mix of charisma, martial prowess and magical invulnerability,[49] a combination that instilled fear in kampong-dwellers as well as commanding their admiration. Anderson in turn based himself on the authoritative publication *Over het bendewezen op Java* (1949) by P.M. van Wulfften Palthe, even though the latter never mentions the word *jago*. D.H. Meijer, however, commenting on van Wulfften Palthe's work and adding supplementary information, does use the term.[50] John Smail too discusses the *jago*, and distinguishes between an urban and a rural type. While the former was in his view very similar to the normal Western criminal, the rural *jago*, operating as the head of a gang, was an entirely different species, someone who possessed an extraordinary range of knowledge and skills and radiated an air of mystery. Rural gangs led by a *jago* could be seen as an institution with their own specific place in society, according to Smail.[51]

Another researcher whose work helped to anchor the concept of the *jago* in the academic literature is Onghokham. This Chinese-Indonesian historian saw the *jago* in colonial Java as far more than an ordinary criminal. In his view, *jago* was a more general term for a broker or someone who mediates in violence. Like Smail's comments on the rural *jago*, Onghokham emphasizes the man's magical powers.[52] However, Onghokham uses a very wide definition of the *jago*, which can include anyone from indigenous administrators to religious instructors and pilgrims on their way to Mecca.

Henk Schulte Nordholt does not go that far, but he nonetheless discusses the *jago* in the terms proposed by Onghokham.[53] Schulte Nordholt too refers to the *jago* as the 'insolent muscleman' as well as a broker or mediator in violence with magical powers.[54] And he too relies on sources that do not necessarily use the term *jago* explicitly, but merely refer to 'devious characters'.[55] Such discussions have had the effect of constantly broadening the definition of the *jago*. Schulte Nordholt posits a link between the behaviour of *jagos* in the Javanese hinterland and the failure of the colonial state to maintain law and order in rural areas.[56] He sees *jagos* as men who occupied the vacuum that arose with the establishment of the colonial state. The indigenous colonial authorities used *jagos* to establish and maintain their authority. According to this theory, it was the state's failure that created the enabling conditions for the rise of jagoism and crime: indeed, *jagos* can be seen as an extension of the authorities, which terrorized and also robbed the local population.

Van Dijk argues that the converse may also be true, namely that it was precisely the state's poor law enforcement mechanisms that compelled the local population to arrange their own protection. In this view, *jagos* and criminals were rather aligned *against* the state. For instance, it may have been they who set fire to estates, the clearest possible symbols of the colonial state. This line of reasoning defines the *jago* not as the oppressors' accomplice but quite the opposite, as the people's resistance hero, the true patriot.[57] Interestingly, the scholar Michael Adas maintains that a similar peasant resistance was found in earlier, pre-colonial, times.[58] This suggests that such action by *jagos* — if we wish to adhere to this term — was not directly related to the colonial state, but was actually characteristic of Javanese society down the ages. According to Adas, colonial states in Southeast Asia probably had better systems for preserving law and order than their pre-colonial predecessors.[59] In this approach to the study of *jagos*, crime and resistance, the focus is less on the colonial state than on the society of the archipelago.

In his enumeration of paraphrases and the use of unclear terminology in the work of other scholars, van Dijk overlooks Robert Cribb. In Cribb's *Gangsters and Revolutionaries* we encounter a certain casualness in references to the different purveyors of violence. He seems to use the word 'gangsters' for people ranging from those who commit petty crime to robbers, but also for estate managers or stewards.[60] This nebulous and inconsistent terminology is not helpful in the context of a debate about crime.

Most of the authors cited by van Dijk adhere to a kind of mafia theory for the rural hinterland, revolving around the figure of the *jago*. How such stewards indulged in robbery 'in their spare time', as it were, is not entirely clear. But as I have argued, the general literature on the mafia shows that robbery was a completely different 'business'.[61]

I would endorse van Dijk's appeal for more clarity in definitions. I too encountered a very different classification of crime in reading the colonial press than in the contemporary literature as briefly reviewed above. However, my own method for testing the validity of the contemporary meanings differs from that chosen by van Dijk. In this book I shall analyze the discourse that shaped the image of colonial (in this case Javanese) crime, in which robbery eventually emerged as an inextricable element of the colonial order. A kind of 'mafia hypothesis' of Javanese society arose quite early, towards the end of the nineteenth century, when the *Bataviaasch Nieuwsblad*, for instance, started including reports on 'our mafia'. The idea that some individuals acted as brokers in violence was adopted by Onghokham, Henk Schulte Nordholt and Robert Cribb.

My own research yields — for Batavia and the surrounding area at any rate — a more differentiated picture of violence, in which there was no powerful 'broker' in the use of force. Rather than placing the *jago* at the centre of the world of crime and violence, this book is predicated on a more varied picture — one that is often proposed by Indonesians themselves — of the illegal or informal side of the society in and around Batavia. The entire concept of the *jago* seems to stem from echoes of the work of a mere handful of writers, most notably van Wulfften Palthe and Meijer, both of whom relied in turn on the late nineteenth- and early twentieth-century discourse on colonial force. Bandits maintained few if any relationships with colonial officialdom. They naturally benefited from its shortcomings, most notably from the lack of a sound law and order system. As we shall see, the genealogy that runs from pre-colonial pretenders to the throne by way of *jagos* in the Forced Cultivation System to social bandits and onward to the Pemoeda youth organization branched out in several different directions.

CHAPTER 4

Firearms

Judging by the available statistics, the Europeans in Batavia had little cause to fear that they might fall victim to robbery. If such a mishap did occur, however, it was certainly not unrealistic to fear that the robbers might use firearms. For the bandits ostentatiously displayed the modern weapons in their possession. The importance of firearms can scarcely be overstated. In the words of one author: 'All the robber needs, in the final analysis, is a revolver.'[1]

This chapter will discuss the trade in firearms as well as the symbolic and functional significance of firearms in the diverse sections of the population in Batavia and the surrounding area. After first exploring the differences in firearm use by bandits and other groups, we shall look at the implications for the role of banditry in the society of the Dutch East Indies.

The possession of firearms

The possession of firearms was very common among the European population of the Dutch East Indies. In principle, only Europeans, their descendants and East Indies officials did not require a licence. All others (*Vreemde Oosterlingen* or 'Foreign Orientals' as well as the indigenous population) were required to obtain a gun licence. And legislation introduced in 1828 made it mandatory to renew this licence every year.

Given the absence of an effective modern police service, the people took it upon themselves to protect their own lives and property. The landowner Du Perron, who lived on his estate a few miles outside the city, had an idiosyncratic way of maintaining security. If he heard noises in the garden in the evening, as he sat reading on the veranda, he would fire several shots with his pistol just above the height of a man's head, so as to frighten away anyone who happened to be there.[2]

Europeans did not have to keep to any rules when it came to the possession of firearms. They were above the law — or more accurately perhaps, the law did not exist in relation to them. To preserve law and order in Batavia, they used their firearms in different ways. They set up a militia, for instance — like those in the mother country — to put down any disturbances that might arise in the city. But the militia in Batavia commanded little respect, largely because Europeans were allowed to hire local servants to take their places in the night watch. In the period under discussion, the role of the Batavia militia was primarily ceremonial, and it was often the object of derision. Still, the tradition of civic vigilance that spawned the militia was deeply rooted in the European community. That became clear during robberies, when armed Europeans would sometimes appear and pursue the perpetrators.

The local population had their own mode of law enforcement, known as *ronda*, a Portuguese loan-word that probably refers to a very old, pre-colonial system. Today, the term *ronda* is used for a neighbourhood watch, in which the male members of the community take turns to serve. It is organized by the local chief, the *kepala RT*, and in previous centuries too, the neighbourhood officer was the driving force behind the *ronda*.[3]

In the latter half of the nineteenth century, a gunfight could be a big boost to a man's prestige. In 1864, the escaped convict Mangoon, a bandit, attacked a police station in the area of Batavia to free other prisoners and to kill certain much-despised police officers.[4] He rallied hundreds of supporters and set about plundering shops and houses in Tangerang, to the west of the city. But towards the evening the crowd dispersed, leaving Mangoon behind with just two of his comrades. This made him an easy target for the 30 soldiers commanded by the Assistant Resident of Tangerang who came to arrest them, and Mangoon was killed in the ensuing clash. Over the following few days, the Assistant Resident proudly went about the city boasting that he had fired the fatal shot himself. The city-dwellers received this news with open scepticism. No one thought it curious that the Assistant Resident sought to enhance his reputation by shooting dead a local bandit; they merely doubted whether he had actually done it.[5]

During one clash between state officials and Entong Gendut, a local rebel who had led a religious revolt in Meester Cornelis in 1916, it became clear that the status and authority of the state's representatives derived from their marksmanship. In fact this relationship was to some extent built into the bureaucracy. Entong received an abdominal gunshot wound when he and some comrades ambushed the police officers Reisner, Bodewitz and Brown. The official report of the incident states:

> The fact that Messrs Reisner, Bodewitz and Brown remained calm and were therefore able to shoot with a steady hand is greatly to their credit. These gentlemen therefore deserve a word of commendation.[6]

The provenance of firearms

Before 1870 firearms were imported on a large scale — pistols as well as rifles and carbines — and changed hands in a lively local trade.[7] They were sold to Europeans and indigenous officials. Around 1870 the arms trade started to pose more of a problem to the colonial authorities, amid the war in Aceh and other conflicts in the Outer Islands that were conquered during this period of colonial expansion. The regions left until last generally put up the stoutest resistance, frequently with the use of firearms. So restrictions were imposed on the legal trade at this point.

In addition, large numbers of firearms were smuggled into the territory by people of various nationalities, most notably Americans, Chinese and Buginese. Proas carrying contraband plied back and forth in the seas around northern Sumatra, Aceh and Singapore.

The Principalities on Java also played a key role in the illegal imports and transit of weapons. In these enclaves of Yogyakarta and Solo, the 1828 ban on gun imports for, and sales to, the local population had never been enforced, since these regions were governed by Javanese rulers.[8] Large numbers of revolvers of Belgian, German and American manufacture thus found their way to the indigenous population.

In addition, many weapons were manufactured locally. The Javanese population had long been familiar with firearms,[9] and it is clear from the earliest reports written by European newcomers to the archipelago that firearms including arquebuses and muskets were common. These probably came from other countries in the region, such as China, Japan, Siam (now Thailand) and Pegu (now Burma/Myanmar).[10] Even in the Mataram era (sixteenth and seventeenth centuries) Javanese smiths had been capable of producing and repairing firearms. In general, it is fair to say that firearms were modernized more rapidly than any other types of objects on Java.[11] The Dutch contributed to this process. In the seventeenth century they had introduced countless new types of firearms, from snaphaunces to pistols.[12] Although initially intended for hunting tigers, these weapons soon acquired other applications. As technological innovation rapidly gathered pace, the use of firearms among the local population also increased, especially in the final century of colonialism in the archipelago, between 1850 and 1950.[13] In that period, percussion weapons became popular.[14] These had been used for hunting in Europe since the early nineteenth century, and in 1841 they had been introduced into the Dutch army. Not long afterwards they reached the Dutch East Indies.

With the advent of breech-loading, firearms became still more effective, but the most important breakthrough came with the invention of the revolver, and, not much later, the repeating rifle, which could fire several bullets in rapid succession. Revolvers were first used in the Dutch East Indies around 1880, and repeating rifles about ten years later.[15] The end result was that within a fairly short space of time, firearms became more reliable and more precise, had vastly increased firepower and were easier to load.

The people of the archipelago tried to keep up with these technological advances, and Java's kampongs had many skilled gunsmiths. The following account in the *Locomotief* might have served as a set of instructions:

> The gangs in Meester Cornelis make their own firearms from sections of gas pipes. They are sealed at one end, after which a hole drilled in that seal serves as the touch-hole, into which a short tube is inserted and fitted with a percussion-cap, the pipe is charged with gunpowder and pieces of old iron and nails, and fired using a quite ingenious mechanism, with a rubber band that makes a nail strike the percussion-cap, causing it to explode.[16]

Many curious firearms of this type remained in use well into the twentieth century.[17] Since Javanese gunsmiths were incapable of making more modern firearms in this period (in particular revolvers), Peter Boomgaard has concluded that only a small proportion of the local population possessed them.[18] He adds that the colonial authorities clamped down on gun ownership by introducing restrictions in 1822. Importing firearms became a state monopoly that year. Guns used for hunting and other 'luxury' weapons were exempted, but even for these a gun licence was mandatory.

The local population had numerous ways of circumventing the restrictions, however, and Boomgaard's assertion that the Javanese did not possess many firearms in this period seems highly questionable. Although they only made relatively primitive firearms, they could acquire more modern weapons through contraband trade, or through acquaintances who were able to buy them legally. Indigenous officials, who were allowed to possess firearms, had a wide circle of acquaintances who were able to exploit this privilege indirectly. Locals could sometimes buy firearms from Europeans who were strapped for cash,[19] and anyone who needed a gun temporarily could generally rent one from a Chinese neighbour with a licence.[20]

Even prosperous Europeans were sometimes willing to furnish their local business associates, for instance, with modern weapons. Newspaper articles and official notices occasionally berated Europeans for their carelessness with firearms, which were left lying about the house (sometimes near the servants' quarters) or in hackney carriages. In 1870, the government conducted an investigation into gun ownership in Semarang — a major supply port for weapons. It emerged that as many as 900 Javanese city-dwellers had firearm licences.[21] Given the prevalence of illegal possession, the real figure must have been far higher. In 1884 an article in the local newspaper the *Java-bode* estimated the number of illegal firearms in the Preanger district at approximately 10,000.[22]

Firearms and rebellions

It seems likely, then, that many villagers had ready access to firearms. Some Europeans regarded this as a social evil. Of course, many of these weapons were used for hunting. Javanese farmers saw the extermination of certain animals as a necessity. Especially at dusk, gunshots would ring out from the kampongs, as farmers fired at the flying foxes or kalongs that were plundering their fruit-trees.[23]

It was also not uncommon for Javanese farmers to use rifles or pistols to rid themselves of an enemy. The columnist 'Opheffer' (the pen-name of the former Resident G.L. Gonggrijp) gives the following account.

> Our Kromo, needing to avenge his honour as a farmer, wanted to shoot his foe dead, but had no rifle. But old Pa Tirto had one, and Kromo went to visit him. After they had rolled and smoked a few cigarettes together, Kromo explained what he wanted: he needed Pa Tirto's rifle for a day, to kill someone. Old Tirto had no objection: 'Certainly, my lad, you can have it' he said, genially. They talked a

> little, and Tirto, who kept his old gun carefully concealed from the police, went to get it.[24]

In the event, however, Tirto decided not to loan his neighbour the rifle after all, since the intended victim turned out to be his own first cousin. So Kromo went off to borrow a rifle somewhere else, and carried out the murder a few nights later.

The Europeans suffered occasional bouts of terror at all the weapons that must be lying around the kampong. But this anxiety affected the Dutch in the mother country more than the colonialists. Now and then, the Ministry of Colonies would ask for precise figures, and often complained about the vagueness of the replies received from the colonial officials at Buitenzorg.[25] The colonial government probably realized that estimating and verifying the real numbers was a fairly hopeless task. That not everyone deplored gun ownership is clear from the indignant messages in the *Java-bode* and the *Bataviaasch Nieuwsblad* about the searches for illegal weapons in the kampongs of the Ommelanden in the year 1903.[26] The journalists wrote that the authorities were abandoning the people of the kampongs to their fate by depriving them of the means to protect themselves from bandits. The *Algemeen Handelsblad* published an editorial on security, calling for a new policy on firearms. Why should all kinds of shifty Europeans and their descendants be permitted to own handguns and not the settled population of the archipelago? He thought that the local residents and 'foreign Orientals' should also be allowed to have firearms in their homes, provided they did not take them off their own land. The writer did not see this as posing any kind of political hazard.[27]

Some Europeans were obviously afraid that the locals might take up their guns and use them in a revolt. But this fear proved groundless. This can be illustrated by recalling two revolts mentioned in earlier chapters. In the 1869 revolt in Tambun, reports noted explicitly that the rebels had used only *goloks* and not firearms. In the most notorious rebellion, on the Ciomas estate in 1888, the difference in weaponry between the rebels and the colonial authorities was greater still. Seventy-five unarmed men in a gorge were shot dead from above. These accounts show that the local population did not resort to firearms in the event of a revolt.[28]

Besides rebellions in pursuit of specific demands, there were wider-ranging revolts against the *status quo* as a whole. It is fair to question the use of words such as 'revolt' or 'rebellion'; in some cases 'demonstrations' might be an apter term. Mass gatherings of this kind were traditional in this region.[29] In earlier times it had been common for the people to go to the sultan, express their grievances, and then go home. The protests inspired by the *Sarekat Islam* (an Indonesian liberation movement founded in 1911–2) were infused with a philosophy of non-violence.

Administrative officials never knew what to expect when they heard news of a revolt. The *controleur* or Assistant Resident would hear from the *wedana* or assistant *demang* that there was unrest somewhere, but not until arriving on the scene would he discover whether there were ten, a hundred or a thousand people involved, and what mood they were in. Sometimes he judged that it was better to negotiate, if only to save his own skin, and the protesters would receive assurances that their complaints would be looked into.

The officials could generally count on being censured however they dealt with the situation. In 1864, when the bandit leader Mangoon unleashed a riot, the Assistant Resident C.N.H. Lawick van Pabst took his wife and children to safety in Batavia before setting off to deal with Mangoon. The government was incensed and reprimanded the Assistant Resident, accusing him of cowardice, even though he had gone on to defeat the armed bandit. In the same period, Assistant Resident de Kuijper was killed in a revolt because he had bravely confronted the rebels.[30] In short, the only way for colonial administrators to achieve glory in the rebellious Ommelanden was by being killed in the line of duty.

Firearms and bandits

All these anecdotes show that the authorities were not greatly troubled by the use of firearms among the local population. But the frequent use of firearms by bandits did give rise to concern. We can infer from newspaper reports that firearms started being used more often in robberies after 1890. It is fair to assume that this was largely because revolvers were now cheaper and more widely available. Although the special mechanism of the revolver, which made it possible to fire six shots in succession without reloading, had been known for centuries, it was not until the technological modifications of the mid-nineteenth century that the revolver became a practical weapon. The same applies to breech-loaders — guns into which the charge was introduced at the breech instead of the muzzle. These too became more widely available in this period.[31]

With Si Pitung, the legendary bandit to be discussed at length in Chapter 8,[32] a new pattern of criminal behaviour emerged. His robbery of Hadji Sapiudin's house in Marunda was accompanied by intimidating gunfire, and Pitung's life ended in an equally dramatic gunfight with the policeman Hinne.

Not until the 1880s were the statistics for *rampok* included in the annual colonial reports. This was probably in part because of the growing use of firearms, which caused *rampok* to be seen as more of a problem for the colonial authorities.

The subsequent decades produced a series of self-conscious 'villains' who used revolvers in assaults on the police and townspeople. In 1892 (in the period when Pitung was still active), a gang plundered the house of a Chinese man in Tanah Tinggi and set off towards the town centre with the spoils. The man who had been robbed shouted for help. First on the scene were the men of the neighbourhood watch or *ronda*, but they were powerless in the face of the gang's weapons. Shortly afterwards, a few Europeans arrived, but their guns jammed, eliciting jeers of triumph from the criminals: 'Madjoe loe Blanda, kaloe berani semoea dalam di Kampong!' ('Come on Dutchmen, if you've got any guts, let's all go to the kampong').[33]

In 1909 an armed robbery took place that displayed many of the stereotypical features of newspaper crime reports. It is therefore worth discussing at some length.[34] A Chinese resident of Batavia had locked up for the night when he heard a knock at the door. When he asked who was there, someone answered in a reassuring tone. Upon opening the door, he was confronted by a band of heavily-armed men, their faces blacked, who pushed him aside and forced their way into the house. He ran into the street and sounded the alarm with a *tongtong*, an instrument specially made for this purpose. But when the neighbours came running, the bandits kept them at bay with threats, some even blocking the road!

Inside the house, the man's wife was told to point out where she kept her valuables. When she refused to do so, a bandit fired at her, and she suffered a bullet-wound to the head. All they found was some money (about 50 guilders) and a valuable batik. By that time the police had arrived. When the bandits heard them, they reacted enthusiastically, 'Come on then!' and fired shots into the air. Every shot was accompanied by a defiant roar. The police immediately retreated, allowing the robbers to carry on with their work. The neighbours fired sporadic shots in the air in the hope of startling the villains, but to no avail. By the time military units arrived on the scene, the robbers had finished what they came to do.

These examples demonstrate the willingness of the people of Batavia to defend their close neighbours from the menace of bandits, and also to fight in defence of their own property. In the meantime, the growing use of firearms had not escaped the notice of the Malay press:

> Theft is very common nowadays in the village of Tjikini. Not an evening passes without something being stolen. The thieves are becoming more and more audacious, since the village headman seldom notices anything and no one dares to come when people call for help, since the thieves carry firearms these days and the people are frightened.[35]

Illus. 6 Tongtong, a wood-block on which warning signals could be made. The meaning of the signals is mentioned on the board: Tjaroek (come to blows) – 1,1; Barang (theft) – 2,2; Kebakaran (fire) – 3,3; Bandjir (flood) – 4,4; Rodjokojo (theft of life stock) – 5,5; Land.Lari (flight from the agricultural institution Pro Juventute) – 2. D.H. Meijer wrote in the article in the *Nederlandsch Indische Politiegids*, in which this illustration was included, that the population believed that the wood-blocks had mystical, deterrent effects that protected the immediate surroundings against disaster. ('Ketongan en veiligheid', pp. 104–7)

To acquire a weapon — the most important instrument of his profession — a bandit either had to have ties with a colonial official from whom he could acquire one or he would have to be a trader of sorts, with sufficient funds to pay for a revolver and bullets. These were still too expensive for ordinary kampong-dwellers. At the same time, Europeans blamed the rise in crime on the fact that at 50 to 100 guilders, guns were too cheap.[36]

Tagliacozzo emphasizes the Europeans' fear of gun ownership among the local population. This may be something of an exaggeration. Most Europeans in Batavia were only troubled by firearms when they were owned by bandits. Robert Cribbs' theory of gangsters as the vanguard of the Indonesian independence struggle is also open to debate. Cribb writes that the gangsters were uniquely able to gain easy access to firearms. But there is reason to believe that even ordinary members of the local population had little difficulty obtaining firearms. The difference, perhaps, is that the bandits possessed more expensive, superior guns, costing more than 50 guilders apiece, which were completely beyond the means of ordinary villagers.

The effectiveness of firearms

In the Batavia of the nineteenth and early twentieth centuries, few bullets actually hit anyone. There was a great propensity for firing into the air, and numerous shots went completely astray. It was far from exceptional for all six shots in a revolver volley to miss their target.

In gun battles with the police, neither side shone in the effective use of their weapons, as is clear from the following passage from the *Bataviaasch Nieuwsblad*. A police patrol happened to pass by in the middle of a robbery:

> The officers concealed themselves at the behest of their commander, while Djamangin shouted at the bandit in sight that he must stop what he was doing or be shot. However, the bandit calmly carried on regardless. He paid no heed even to the third such injunction, upon which Djamangin ordered his men to shoot the villain. The shot boomed and the bandit fell to the ground. At the same time, a volley of shots rang out from the bushes and bullets whistled past the heads of the policemen, fortunately without hitting any of them. At this point, someone insolently asked the officers whom they had come to assist, the Chinaman or the bandits. At the same time as this contemptuous enquiry, a

> new bandit appeared in front of the house to take the place of his fallen comrade.
>
> ...
>
> The proposed *rampok* now became a formal gun battle between three police officers and twenty robbers, all of whom possessed good revolvers and four of whom must also have been using fine breech-loading rifles, judging by the rapidity of the shots. Meanwhile, the gang had not given up the robbery. A bullet from one of the robbers' rifles penetrated doors and wall partitions in the Chinaman's home but fortunately did not cause any injury. In the meantime, there was a flurry of hatchets. The fighting took place in almost pitch darkness, since only a few feeble rays of light penetrated the bushes. Occasionally one would glimpse a burst of gunfire from a revolver or rifle.[37]

All too often, the bandits were better armed than the police. The robber Gantang was quoted as saying derisively (in 1903) that in the next gun battle, he would lend the police some of his ammunition.[38] Almost 40 years later, things had not greatly improved:

> The military police inspired so little fear or respect in the bandits that on one occasion when a patrol happened on a gang in the middle of a *rampok* and answered the demand 'Who is there?' with the words 'The police!', the bandits replied, 'Just the people we were waiting for!' and received them with a hail of bullets that forced them to retreat.[39]

One explanation for the relatively small number of people killed or wounded in robberies is that it was generally not to the bandits' advantage to kill their victim. After all, they needed information on matters such as how to open the safe and where the valuables were kept. After intimidating the victim into a state of shock, the bandits had to get him to cooperate.[40] They were interested in the loot, not the victim.

If one assumes that the bandits went to work in a calculating way, one would expect them to reason that the use of extreme violence or even terror would be counter-productive, since it would lead to a more forceful police response and harsher sentences. It is not clear to what extent the robbers were aware of these distinctions during their robberies, but the courts explicitly distinguished between robberies with fatalities and those in which only stray shots had been fired. If a victim had been killed, the bandit was often sentenced to death. This is partly because until an effective prison system was introduced, around 1910, the alternative

— forced labour — was believed to pose an unacceptable danger to society, because of the risk of escape.[41]

Another reason for caution was the bandits' reluctance to jeopardize the goodwill they might enjoy in their own community. There is some evidence that kampong-dwellers were ambivalent in their attitude to bandits, and their sympathy could soon turn to resentment. It also seems that bandits had a certain fear of the local population. It was this fear that prompted Kesen to give himself up to the police voluntarily. Bandits who fell into the hands of incensed locals were sometimes beaten up savagely.[42]

It has been noted before, in Florike Egmond's study of banditry in the French period, that the brigands were often less vicious and bloodthirsty than their contemporaries were apt to maintain in newspaper articles and pamphlets. Out of 105 robberies carried out by the 'Great Gang' (*Grote Bende*) that roamed Limburg, she finds that 'only five fatalities' resulted. And in the robberies of the 'Holland Gang' (*Hollandse Bende*), not a single person died. Egmond also notes that Richard Cobbs's study of the *bande d'orgères* in France reveals that in the course of 95 robberies, as many as 75 people died. French gangs, unlike their Dutch counterparts, frequently indulged in ritual violence.[43] Clearly, the amount of violence used by gangs of robbers at different times and in different places varied immensely.

In addition, newspapers will have been inclined to exaggerate the use of violence in order to provide sensational news. And rumours — on which journalists sometimes based their reports — tend to become inflated. For instance, in 1937 a rumour spread that a Chinese couple in Batavia who had been robbed had died of their injuries in hospital. A few days later, however, it was impossible to avoid noticing that the couple were busy repairing the damage to their shop.[44] In Appendix IV, however, we see that fatalities did sometimes occur. The newspapers also contain reports of people being gunned down by bandits for offering resistance. Incidents of this kind caused public outrage. The accuracy of estimates of violence in newspaper articles, pamphlets and other written sources is hard to assess. Unfortunately, in the substantial literature on robbers' gangs, we find few authors who have ventured to compile a statistical survey.

Notwithstanding the lack of figures, Anton Blok's study *De Bokkerijders* and surveys of banditry in South America give the impression that banditry was more violent in the eighteenth century than in later periods.[45] Paradoxically, the firearms that became so popular among bandits in the nineteenth century appear to have reduced the degree of violence because they posed such a potent threat.

Bandits in the Dutch East Indies appear to have been less violent than those in other parts of the world. When they did use force, it was often 'functional'. In *Een ketjoegeschiedenis*, which deals with robberies in Central Java, the author I. Groneman maintains that most bandits allowed their victims to leave unharmed and that they seldom indulged in acts of arson or unnecessary vandalism.[46] In 33 robberies in the Buitenzorg district in 1903, only three people sustained gun injuries, two of whom were robbers shot by their own comrades.[47] A similar pattern was reported in Meester Cornelis. One police officer died in this district, in a gun battle in which two or three robbers were wounded.[48]

A different account, one that lends itself to interpretation either as an escalation of violence or a case of restraint, concerns a robbery that took place in Babakan Bekasi. One Saturday night in October 1920, a group of about 20 indigenous people converged on the estate of Babakan. The wealthy landowner heard them coming and ensconced himself in the attic with four rifles. From there he took aim at the marauders, killing one and wounding five others. The remaining bandits stormed the attic, where a scuffle ensued. When the attic's zinc floor collapsed, the fight continued on the ground floor. The owner was tied up, threatened with a pistol and ordered to hand over the keys to the safe. When he refused, the robbers broke it open and made off with a booty of 1,000 guilders. The final toll of casualties in this spectacular clash, which involved numerous firearms and other weapons, was one fatality among the bandits and eight men wounded. These included the owner, who suffered five machete blows to his head, none of which, miraculously enough, was serious.[49] Was this a question of chance? Were the robbers capable of exercising restraint, so as to limit the number of deaths and injuries?

Judging by newspaper reports in Batavia, the violence related to robberies pales into insignificance compared to the number of deaths that resulted from honour and revenge killings, quarrels within Chinese circles and crimes of passion. Then there was the almost unremitting background noise created by the vandalism and violence of drunken soldiers and sailors. One police officer asserted in 1917, and he may well have been right, that many more lives were lost in Batavia each month as a result of poor hygiene than in a hundred years of *rampok*.[50]

All in all, when it comes to trigger-happy bandits in the Dutch East Indies, we can conclude that this may have been one of the few places in the world where robberies ended up causing more deaths among the bandits than among those they robbed.

CHAPTER 5

Jagos, jimats, and *dukuns*

Bandits had other weapons besides firearms. They were also feared for their magical powers and physical strength, fears that escalated and spread among the European and Eurasian populations around 1915. The European colonialists became obsessed with amulets or *jimats*, which they saw as symbols of a wider conspiracy against them. Some tried to allay such fears, with reassurances that the possession of amulets did not make the robbers any different from the rest of the population — even the Europeans. Similar reassuring claims were made about other features associated with bandits, such as martial arts and supernatural powers. In spite of such efforts, however, indigenous bandits were increasingly seen as charismatic figures who could communicate with a mystical world.

Jagoism

While all bandits were *jagos*, not all *jagos* were bandits. Bandits possessed many qualities labelled 'masculine' in the West, such as audacity and a strong sex drive.[1] This Javanese form of what Westerners call 'machismo' was an essential part of the bandit's identity. Novellas and newspaper accounts of bandits frequently allude to their sexual activities, noting that they made women the objects of their 'foul lust'.[2] We shall return to the sexual preoccupations of those who wrote about indigenous robbers in Chapter 6. It is not easy to assess the prevalence of sexual violence. The topic is seldom discussed in reports of *rampok* incidents. But bandits were sometimes accused of forcing men in the kampong to loan them their wives for a few weeks, with all the sexual intimidation this undoubtedly entailed.[3] The prevailing view was that Batavian robbers could not keep their hands off women.[4]

Meanwhile, the bandits' wives expected them to behave with a certain masculine aggression. One journalist wrote that when a group of wounded robbers stumbled home from an abortive robbery, their wives met them with jeers of contempt: 'A fine thing! To go out on a night of *rampok* and to come back with men wounded and no booty!'[5]

Accounts of bandits also dwell on masculine qualities such as courage and audacity. When Si Pitung was seriously wounded, for instance, he sang a merry song and asked for a glass of sake as he was being taken to hospital. And one young robber threatened with the hangman's noose answered coolly: 'Well go ahead and hang me then!' The robber Lias sent his distraught family away just before his death. Even the few female bandits were fearless:

> Two miscreants knelt before the lord of the estate. A sturdy young man with an insolent gleam in his eyes, his clothes in tatters, suggesting that he had been manhandled during arrest, and a young woman, saucy but with a pleasing appearance.
>
> 'Yes *kandjeng*, they were caught red-handed early this morning.'
>
> The lord of the estate took over the interrogation, from which it emerged that the two culprits (the woman in men's clothing), armed with a good Colt revolver, several *goloks* and a *piso raout* [knife], had been caught plundering a goat stable in the field. The woman spat contemptuously on the floor now and then, and when the lord of the estate asked her calmly why she was willing to be party to such an exploit, she replied impertinently: 'Ha! You've got me this time, but once I'm free, there will be a merry *rampok* here!'[6]

Female bandits were fairly unusual.[7] But some women were referred to as *jagos*. One worried man wrote a letter to the editor about a girl in a village he had seen on his way to work. Tall and dressed as a grown woman, she was quarrelling with the other villagers. From scraps of information he picked up he inferred that everyone in the village was afraid of her, and he concluded his letter, 'This was truly a *jago besar*!'[8]

These anecdotes suggest that it would be overly simplistic to refer to jagoism as a Javanese form of machismo. Qualities such as boldness and honour that are associated with masculinity — in the Mediterranean world, for instance — are often rooted in physical strength. It is by demonstrating his ability to protect himself and his property that a man in the Mediterranean region upholds his honour. Women are excluded from this; they cannot present themselves in the same way.[9] But the boldness, courage and potency that are associated with the *jago* have more to do with spiritual powers. In the Javanese conceptual world, this spiritual power hovers above the material world, and men and women alike can draw on it. Several authors, including Anderson and Errington, have pointed out that the cultures of Southeast Asia have no mechanisms that link prestige or power to gender or make it hereditary. Anyone can potentially acquire spiritual power. Consequently, many professions that are exclusive to one gender in the Western mindset are practised by both men and women on Java.[10]

It must be added that Javanese ideology does draw distinctions between men and women.[11] Men are believed to be more inclined to spirituality and keener to assert their prestige. Women are considered to be more focused on earthly affairs and to be more direct in expressing their emotions. Because of these qualities, many women are found trading at the marketplace.

Illus. 7 Wayang golek puppet representing Si Pitung as a typical 'jago'. (Private collection Max Rijkschroeff)

Applying these considerations to professions in the illegal circuit, one might reach a number of different conclusions. One would be that the qualities described above do not necessarily exclude women from banditry. Indeed, women appear pre-eminently suited to some of the functions that are related to banditry, such as that of *dukun* (counsellor, religious leader) and healer. For given that woman are less swayed by matters of prestige in Javanese ideology, they can draw on a wider range of communication styles than men. The ability to communicate freely is crucial to intermediaries such as the *dukun*, who mediates between the higher spiritual powers and ordinary human beings. The same applies to healers, who need to have a wide network of relationships as well as knowledge of the market. We therefore find both male and female *dukuns*, healers and *jagos* in Southeast Asia.

Male and female bandits alike formed a dissonant note in colonial ideas about the Javanese. The encyclopaedia *Geïllustreerde encyclopaedie van Nederlandsch-Indië* describes Javanese people as 'mild, quiet and generally meek'.[12] In the prevailing colonial discourse, the Dutch liked to see the Javanese people they governed as feminine and docile, seeing themselves as resolute fathers or elder brothers. The people of the Ommelanden did not fit this stereotype, and the bandits were more extreme still. With their confrontational behaviour, they not only defied the standards that the colonialists sought to impose, but they also deviated in some areas from the rules of their own society.

Their attitude to children is one good example of this. Having offspring was an important aim in Javanese peasant society. But it is clear from the *rancak* 'Si Pitung' that peasants saw themselves as different from bandits/*jagos* in this respect. Notwithstanding the *jagos*' numerous sexual adventures and their many mistresses, children played no part in their lives. This places their sexuality — which was not geared towards producing offspring — partly outside the prevailing norm.

Mysticism

According to the prevailing beliefs about Javanese crime around 1915, to commit a successful robbery it was essential to possess an amulet and to calculate the right time to strike as well as the appropriate method. To arrange these matters, one had to visit a sorcerer or counsellor known as a *dukun*. Robert Cribb writes in his book *Gangsters and Revolutionaries* that the *jago* and the *dukun* were frequently one and the same. He bases this conclusion in part on a study of the 1924 revolt in Tangerang, in which a number of *dukuns* were in the vanguard.[13] But I have been unable to find any other instance of *dukuns* being directly involved in revolts or robberies (except as victims), so the example cited by Cribb can scarcely be regarded as typical. My own findings suggest that the *jago* (who in this context is a bandit) and *dukun* were quite distinct. Bandits needed to consult a *dukun* to obtain an amulet, for the complicated calculations that had to be made, and for advice on how to stay ahead of the police. The *dukun* might be male or female. In the 1930s, a female *dukun* living in the vicinity of Buitenzorg was known for the help she gave to criminals.[14]

A report dating from 1888 (which refers to Central Java rather than Batavia), describes a visit to the *dukun*. At his first visit, the client handed over a 50-cent coin from which an amulet would be forged. During this and subsequent visits to the *dukun*, incense would be burned and incantations recited from a *primbon*, a Javanese book of mysticism rather like an almanac. Although the consultation was free of charge, the *dukun* would urge the aspiring miscreant: 'Remember the old *dukun*.'[15] The account states that *dukuns* tended to be quite prosperous as a result, and could pay the 60-guilder fine imposed for these disreputable practices without blinking.

Robbers' amulets were steeped in mystery. The *Bataviaasch Nieuwsblad* reported that some came from the region of the Badui, an enigmatic tribe that to this day lives in relative isolation in the hinterland of Western Java.[16] When arrested, robbers were often found to be carrying amulets in the form of scraps of paper bearing Arabic inscriptions, which also came from a *dukun*.

Amulets often made bandits overconfident, even in a court of law. They were thought to protect the owner from the consequences of lying under oath. This made amulets undesirable in the authorities' eyes. Even so, C. Snouck Hurgronje had warned back in 1890 that amulets were so widespread among indigenous people that seeking to ban them was fairly pointless.[17]

In the years leading up to the First World War, the colonial authorities were gripped by a renewed fear of amulets, as emancipatory movements inspired a wave of revolts in the Javanese countryside. The rebels' fondness for amulets greatly boosted trade in them. This was a lucrative business, and the colonial authorities saw the *dukuns* as swindlers. In one branch of the *Sarekat Islam* in the Preanger region, members were pressured to purchase amulets at 15 guilders apiece.[18] The debate on the need to suppress the possession of — and trade in — amulets flared up once again. In this debate, two writers, Noto Soeroto in the daily newspaper *Het Vaderland* and S. Soeriokoesoemo in his periodical *Wederopbouw*, again urged the authorities to be more tolerant of amulets. They pointed out that amulets might take many different forms.[19] A dried sea-horse brought luck to someone who owned horses, dried herbs gave good health, and Arabic inscriptions averted disaster. The writers added that the Europeans too used amulets: some had chestnuts in their pockets to ward off rheumatism or tiny effigies of the Virgin Mary in their purses. The upshot of the debate was that it was prohibited to have an amulet on a person during a court hearing or to be in the possession of an amulet intended for some criminal purpose — something that was obviously difficult to prove.

Bandits also needed a *dukun* to make certain calculations to assure the success of their robbery. In an article entitled 'Animisme in de Javaansche dievenwereld' ('Animism in the world of Javanese thieves'), published in 1929, W.G. Vergouw wrote that bandits could be divided into three categories. The first category was the *maling krowodan*, 'thief of crops' or occasional thief. The second, the *maling tengah* or 'middle thief', was a professional thief. And the third, the *maling ketoet* or 'muscular thief', was the category discussed in this book — the bandit. Occasional thieves did not concern themselves with calculations, but to the other two categories these were crucial. To guide these calculations, which were designed to assure the success of their ventures, they used tables inscribed on a *radja moekah*: *radja* means 'ruler' or 'distinguished person', in this case 'master thief', and *mukah* means 'rip apart with violence'. So the *radja moekah* — a small piece of wood inscribed with various symbols and hieroglyphs, which also served as a talisman — was intended to protect the thief from violence. Readers who are curious to see how this worked may refer to Appendix III.[20]

The most important part of the calculations was predicting the level of violence that might occur in the course of the planned robbery. Meanwhile, the robbers' adversaries, the police and their intended victims in the villages, did not stand idly by. The indigenous police officers — to the despair of their modern European counterparts — enlisted the help of *dukuns* to identify thieves from the earth in their footprints. The villagers too had their own methods, and they too consulted *dukuns*. Furthermore, numerous omens were taken to predict the arrival of thieves and robbers, from the sound of certain birds to the presence of many small objects such as sticks (that might be used to pick a lock) round about a house.

The villagers believed that 'if the small portents are seen, the thieves will soon follow'.

One important caveat should be added to these accounts of the calculations made by thieves and the police: even the experts conceded that many shrewd thieves would set off to commit robberies on 'unsafe' days, taking advantage of the slacker vigilance of police and villagers alike.[21]

Pencak silat: Indigenous martial art

Ideally, bandits were adepts of the indigenous martial art *pencak silat*.[22] This sport originated in the Minangkabau, where it was called *mentjak*. According to one legend, a woman from this region was washing her clothes in the river one day when she saw a tiger and a bird fighting. When she subsequently arrived home later than expected, her husband went to strike her, but she deftly avoided the blows in the way she had seen the bird avert the tiger's thrusts.[23] This success propelled her to prominence as the first instructor in the art of *pencak silat*. This anecdote serves to highlight the role of women in *pencak silat*. On Java, for instance, one of its primary exponents was the legendary Si Mirah from Marunda.

In 1913, *pencak* was described as a cross between boxing and wrestling, similar to *ju-jitsu*. In the area of Java's northern ports in particular, the 'Malay' *pencak silat* was greatly influenced by Chinese martial arts.[24] For this reason its practitioners are generally assumed to be unarmed, but this is certainly not always the case; we often find a fetishistic attachment to daggers, knives and pick-axes.[25]

Prize fights were a common feature of the *pasar gambir* (market or fair). Ucee's crime novel *De schoonste triomf van de Indo-detective* ('The Indo detective's greatest triumph') contains an account of one such prize fight between a number of *jagos* from Batavia. The prize money is 500 guilders. The contestants begin by challenging each other in a war dance or *tandak*. Their fists are treated with chalk, so that each blow will leave an imprint on their opponent's body. Fights of this kind were prohibited on private estates, since they tended to generate feuds. Europeans considered *pencak* (also known in Batavia as *pukulan*) to be devious, since it was so unlike the European-style boxing with which they were familiar. In 1913, the bandits Si Pitung, Gantang, and Dji-ih were all described as masters of this martial art by the Indonesian journalist Rudi Veha.[26] In today's Jakarta, an important element of traditional *lenong* performances (an indigenous form of theatre) consists of a stylized *pencak silat* dance involving two figures:

the man guarding the private estate and the defender of the people — the *jago*, in the eyes of the audience.[27]

Nowadays *pencak silat* is viewed as an Indonesian or Asian martial art. But an editorial written in the 1930s emphasizes the Eurasian influences that helped to shape it. The newspaper *Het Nieuws van den Dag voor Nederlandsch-Indië* complained that *pencak silat* had become a veritable cult among local boys in the margins of society. The writer urged the need for more useful activities to occupy these boys' time.[28]

Pencak silat was popular among men on Java, especially among those whose profession involved force of some kind. The local guards who worked in the plantation economy of the Dutch East Indies did much to distribute its finesses throughout the island.[29] Mastering *pencak silat* was comparable to a present-day criminal's daily visits to the body-building gym.[30] But *pencak silat* was not the sole prerogative of bandits. Its techniques were seldom of any use during robberies, which tended to be dominated by the use of firearms. But a mastery of *pencak silat* may have been useful in escaping from prison or in the period immediately following arrest, besides which its meditation techniques would have helped to sustain bandits during their term of imprisonment.

Clearly, bandits were not alone in practising the art of *pencak silat*, nor were they the only ones on Java to concern themselves with the supernatural. Even so, an aura of mystique clung to the indigenous bandit, and Hobsbawm writes:

> Thus the traditional Javanese 'rampok' band is essentially a 'group formation of a magical-mystical nature', and its members are united, in addition to other bonds, by the ilmoe (elmu), a magical charm which may consist of a word, an amulet, an adage, but sometimes simply personal conviction, and which is in turn acquired by spiritual exercises, meditation and the like, by gift or purchase, or which comes to a man at birth, designating him for his vocation.[31]

While Hobsbawm elaborates on the magical powers of Indonesian bandits, he adds that bandits active in other places and times have a similar reputation. It is interesting to look closer at the basis for this reputation. After all, given the hazards inherent in the robber's life, he will naturally take refuge in reassuring rituals. James Hutton's account of the dacoits and thugs of India in the mid-nineteenth century includes several pages on their superstitions.[32] Even American robbers in the 1960s were deeply fatalistic, and thought that only rituals could provide a degree of protection. But that did not stop them planning their robberies in a wholly rational way — as did the bandits of the Dutch East Indies 50 years earlier.[33]

In conclusion, we can say that criminals were no different from the rest of the population in terms of the possession of amulets, calculations of time, or skill in the martial arts. Almost every inhabitant of the Dutch East Indies, with the exception of European newcomers or *totok*, made calculations to determine the propitious time for an important event and assured himself of an amulet. If the calculations and amulets of criminals were cloaked in mystery, this was merely because they were associated with an activity that had to remain concealed.

Subversion, inversion, and tactics

Seizing someone else's property by force violates the laws and moral codes of most societies. The perpetrator may be accused of subversion if he declares that the former owner had no legitimate right to this property in the first place. All sorts of conscious and unconscious utterances and actions could be taken as signs of subversion. Such behaviour might include the decision to distribute the proceeds of crime to the poor, or acts of vandalism committed in the course of a robbery — a type of behaviour that was also seen in the Ommelanden.

Robbers often challenged the authorities. Later on we shall see that criminals threatened the police chief Hinne from their prison cells. And police chief Misset, who set about designing the new police apparatus immediately upon arrival from the Netherlands, incurred the collective wrath of the robbers when he unwisely interfered in a robbery near his home and killed one of the bandits, even though he was not on duty. Not long afterwards, he was warned that the bandit chief 'couldn't let this pass'. One night, when Misset was away from his idyllic home in the Ommelanden, he returned to find the place ransacked and vandalized. The robbers had left their excrement in a dish on the dining-table, with the police chief's calling cards poked into it as little flags.[34] This incident provoked a flurry of indignant responses in the press, and had serious repercussions on the plans to modernize the police force.

It is interesting that the robbers did not resent Misset for trying to catch robbers; as a police officer, he was expected to act in this way. What incensed them was that he should have done so in his free time. It therefore makes little sense to call the bandit chief's actions subversive, since he clearly saw criminals and police as each other's 'natural' adversaries.

One specific form of subversion is the inversion of prevailing definitions. This is described at length in Anton Blok's book *De Bokkerijders*, which deals with the gangs that held sway in the Netherlands in the eighteenth century:

> We have also seen that secret societies often bolster their image and justify themselves by highlighting ways in which they differ from society at large and invoking traditions that are diametrically opposed to prevailing religious views. Their ideology and rituals can therefore only be understood in terms of the social order against which these societies rebelled. This is also seen in the initiation rites of the Bokkerijders. These consisted of a configuration of numerous oppositions and inversions, most notably the desecration of Catholic relics and sacred places. Thus, they defiled the chapels where they met, used a form of Holy Communion as an initiation rite, kicked and spat on crucifixes and reversed God and the Devil....
>
> Ritual thus served to create a bond of solidarity and to draw clear lines between members and non-members.[35]

It should be added that most bandits in and around Batavia had a different value system from that of their victims, in that they were Muslims and many of their victims were Chinese and Christians or Confucians. Indeed, it was common for robbers to emphasize their religion. They sometimes wore white turbans or headscarves. Many were *hadji* (that is, Muslims who had made the pilgrimage to Mecca), a status that earned them the respect of the local community and the suspicion of the colonial authorities. Many robbers were called *dji*, a name that was evidently reserved for bandits and was an abbreviation of the word *hadji*.[36]

The bandits' Islam had numerous specifically Javanese features, but did not differ in this respect from the religion of the local community. It is interesting to see that in an entirely Islamic environment, in which the victims as well as the perpetrators of *rampok* were Muslims, we do find a certain reversal of Islamic values. For instance, in Central Java, robbers who approached a house intending to commit *rampok* (or *ketjoe*, as it was called there) customarily announced themselves as dogs or pigs, animals that are regarded as unclean in Islam. They decorated themselves with *janur kuning*, leaves that were believed to symbolize evil.[37] In the Ommelanden too, the robbers sometimes employed shock tactics, such as painting their faces black before a robbery or appearing naked.

Batavian robbers often dressed up in the uniforms of the colonial police or army, women's clothes, or carnivalesque costumes copied from adventure tales or films. Frances Gouda gives a detailed account of young Indonesian freedom-fighters and their imitations of cinema idols. It was not uncommon for young *pemuda* militants to dress up as cowboys and to adopt the names of Wild West heroes.[38] Bandits too followed the latest fashion in plays and films and adopted similar guises and names. The relationship between *stamboel* performances and the seamy side of Batavia's society was remarked in an earlier chapter. In 1896 the newspaper *Hindia Olanda* published a complaint about the terrible din of pistols being fired in the kampong that unfailingly followed every *stamboel* performance, keeping everyone in the wide vicinity awake. The authorities viewed *stamboel* theatre with deep suspicion, as a 'realm of passion and violence',[39] and the unrest that followed the performances of the troupe *Sri Stamboel* prompted the Assistant Resident in Batavia to revoke the troupe's licence.[40]

Westerns were the most popular genre in the early twentieth century,[41] and in the 1920s there was a craze for actors such as Douglas Fairbanks, leading to an abundance of imitations among Batavian *jagos*.[42] This was a source of concern for the colonial film censors, who laboured to purge the screen of images of European women in 'bathing costumes' and where possible of murder scenes. The aim was to eradicate the 'atmosphere of crime'.[43] But real scenes of robbery were just as spectacular as those seen at the cinema. In the furore of the robbery near the home of the police chief Misset, when Misset shouted at the servants and other members of his household to go inside and lock the doors, the *babu* refused to budge from her place on the steps of the veranda, saying, 'It's just like the cinema!'[44] On the other hand, films and plays may have actually tempered the violence: they showed a great deal of shots fired into the air, an example that the bandits emulated.

In the *stamboel* performances and the colony's earliest films, social and ethnic differences were explored and dramatized. But these were not the only places where people took a playful look at the changing fabric of society; similar games were played at fancy dress parties, for instance. In a variation on Rudy Kousbroek's description of the Dutch East Indies (in *Het Oost-Indisch kampsyndroom*) as 'one big open insane asylum', one might say that it was 'one big masked ball'. The robber Gantang liked to dress up as the Assistant Resident. One of his comrades was reported to be going around in an *Aimard* suit made of red material with an abundance of trimmings.[45]

Gustave Aimard (a pseudonym used by Olivier Gloux, 1818–83), was a French adventurer and writer of picaresque novels whose style of dress was evidently much admired by bandits. Conversely, the European men in the colony liked to identify with Gantang. While Gantang himself liked to don the uniform of a European soldier, several European men set off for a masked ball in a Gantang outfit; they fired several loud shots at their entrance and ended up winning second prize.[46]

In seeking to explain Batavian bandits' penchant for fancy dress, we should look at the frivolity associated with Javanese robberies. It may seem odd to see something as serious as a violent attack on people's property in a playful light. But in an entirely different context — the religious violence in Pakistan in the 1980s — Oscar Verkaaik has shown a similar mechanism at work.[47] He argues that playful kinds of behaviour, which sometimes had the effect of humiliating the victims, enabled young men to express their ambivalent feelings by taking on different roles, at the same time as providing a kind of competitiveness to test each other's courage and creativity.

We have already seen (in Chapter 3) that in Meester Cornelis, quite near to Batavia, robberies were widespread and that many people took part in them. One can easily imagine that a certain atmosphere of competition existed among men — the region had a high percentage of single men — as to who was the most audacious and who could find the most creative ways of humiliating his adversary.

In addition, dressing up may well have been a tactic designed to induce a state of shock in the victims, so that the robbers could strike and make their getaway as quickly as possible — and without being identified. An imaginative disguise is often a more effective way of confusing the victim than covering the face. Another favourite tactic of local bandits was the *Köpenickiade*, named after the famous exploit of Wilhelm Voigt, better known as the captain of Köpenick, who robbed the mayor of Köpenick (near Berlin) in 1906 by posing as a Prussian army officer. This kind of trickery was extremely successful in the Dutch East Indies, and has indeed been called a 'typical' crime of the region.[48] The victim would open the door to men dressed as officials who turned out to be robbers in disguise. The villagers were often so impressed by the uniforms that they failed to notice anything wrong.

Even the bandits' custom of sometimes appearing naked at the house they intended to rob — a detail that was mainly reported in the press when the victims were women — may have been in part a precautionary measure. They generally owned very few clothes, so that any garment worn during a robbery would be recognized and might be produced as evidence if lost.

The bandits' activities placed them outside society, but the magical powers and eccentricity imputed to them were exaggerated. This was part of a general discourse around the turn of the century that highlighted the supposed contrast between the civilized city and the backward rural regions.

THE CITY-DWELLERS

CHAPTER 6

Progress and Degeneration

In the early twentieth century, progressive politicians and leaders of public opinion sought to improve the poor social conditions in the Ommelanden through new infrastructure, a more effective police force, and changes in ownership structures on the private estates. Increasingly, the Ommelanden were viewed as the antithesis of civilized existence in the colonial capital of Batavia. The popular media in the colony, including the Indonesian press, were clearly influenced by the late nineteenth-century discourse on progress and its dark side, degeneration. This discourse, which cannot be seen in isolation from the rising urban middle class, had a profound influence on later descriptions of bandits, up to and including Hobsbawm's well-known study.

Progress versus degeneration

In the colonial period, the metaphor of the family was used to distinguish among the world's peoples. Skin colour ('race') was seen as parallel to gender; whites were superior to coloured people, and men took precedence over women.[1] White men were at the top of the hierarchy and coloured women at the bottom.

Until the nineteenth century, differences between peoples were explained in terms of degeneration from the ideal, which was the white man Adam. By drifting away from this common ancestor, some people (under the influence of a different climate, for instance) had become ever further removed from the ideal. A competing theory postulated that mankind had been created not in one place (the Garden of Eden), but in many. Some parts of the world had produced less perfect races.[2]

In the late nineteenth century both of these creationist views were challenged by Darwin's theory of evolution, first published in 1859. This new theory made it even easier for scientists to devise explanations for purported differences between races. For instance, it seemed only natural that races which had occupied different parts of the planet for long periods had followed different evolutionary paths and therefore differed from one another physically. Moral and intellectual differences could be explained in the same way. Not only evolutionary theory was used to support these conclusions, but also statistics. Scientists began measuring and comparing all sorts of physical traits, identifying a biological basis for social differences. A hierarchy of human races was developed on the basis of anatomical criteria:[3] at first, mainly cranial features, but later, limbs, ears, eyebrows, and other body parts as well.

Anatomical features were used to deduce the character traits of different races, but not only for that purpose. They could also provide insight into the roles of individuals and groups within their own races. They were used to identify 'backward' (or 'degenerate') people and groups within European societies, such as prostitutes, Jews, lunatics, the unemployed, and criminals. The major scientists in this field, known as eugenics, included its founder, Francis Galton, and the surgeon Paul Broca, both of whom claimed that the geometry of the body determined the form of the psyche.[4]

Cesare Lombroso is often mentioned in the same breath as Galton and Broca. An Italian physician, he postulated that thieves and murderers differed fundamentally from ordinary people. According to Lombroso, you could distinguish criminals from other people through their physical traits. He introduced the idea of the 'born criminal' — a person who, for reasons both hereditary and environmental, was destined to stand outside the social order. Lombroso's key term was 'atavism', meaning a kind of primitive relic.[5] He arrived at his theory after seeing the skull of the notorious bandit Vilella:

> At the sight of that skull, I seemed to see all of a sudden, lighted up as a vast plain under a flaming sky, the problem of the nature of the criminal — an atavistic being who reproduces in his person the ferocious instincts of primitive humanity and the inferior animals. Thus were explained anatomically the enormous jaws, high cheek bones, prominent superciliary arches, solitary lines in the palms, extreme

> size of the orbits, handle-shaped ears found in criminals, savages and apes, insensibility to pain, extremely acute sight, tattooing, excessive idleness, love of orgies, and the irresponsible craving of evil for its own sake.[6]

During his own lifetime, Lombroso saw his theories come under fire. Even so, he influenced many politicians and authors, such as Joseph Conrad and Arthur Conan Doyle, as well as the authors of many varieties of Gothic literature.

Lombroso's theory cannot be understood in separation from the political situation in European nation-states in the late nineteenth century. Like many other city-dwellers, Lombroso was frustrated by the stark contrasts within the Italian state. There was a gap between the urban population in the north and the small farmers in the south, who were still living in a kind of serfdom. In other nation-states in the throes of modernization there were similar figures, who also saw the 'backward' countryside and its inhabitants as problematic. In *Peasants into Frenchmen* (1986), Eugen Weber describes in detail what city-dwellers thought about 'primitive' rural areas. Against this backdrop, it is not surprising that around 1900 Lombroso's ideas were attracting a good deal of interest in Batavia's middle-class circles, where they formed a topic of open discussion. As discussed below, the Ommelanden had everything that the inhabitants of modern cities tend to hate: bad roads, uneducated tenants, spreading country estates, and a lack of modern state institutions.

Like the almost impassable roads and poor social conditions on the estates, the bandits were seen as a problem to be solved. In the late nineteenth century, the positive connotations of masculinity and bravery that banditry had once carried were completely overshadowed by its associations with the primitive, backward, and criminal. In writings by scholars and public officials on the problems in the environs of Batavia, Lombroso's theories were used to explain the high levels of crime. A pamphlet by W. de Veer about private estates and public security in and around Batavia describes the widespread banditry in the Ommelanden as a result of the region's long history of wars with Bantam, which led to the depopulation of the rural areas around the capital and the emergence of roving, predatory bands. Indonesian soldiers and bandits, sometimes working together, took advantage of the situation to make life difficult for the authorities, who were hamstrung by the wars and could do little to retaliate. De Veer argues that this resulted in 'a natural predisposition to disorderliness in the constitution of the population' of the Ommelanden. Though he noted that this tendency had decreased somewhat after the wars, as the colonial authorities strengthened their grip on the Ommelanden, De Veer concluded (writing just after 1900) that 'in Kabajoran and the adjoining part of Bekassie, even today specimens of the *criminel né* are born that would make a Lombroso thrill with delight'.[7] De Veer buttressed this argument with observations from public officials who believed that the indigenous inhabitants of that region regarded robbing and stealing as a sport, and were instinctively drawn to danger.

In the case of Bekasi, colonial officials found an explanation for the superstitious and criminal nature of the locals. They claimed that around 1825, a large number of 'bad elements' had been dumped in the Bekasi area by the Sultan of Cirebon. The sugar factories, which had been established not long before, were in need of workers, and the regents under the Sultan of Cirebon supplied them, thereby ridding themselves of the biggest troublemakers on their territory.[8]

Reference was often made to the mixed blood of people in the residency of Batavia, and of the bandits there in particular. Bekasi was regarded as a den of thieves not only because of the 'legacy' of the Sultan of Cirebon, but also because none of the original population was still present.[9] The people of Tangerang were thought to be aggressive and quarrelsome because their blood had been mixed with that of the Chinese.[10] The Resident of Batavia, H. Rijfsnijder, wrote about his residence:

> One result of this mixture of races is that one has to contend with a most peculiar, difficult, and disobedient local population, whose members have many bad qualities and few good ones.[11]

As far back as the early nineteenth century, a description of the Ommelanden claimed that many sons of European mandoers (overseers) and Indonesian women chose the path of the bandit:

> Because these children, raised in sin among the slave women, usually grow up in the wild without care or instruction, in freedom, idleness, and all sorts of vices and villainies, the sad consequence, as experience teaches us, is that it is often the adult sons of mandoers who form a threat to public safety, lead the robber bands, commit crimes on public roads and in the kampongs, and then hide out on the vast estates.[12]

Until well into the twentieth century the word *buaya*, which normally refers to pubescent Indo boys, was also used to mean *rampokker* (perpetrator of *rampok*, a type of robbery; see also Chapter 2).[13] Likewise, the word *preman* is used to this very day to refer to a particular type of bandit. This term comes from the Dutch *vrijman*, used for freed Asian slaves in the seventeenth and eighteenth centuries.[14] *Preman* bandits were known for wearing a moustache and a beard, and unlike most of the archipelago's indigenous people, they tended to be tall. The bandit Oesoep, who was active around 1920, is a good example of cultural blending. The European press described him as *menak*, a Sundanese word for distinguished or aristocratic. His skin was fairly light in colour. He had received a good upbringing, and could speak, write, and read Dutch, Malay, and Arabic. Some even said that he read the newspapers to find out what was being written about him.

Stories like these reflect the late nineteenth-century discourse of social Darwinism and Lombrosian criminology, in which mixed blood is a sign of degeneration. In the nineteenth-century Dutch East Indies (as in British India in an earlier period), there was a growing belief that people of mixed European and indigenous blood would slip to the bottom of the social hierarchy and then utterly vanish into indigenous society.[15] Pauperism among Europeans, for instance, was said to be the result of racial mixing. This 'slippage' was seen both in biological terms (it was thought that mixture of races would eventually lead to infertility) and in social terms (through the lens of Spencerian social Darwinism).[16] Conversely, of course, to move up in the world one had to avoid racial mixture. It became advisable to be a 'full-blood', to use a word typical of the period.[17]

The phenomenon known as pauperism was regarded as a problem. In the early twentieth century, a commission was appointed to determine what became of Europeans and Eurasians who 'slipped' down the social ladder; its findings filled several bulky volumes. This group certainly was poor and lacking in opportunities, but only relative to the affluent, 'modern' lifestyle of the new colonists who were arriving from the West in growing numbers. After all, since the Dutch had first colonized to the region, there had always been a large group of Europeans and Eurasians who had 'gone native'.

Tales of real or supposed bandits in the Ommelanden reveal the same preoccupation with their physical appearance, in which the traces of degeneration and a predisposition to crime were thought to be visible. This belief that criminals were primitive, animalistic beings influenced reporting in both the Malay-language and the Dutch-language press. The Malay newspaper *Bintang Barat* described one robber as having 'the genuine look of a thief, with bloodshot eyes and a face like a tiger's'.[18] Another example can be found in the Malay book about the Batavian robber Si Tjonat.

> He had a beard and moustache now, and his eyes were sunk in their sockets, his cheekbones protruded, and anyone who saw him was certain to take fright. He was always quick, too, though clearly lacking in strength.
>
> Do you recognize this man, dear reader? I would not have done so myself, had I not seen his restless eyes. It was none other than Si Tjonat, whom Si Bohong and Si Gondit had murdered, and who had taken his pleasure with njai Saipa, Mr Opmeijer's sweetheart, before making off with her jewels and his money.[19]

The robber Gantang was described as tall, hairy, full of scars, and pockmarked by venereal disease.[20] Gantang also bore the marks of the colonial penal system; that is, the stripes of the cane.[21]

City-dwellers believed that even apart from well-known robbers such as Kesen, Tjonat, Gantang, and Pitung, the Ommelanden were full of 'born criminals'. A reporter from the *Bataviaasch Nieuwsblad* who was visiting the area wrote:

> The people of this region are surly and unresponsive to Europeans, with a hint of that crude *sans gêne* that can be so jarring in an otherwise mild-mannered native. They truly have the phizzes of thieves, as one of our party worded his opinion.[22]

In the Dutch East Indies (as in most other parts of the world), criminals were the objects of scientific study, which was aimed at determining how their physical features differed from those of ordinary people. This fact was well known to the indigenous population and prompted the following verse of the *rancak* entitled *Si Pitung*:

> Si Pitung is dead; and his relatives have been told.
> His bier was carried from Krekot; he was buried in Penjaringan.
> I know someone in the hospital who spread the story
> That his guts were preserved in spirit.[23]

Hobsbawm was no better able to escape the discourse described above. It is fascinating how strongly Hobsbawm's words echo nineteenth-century sentiments about violence in rural areas:

> Nowhere more so than in those peasant insurrections and rebellions which have failed to turn into social revolutions, and whose militants are forced to fall back into the life of outlaws and robbers: hungry, embittered and resentful even against the poor who have left them to fight alone. Or, what is even worse, among that second generation of 'children of violence' who graduate from the ashes of their homes, the corpses of their fathers and the raped bodies of their mothers and sisters to the life of outlawry.[24]

This illustrates how nineteenth-century theories about degrees of civilization resurface in modern accounts of bandits, *jago*s, and *preman*s.

Sex in the Ommelanden

Given that racial distinctions were central to the mental life of the Batavian public, it is not surprising that they were fascinated with interracial sexual contact. Newspaper articles about banditry in the Dutch East Indies contain a great deal of sexual innuendo. Bandits like Pitung and Gantang generated a great deal of excitement in colonial society. One journalist wrote:

> We saw a considerable number of Europeans, and even young ladies, on their way to the pasar of Tjelilitan [Cililitan – MvT]; they all wished to see the Chinese shopkeeper who had found himself in such difficulty when he was robbed; they all had to see the shop door that had been so heavily damaged by axe blows and bullets; and perhaps they hoped — and now I am referring to the young ladies — to see Gantang suddenly emerge from the bushes by the road, shouting wildly. It's all about emotion these days.[25]

Descriptions of the underworld of robbers around Batavia generally had strong sexual undertones. For instance, the press reported that Gantang and his band organized banquets in the kampongs which were eagerly attended by indigenous women, and that some time later these women, in the words of the *Java-bode*, gave birth to 'little Gantangs'. The relationship between robbers and women was described in peculiar terms: 'The men were stripped of all their valuables and the women were raped, though without any suffering on their part.'[26] The one female bandit that was captured was described in terms such as 'saucy but well-proportioned'. Newspaper readers were also treated to a report about female police spies who had tried to arrest Gantang. They were said to be 'most beguiling',[27] and Pitung was described as having just 'one weakness': women.[28]

Robbers are not always thought to have an exuberant love life, even in the romantic tradition. Hobsbawm claimed that robbers were usually chivalrous and restrained in their dealings with women.[29] The Brazilian robber Lampião was said to have had puritanical sexual mores,[30] and the Sicilian bandit Giuliano Salvatore was rumoured to have been asexual. Regardless of whether bandits in the Dutch East Indies were actually all that interested in women, the stories about them evidently fulfilled a craving among newspaper readers for sexual titillation, or a desire among journalists to describe bandits as engaging in vigorous sexual activity.

In his book *Empire and Sexuality* (1990), the British historian Ronald Hyam described sexual urges as a driving force behind colonialism. According to Hyam, the repressed sexual climate in Europe gave Europeans a motive to conquer new territories, where they could enjoy more liberated sex lives. Hyam studied the situation in British India, but his description of relative sexual freedom is just as applicable to nineteenth-century Europeans in the Dutch East Indies.

Towards the end of the century, attitudes in European colonies gradually shifted. Rather than sexual liberation — such as Europeans had permitted themselves at Majoor Jantje's parties on the estate of Citrap (see Chapter 1) in the mid-nineteenth century — control over sexual relations became increasingly important as a pillar of colonialism. In French colonies, sexual conduct could even be a reason for refusing citizenship to members of the indigenous population, and thus denying them any real say in the colonial administration.[31] Of course, all this also meant that Europeans could no longer lead such licentious lives. In the old days of informal colonialism, the authorities had allowed Europeans great liberty in their relations with indigenous women, but the subsequent formalization of colonialism created unwritten rules for sexual congress between Europeans and locals. The arrival of large numbers of European women put great strain on the multi-ethnic household, which had been a part of life in the Dutch East Indies since the seventeenth century.[32]

Against this background, the pronounced sexuality in tales about robbers is less surprising. In the colonies, sexual conduct departing from European norms was pushed ever further into the margins, and debauchery was limited to masked balls, sensational stories about robbers, and 'great literature', such as Louis Couperus' novel *The Hidden Force*. For colonial journalists, stories about robbers' romantic, decadent love lives killed two birds with one stone. On the one hand, they met the popular demand for a kind of furtive amusement, by portraying the degenerate robber as the antithesis of progress, and on the other hand, they served as a warning to their readers, by showing how the robbers' questionable sexual mores led to violence, quarrels over women, and a hunger for wealth.

The most exciting feature of such stories was that the robbers challenged the greatest taboo in colonial society, namely the prohibition against sexual contact between indigenous men and European women. Ann Stoler has described the ever stricter control to which European women were subject in the late nineteenth and early twentieth centuries in all European colonial territories. Keeping the European community unified and 'pure' required new boundaries between the colonized and the colonizers. In addition to the above-mentioned condemnation of relationships between European men and Indonesian women, and the contempt shown for Europeans who acted too much like Asians, European women were protected from the attentions of Asian men. At the same time, women were expected to defend their own moral integrity and physical health.[33] They thus formed the boundary markers of the colonial empire.[34]

It did not take long, however, before this 'policy' was undermined by numerous varieties of conversion and fetishism.[35] The dominant rhetoric of the chivalrous white man as leader was mocked at colonial balls, where a man dressed as a poodle might leap onto the laps of the women present. There were also European gentlemen who visited these parties dressed as robbers. The remarkable popularity of masked balls in the Dutch East Indies is in itself a sign of how deeply the colonists desired to escape their social roles, if only for an evening.

The eagerness with which the newspapers described 'encounters' between indigenous men and European women reflects the same mentality. The following story, for instance, took every opportunity to play on the fear among European men that a European lady might be approached by an indigenous kampong-dweller. Mrs Giesberg, a European widow staying in her parents' pavilion on Koningsplein, was caught by surprise one night by a robber with a long knife who had crept through her bedroom window. Although there was a great deal of jewellery in her room, she was able to manipulate him, so that in the end he left with only two and a half guilders. Mrs Giesberg then raised a loud alarm, trying to call Batavia's sheriffs (*schouten*) to her assistance. None of them were home, however — they were all on duty. The wife of the Tanah Abang district sheriff interceded, however, sending out several indigenous assistant police officers. Once this type of pressure was brought to bear, the watchman at the home of Mrs Giesberg's relatives soon confessed that his brother was the culprit.

When the man was arrested, Mrs Giesberg said that she could only identify him if she saw him as he had been when he entered her room, namely naked, 'clothed' only in a bandanna. This was no sooner said than done; the man was ordered to undress entirely so that he could be identified. And as the newspaper reported, when the sheriff came home from work at 5 a.m., the incident had already been dealt with.[36]

Case study: Si Kesen

One instructive example of how tales about robbers generally conformed to the discourse described above is the story of Si Kesen. There are three versions of Kesen's adventures: first, a report by the Assistant Resident of Tangerang; second, the Dutch-language reporting on his exploits in the *Bataviaasch Nieuwsblad*; and third, two almost identical stories: 'Uit de Indische rechtszaak: een rampokker' (Court case from the Indies: a *rampokker*) by Judex in the *Java-bode* and 'Si Kesen' in the Malay-language paper *Bintang Betawi*.[37] This section examines how the newspapers altered and retold the bandit's story, transforming the narrative in the official report to present a certain image of the social environment in Batavia and the Ommelanden. In the Malay press, Kesen's story is full of moral lessons emphasizing the friction between a bandit and his environment.

Let us begin with the Assistant Resident's official report,[38] which states that Kesen came from the village of Rawa Bokor near Tangerang, about 20 kilometres to the west of Batavia. At one point he was suspected of involvement in several robberies and murders around Batavia and on the Pulau Seribu ('Thousand Islands') north of the Batavian coast. He also forced local fishermen, owners of rice fields, and landowners to make regular payments to him. The *demang* (district head) in the village of Mauk informed the Assistant Resident of Tangerang that Kesen planned to marry a woman from the village of Dasah. The Assistant Resident ordered the *demang* and his men to arrest Kesen at the wedding. Kesen was married according to plan, but to the Assistant Resident's disappointment, he was not arrested. In fact, it appeared as if the *demang* had been undermining the efforts of other local law enforcement officers to arrest Kesen.

The tension mounted when a number of mandoers and *oppassers* (constables), under the command of a person named Adiwaris, set out to arrest Kesen. During this expedition, they stopped at the home of the mandoer Noman, where they were warned that Kesen was coming for them, along with eight companions, all armed with pistols and rifles. They had just enough time to bar the door to the house before Kesen arrived and invited them to step outside. When they declined this invitation, the bandits started hacking at the door with axes.

In the fight that followed, men on both sides were killed, and Kesen himself was injured. He fled, with Adiwaris and his men in hot pursuit. But when the *demang* was informed of this chase, he ordered that it be called off. Even more surprisingly, when Adiwaris returned and reported to his superior, the *demang*, he received an official warning. This prompted the Assistant Resident to assume personal responsibility for the matter. He began an organized manhunt for Kesen, following a trail of footprints in the jungle, fresh banana peels, and the like. Kesen managed to escape his pursuers, however, and the Assistant Resident eventually gave up, profoundly disappointed in the *demang*. During the chase, two members of Kesen's band had been hit by bullets. His brother-in-law, a former mandoer, had been taken prisoner, along with another mandoer. The three other prisoners included a *dukun* (traditional healer). Kesen himself and two or three of his companions (including one Chinese man) were still at large.

To find out how Kesen was finally captured, we must consult the Dutch-language newspapers: the *Bataviaasch Nieuwsblad* and the *Java-bode*.[39] These papers also gave inside information about Kesen's motives. Apparently, the bandit had gained the confidence of a religious leader and borrowed a *golok* (machete) with magical powers. Kesen later gave this *golok* to his associate Ong, who used it in a robbery in Batavia. On that occasion, however, the weapon fell into the hands of the police, to the indignation of the religious leader, who held Kesen responsible. Accompanied by other religious leaders, he went to the house where Kesen was then staying. The bandit seemed indifferent to the whole affair, and even fired a round of shot into the religious leader's face. This made Kesen *persona non grata* in his own community.

According to the *Bataviaasch Nieuwsblad*, it was not primarily the efforts of the Assistant Resident and the police that had led to the bandit's arrest. Kesen, it was reported, had been under pressure to turn himself in from other prominent local figures, including religious leaders, a landowner, and even his own family. The *Bataviaasch Nieuwsblad* reported that Kesen had turned himself in, using a landowner as intermediary, for fear that he would otherwise be mistreated by the police.

The colonial authorities vigorously disputed this account arguing that it was pressure from the police which had ultimately led to the arrest; after all, it was the police who had blocked the roads around Kesen's hideout and held several of his family members hostage. This is the extent of the information in the official report and the Dutch-language press.

Six months later, several Batavian newspapers published articles about Si Kesen. One of them, *Bintang Betawi*, ran a five-part serial about the bandit from 29 January to 4 February 1904.[40] At that time, J. Kieffer was both the editor and the publisher of *Bintang Betawi*, which was aimed at the Chinese, Malay, and Eurasian middle class.

Beyond the names of Kesen, his friends, and his enemies, and the fact that the story is set in Tangerang, it is hard to find anything in this story that corresponds to either the Assistant Resident's report or the account in the *Bataviaasch Nieuwsblad*. The story does, on the other hand, tell us a great deal about how European and Eurasian city-dwellers saw rural life in the environs of Batavia. In this version of the story, entitled *Tjerita Si Kesen satu kepala penjamu di Tangerang* (The story of Si Kesen, leader of a band of robbers in Tangerang), Kesen's ill-fated life begins at the moment of his conception. One evening, as Kesen's mother is coming home from the market, she is raped by a tall Muslim man who emerges from the bushes. In other words, Kesen is the son of a *jago*. This explains why, as a child, he steals anything in the village that he can get his hands on. The village chief, Nomo, warns Kesen's mother not to spoil the child, and to try harder to keep him under control. According to the story, Kesen hates Nomo even as a child. Later, when Kesen is old enough to become a *jago*, he starts dressing like one and becomes 'a *jago* for all the young girls'.[41] Because the women are on Kesen's side and use their wiles to protect him, it proves difficult to arrest him.

Old Nomo's young wife also falls for Komo's charms. From this point on, the story leads inevitably towards a confrontation between Nomo and Kesen. When Nomo catches wind of the affair between his wife and Kesen, he has the younger man arrested. Kesen is condemned to a year of forced labour, but he escapes to become the leader of a band of robbers, armed with amulets and guns. He is now ready to take revenge on Nomo. Kesen goes to Nomo's house, beats him up, and ransacks the place. The remainder of the story proceeds along the same lines as the official report. The *demang* becomes fed up with Kesen, and sends Adiwaris and five *oppassers* to arrest him. Adiwaris has difficulty carrying out this assignment, however; in the words of the story, 'all the men feared Si Kesen, and many women were in love with this robber chief'.[42]

But Kesen cannot shake off Adiwaris. While Adiwaris is at Nomo's house, a shoot-out takes place. In this version, Kesen is ultimately apprehended by a sheriff from Batavia. At the end of the story, he is in prison, serving a 20-year sentence. There, his true nature comes to the surface; he torments his fellow prisoners, and his cellmate dies under suspicious circumstances.

Other tales from the same period, such as those of Si Gantang and Si Pitung, contain many elements of typical bandit stories as described by Hobsbawm. The heroes of these tales steal from the rich and help the poor, while seizing every opportunity to poke fun at the authorities. But the story of Kesen is not like that. From start to finish, he is described as sinister, bad, and concerned with nothing but personal gain.

CHAPTER 7

From Bandit Novels to Detective Stories

The years 1915–20 in the Dutch East Indies have been described by some authors — such as the historian Henri Baudet — as the watershed between the modern age and the legendary *tempo doeloe*, the good old days. The attitudes of European colonists towards the locals changed in this period: they grew interested in learning more about the colony's indigenous people, in part so that they could control them better. For centuries the city of Batavia had been cut off from the surrounding countryside, not only physically but also by its laws; for instance, all the inhabitants were obliged to carry travel documents when leaving the city.

Around 1880, Batavians started to lose their patience with the uncivilized rural areas around the city. A couple of decades later, there were attempts to reorganize both the governance and the infrastructure of the Ommelanden. This was a job for specialists, who were brought in from institutes of higher education in the metropole. The arrival of these new Europeans in the archipelago made practical experience of colonial administration an increasingly rare commodity. As a result, Europeans began to rely on intermediaries who understood the indigenous culture. These intermediaries also played an important role in gathering information about crime, including banditry.

The modern age

It is certainly true that after the First World War, there were many new elements of the political and socioeconomic landscape, elements which had not yet existed ten years earlier. First came the colony's early political independence movements, such as Sarekat Islam and Budi Utomo. Social services also began to bear fruit, with credit banks, agricultural programmes, and a growing variety of educational offerings. The entire street scene was transformed, as motor vehicles gradually replaced horses and carriages, and the modern shopping streets filled with European customers.

One representative of the modern age is A.F. Tillema, who is sometimes said to have ushered in the antithesis of *tempo doeloe*. Born in Friesland in 1870, Tillema left for the Dutch East Indies at the age of 26 to work as a pharmacist. In Semarang he converted a small business affiliated with the pharmacy where he worked into a modern soft drink factory. Tillema believed that pure, clean drinking water was the basis of good health. He put up a slogan for his own brand of mineral water ('Hygeia-water-lemonade are unequalled.') on a large billboard displayed prominently in the centre of Semarang. When the city council forced him to remove it, he had it suspended from a hot-air balloon and flown over Semarang. But even more than hygiene, photography was Tillema's true passion. After he made his fortune with drinking water, he used it to publicize the poor living conditions of the indigenous population. Like Multatuli's famous novel *Max Havelaar*, Tillema's photographs documented the lives of local people.[1] He was especially interested in prisons, criminals, and the margins of society.

Europeans were eager to penetrate deeper into Indonesian society. Around 1900, rapid development in Europe lent new ambition to the colonial project. As part of its 'modern imperialism', the Netherlands expanded the territory under its control, and the influence of local rulers over governmental affairs was gradually diminished. One consequence of this was that the colonial authorities had no choice but to learn more about their indigenous subjects — after all, knowledge was power. A whole series of *adat* collections were published, detailing the customs of the archipelago's people. In *De indologen* (an *indoloog* was a European expert in the cultures of the East Indies), Fasseur describes how students of colonial administration were given a thorough grounding in the archipelago and its people, to prepare them for their future careers and teach them how to maintain 'order and tranquillity' (*orde en rust*) in the colony.

The new science of anthropology was used by the authorities to gather more and more information about the colony's people. Yet this information did not suggest many strategies for keeping urban and semi-urban areas under control. The colonial administration was confronted with major new problems, especially in and around Batavia, a veritable mega-kampong with a population of approximately 150,000. There, the ambiguities in the relationship between the state, its subjects, and its citizens were more likely to bubble to the surface than in other parts of the archipelago. Batavia was home to a rich variety of groups, all of which had economic opportunities. This encouraged the continuing growth of an urban middle class that included people of diverse backgrounds, all under the scrutiny of the burgeoning mass media.

When elements of the Indonesian population committed crimes or acts of defiance, the authorities' need for knowledge and control became even greater. It is only logical that, in the 1912 volume of the *Koloniaal Tijdschrift* (Colonial Journal), G. de la Valetta, a former Resident, cited the eighteenth-century French leader Joseph Fouché as his role model when it came to policing. The former Resident argued that officials in the Dutch East Indies, who all had to manage police officers at one time or another, should familiarize themselves with Fouché's ideas and working methods. Fouché, whom de la Valette called 'the canniest, most competent user of the police that any state has ever possessed',[2] was the French Minister of Police under three successive regimes: the revolutionary government, Napoleon's reign, and the restored French monarchy.

Fouché established a very large, well-equipped modern police force and instructed his men to gather certain information and pass it on to him. Each individual policeman tended to have only partial information about any given case; Fouché was the only one who possessed all the information and could therefore see the big picture and take appropriate action. This system required that many thousands of pieces of information be recorded for short- and long-term use. Fouché developed an atlas of crime data for this purpose, known as the *topographie chouannique*, which contained all the geographical information relevant to their work, such as the locations of houses, inns, caves, and other lodging places where suspicious characters were known to have stayed, and of their secret routes and meeting places for attacks and raids. This atlas was accompanied by a biographical file with hundreds of cards, each corresponding to a suspicious person. The atlas and the biographical file were updated each day, so that the police had a record of every action taken by these individuals. All convicts were systematically added to Fouché's atlas, so that they could be spied on until they died or disappeared behind bars forever. As soon as Fouché decided the time was ripe for action, he would order his subordinates to arrest the suspect in question.[3]

Fouché's principles inspired a great deal of imitation in many parts of the world, including the Dutch East Indies, where the authorities used policing and investigative techniques to monitor and control the local population. They learned, however, that the eye of a detective is difficult to reproduce by rational, scientific means. In the remainder of this chapter, I explore the paradox of the simultaneous emergence of two diametrically opposed phenomena: on the one hand, the idealization of the all-knowing, intuitive detective and, on the other hand, faith in progress in the form of new, scientific police methods, including dactyloscopy, the science of fingerprinting. Ultimately, public servants tried to create a written, bureaucratic record of what they believed to have been the intuitive knowledge of old-school colonial administrators, many of whom had come from the vanishing mixed-race world. This method of information-gathering yielded a treasure trove of new insights into the world of banditry, information that went beyond the romantic image of bandits which had taken shape around 1900. The focus of public interest shifted from bandit novels to detective stories, which emphasized not sex and violence, but the quest to discover the working methods, motives, and identity of the criminal. Fear and control became the watchwords, and indigenous people were dreaded and distrusted for their supposed magical powers. More than in the past, bandits were imagined to possess mystical knowledge.

Impenetrable wilderness

Despite the dawn of the modern era, travel in the Ommelanden was still virtually impossible. This emerges most clearly from an article by a number of European and Eurasian journalists at the *Bataviaasch Nieuwsblad* about a trip that they took to the Tanjoeng-Oost (East Tanjoeng) estate in 1916 to report on an uprising led by Entong Gendut. It is fascinating to see how the journalists continually contrast modern urban life with backward rural areas. Somewhere along the road to Buitenzorg they entered the kampong:

> On and on, down the hill. Then we found ourselves slipping and sliding. It was the worst kind of mud: thick, pasty muck that clung to your shoes and soiled your trouser legs from bottom to top. But for the time being, we still had a wide view. There were little ponds to the left and right, and wild streamlets coursed between the bushes. Beautiful birds in dazzling shades of green, red, and yellow rose into the air, chirping in outrage at the repeated interruption of their sleep.

> In a nearly dry *kali*, which we had to cross, lay a huge devil of a snake glaring at us with its head held high.[4]

Despite this unpleasant surprise, the journalists continued on their way,

> Onward, ever onward, and the longer we went on, the harder the journey. Almost crawling over the ground, we groped our way through a patch of jungle that was cold and clammy under the dense canopy of leaves. Up to our ankles in mud, we searched for living beings. Nothing, nothing! … In the distance, on the main road, a car raced past, tooting its horn loudly! A shudder ran through us, and in the darkness of the jungle we suddenly felt alone and abandoned. Suppose there were fellows lying in wait for us … a fat lot they would know about the paper … would they believe that our intentions were entirely peaceful? We couldn't help but laugh — it was such nonsense, there was nobody there.

The party was lost, even if the main road was still audible in the distance. And the 'native' they ran into could not help them either.

> We asked if he could point out the quickest route to the *djalanan besar* [main road – MvT]. He pointed behind him, uttering incomprehensible sounds. He would not accompany us, so intense was his fear of being nabbed.
>
> After wandering around for almost two hours, we finally made it back to the main road and stopped in a *waroeng* [small eating house] where many natives were gathered. Our colleague had to return home. It was already quite late, and after all, the essentials of what had happened still had to be reported in the newspaper. Off whooshed the car, raising great clouds of dust as it sped away.

Europeans were not the only ones who considered the Ommelanden a dangerous territory. Urban kampong-dwellers were equally ill at ease there. An older inhabitant of Kebun Kacang described how perilous a trip from Tangerang to Batavia was thought to be, even as late as 1925. The dangers included bandits, European soldiers, and *tjoeliks*,[5] little supernatural creatures who spread sickness and ruin according to Batavian folk tales. *Tjoeliks* were a violent fantasy that sometimes became gruesomely real, as two travelling Japanese salesmen found out in 1909 when looking for a place to stay in the village of Batoetoelis. They were soon being trailed by a crowd of people, who grew menacing and repeated the word *tjoelik*.

The Japanese apparently fit the popular image of these mythical creatures. None of the village's householders wanted to let the Japanese men inside. After trying and failing to find someone at the tram stop who would take them in, the two men returned to the village, where they were so viciously attacked with machetes that one of the two died.

When the perpetrators were sentenced, it was considered an extenuating circumstance that the Japanese men had been so careless as to venture into a rural village at a time when the fear of *tjoeliks* had such a strong hold on the people there. This fear was said to stem from a cholera epidemic in the area. The authorities decided that it was therefore understandable that the local population had panicked.[6] In traditional stories, bandits and *tjoeliks* were often mentioned in the same breath. They had little to do with each other, but did set off the same kind of mass hysteria.[7]

In the Ommelanden, not only were the authorities grappling with a wilderness landscape, but it was also entirely unclear who lived there. Identifying individuals was an issue of growing importance to the police. In a randomly selected newspaper from this period, the identification of a 'native' was a significant element of four of the ten stories in the police news section. The aim might be to track down 'unfaithful' (that is, runaway) household servants or fugitive *contractkoelies* (indentured labourers of indigenous or Chinese descent), or to identify the corpses of vagrants.[8]

Colonial officials had the most difficulty identifying indigenous people. The former Resident Gonggrijp, who wrote a series of ironic letters about life in the colony in the *Bataviaasch Nieuwsblad* under the pen name *Opheffer* (roughly meaning 'Civilizer'), was puzzled by the following description of a suspect still at large:

> Name: Kromo
> build: medium
> face: oval
> hair: black
> eyebrows: black
> colour: brown
> eyes: ordinary
> mouth: ordinary
> nose: ordinary, a bit flat
> distinguishing features: scabies scars on his legs. Why, if the man had *not* had any scars, I would have tried my best and put the police to work, with some hope of success, but finding a Kromo *with* scars on his legs? Oh no, that'll never work; they all have those.[9]

The public and the authorities also had a good deal of difficulty identifying bandits. This became clear in the press coverage of the mysterious bandit Sakam, who had terrorized the Ommelanden in 1886. His trial involved a series of mistaken identities.[10] The confusion about Pitung and Gantang and the tendency to blame them for all the crimes in the region is discussed in Chapters 8 and 9.

Identity

The colonial authorities in the Dutch East Indies were not the only people wrestling with this problem. In the late nineteenth century, attention to detail — to a person's individual characteristics — took on a more prominent role in scientific inquiry. A case in point is Freudian psychoanalysis, in which seemingly meaningless trivia are the subject of an investigation aimed at curing the patient. In the literary field, we see the rise of detective novels, the best known of which are the tales of Sherlock Holmes by Arthur Conan Doyle. In these books, Sherlock Holmes' keen ability to interpret details such as footprints is instrumental in catching criminals.[11]

A fascinating essay by the historian Carlo Ginzburg links this growing interest in individuals and details to late nineteenth-century social changes that may also account for the popularity of detective stories in the Dutch East Indies. Ginzburg's term for attention to detail, as a means of obtaining knowledge, is 'the evidential paradigm'. He points out the increasing difficulty of identifying individuals under the pressure of changing modes of production. Changes in the concept of criminal behaviour brought about a tendency towards prison sentences and away from corporal punishment, making it necessary to find ways of identifying criminals, especially recidivists. In addition, urbanization and industrialization dramatically increased many people's social and geographical mobility, making it easier for people to hide from the police.

All these factors were present in the Dutch East Indies after the abolition of the regime of forced agricultural labour known as the *Cultuurstelsel.* In the new legal order, employment relationships were more likely to be governed by contract, and breaches of contract created a great deal of work for the authorities. The colony's infrastructure expanded, so that people became much more mobile. Prison sentences replaced corporal punishment. In earlier days, lawbreakers had been identifiable by the scars of the rattan cane. Once the prison system was established, the only way to keep track of offenders was by maintaining records of their personal details.

Let us now briefly turn to one illustration of how the above-mentioned developments forced the colonial authorities to learn more about their territory and its people: the activities of Sarekat Islam in the Ommelanden, and the government's response to them. Sarekat Islam had been founded in 1912 in Solo to promote the interests of indigenous traders, but it soon became a kind of liberation movement with a religious character and protested against mistreatment of its members in the Ommelanden by landowners and Chinese usurers. All sorts of internal conflicts also arose within the indigenous population: between members of Sarekat Islam and non-members, for instance, or between Sarekat Islam and other associations such as Kong Dji Hin or Djoemiatoel Islammya. These conflicts were generally about trivial matters: a labour dispute, a quarrel over a house pet, or a party that had disturbed the neighbours. Since the authorities approved of Sarekat Islam — at least officially — public servants tried to resolve these conflicts without using too much force. As part of this diplomatic approach, they produced voluminous reports on villagers, their backgrounds, and their past conduct.[12]

Around the same time a number of new methods of identification were being developed in Europe as a response to changing social structures and geographic mobility, and such methods attracted growing interest in

Illus. 8 Mantri police class, probably 1928. Watch the paintings on the back wall, serving as learning material during the explanation of an identification system. (Collection Arie Hoorweg, IFA)

the Dutch East Indies. Alphonse Bertillon devised a system involving precise measurement of body parts, and the first photographic archives were created, but the best-known of these new methods was fingerprinting (also known as dactyloscopy) which met with great enthusiasm in the colonies. Colonial officials now had a way to tell apart their uncooperative indigenous subjects, who 'all looked the same'. And as Ginzburg notes, 'thanks to the fingerprint, even the least inhabitant of the poorest village of Asia or Europe was now identifiable and controllable'.[13]

In the Dutch East Indies, dactyloscopy became popular around 1915, a remarkably late date considering its much earlier introduction in British India. This difference probably has historical roots. In the Dutch East Indies, precise control of the indigenous population had been just as important in earlier times — the days of the Cultivation System, for instance — but it had been exercised by indigenous chiefs who could tell their subjects apart. The impact of early twentieth-century efforts to establish the identities of individual Indonesians is not hard to see if we read the colonial newspapers. Before 1910, reports of robberies and their investigation rarely include the names of the perpetrators. Such crimes are attributed to legendary bandits such as Sakam, Gantang, and Pitung. In contrast, reports on the crime wave that occurred around 1919 give both the robbers and the victims human faces: their names and occupations were reported widely in the newspapers.

The authorities also did their best to understand the perspective of indigenous criminals. The 1929 volume of *Koloniale Studiën* included the article 'Animisme in de Javaansche dievenwereld' ('Animism in the world of Javanese thieves', mentioned in Chapter 5), in which Vergouw describes how Javanese bandits prepared for their crimes: they took a combination of the Javanese and European calendar, added the safe and unsafe times on the day in question, and so forth. Bandits often worked with *dukuns*, experts in Javanese animism, to ensure their success. Calculating the right date for a professional burglary was quite complicated, but the article nevertheless concludes that:

> for a policeman who is aware of this set of 'superstitious' customs, it is often very easy to pick up the trail of the perpetrator, whether of a straightforward or complicated theft, by means of simple arithmetic.[14]

Whether or not any of this is true, we should not be surprised by the nostalgic longing for a good old-fashioned colonial official who knew all these things intuitively or had learned them at his mother's knee. In the 1920s, the colonial press reported that *Schout* Hinne (see next section) was well informed about Oriental superstition and knew the *dukuns* personally.[15]

Yet traditional knowledge was like a mirage; whenever any official approached the ideal of total harmony and omniscience, that ideal seemed to retreat further into the past. After 1915, in the period when new police methods were coming into use, there was a kind of longing for *tempo doeloe*, when colonial officials had supposedly had more influence over the locals thanks to their intuition and deep-rooted cultural knowledge. It was paradoxical; just as the police were amassing a body of evidential knowledge; the perceived need for traditional knowledge was growing.

Detective novels implicitly describe methods of obtaining knowledge and emphasize the importance of detail, much like traditional stories of hunters who track down their prey by following footprints and tufts of hair. Around the 1920s, such novels became tremendously popular in the Dutch East Indies; the reading public devoured both original 'Indo novels' and translations of European detective stories.

Commissioner Hinne: An Indo detective

The *schout* (sheriff) A.W.V. Hinne served in the Batavian police force for about 30 years, from the late nineteenth to the early twentieth century. He was a conspicuous member of Batavian society during his lifetime, and after his death, his name had a legendary ring for the people of the city. During his career, his name was frequently mentioned in crime journalism. In 1932, his adventures were even broadcast by the Nederlands-Indische Radio Omroep Maatschappij (NIROM), to entertain radio listeners. *Schout* Hinne also played an important role in the oral tradition of the indigenous population and appears in their stories to this very day.

Who was he? According to the colony's official records, Adolf Wilhelm Verbond Hinne (born in Borneo in 1852) was the son of a French infantry captain. Hinne himself claimed that he was the captain's adopted son, born under the name of Scipio. It was said that as a child he had been kidnapped by Acehnese pirates and lived with them for six years.[16] When he returned to civilization, he began his career at a Residency office in Padang, West Sumatra. His later positions included postmaster for the island of Ternate and forester in Central Java. Although we do know of a few early triumphs, such as Hinne's capture of the pirate Medomo, his

Illus. 9 A.W.V. Hinne (1852–1915), who served as a police officer in Batavia from 1887 until 1911. (Private collection Chris Hinne)

unmasking of the pseudo-sultan Adil of Halmahera, and his arrest of 'jungle thieves', it is reasonable to conclude that when Hinne became a police officer in Batavia in 1887, the only relevant job experience he had was his period as a forest ranger.[17]

Hinne started out as an *onderschout* (deputy sheriff) in the Batavian district of Tanah Abang. After shooting and killing the famous bandit Si Pitung in 1893, he was promoted to the rank of *schout* and made responsible for the entire Residence of Batavia. His exploits were reported regularly in the press. One day he might be shutting down a Chinese-run gambling operation with his sabre drawn,[18] and the next he might be assigned to a special unit responsible for ridding the Ommelanden of bandit gangs.[19]

The underworld took Hinnes' interference quite personally, as we see in the article 'Een samenzwering in de boei' (Conspirators cuffed), published in the *Java-bode*:

> On Friday the *commandant* at Mangga Besar received an anonymous letter informing him that the perpetrators taken into police custody for the murder of the Chinese man Ko Haij Soei, an inhabitant of Petodjo, and several others — natives accused of serious crimes — had formed a plan to escape from prison and rid themselves once and for all of *Schout* Hinne, by the simple expedient of murdering him.

An investigation was launched, which determined that the anonymous writer had been correct. But the newspaper also had good news: 'We have learned that *Schout* Hinne is not in the least concerned about this pack of thieves' dire plans for him.'[20]

Bandits had a great deal of respect for Hinne, who was said to be invulnerable. In 1913, during his lifetime, the *Bataviaasch Handelsblad* published a serial entitled 'De Indische Sherlock Holmes' (The Indo Sherlock Homes), whose protagonist was modelled after Hinne.[21] It describes how Hinne, disguised as a *dos-à-dos* coachman, arrests Gantang.[22] Gantang escapes from prison not long after, creating an opportunity for another spectacular arrest. The serial also describes how Hinne once shot down Pitung by luring him to a celebration in Kebayoran, a story which is also told in the *rancak* about Si Pitung. It is fascinating to see that during Hinne's lifetime there were already so many versions of his killing of Pitung. In the press, Hinne was portrayed as courageous and plain-spoken. He was the only one to take a stand against the wildly excessive use of spies by the Batavian police, as we see in the coverage of the Fatima affair, a *cause célèbre* in the colonial press. Fatima was a woman who was robbed and murdered on the estate of an Arab landlord. The newspapers presented Hinne as the only honest police officer on the case. He opened an investigation of the police force's failure to take Fatima's murder seriously. After the landlord complained, Hinne was assigned to investigate the crime. When he arrived on the scene, however, he learned that the house had already been searched on the orders of the police controller W.H.L. Johan. No potential evidence was found in the house, but within a week Hinne nevertheless managed to round up five suspects, including one spy working for Johan. Further investigation showed that a great deal of evidence had been destroyed by Johan's men.[23] Apparently, the newspaper articles about the case irreparably damaged the relationship between Johan and Hinne. Johan tried to clear his name in the press,[24] but the readers of the *Bataviaasch Nieuwsblad* had made up their minds long before that he and his spy had suspiciously strong ties to Batavia's criminal world.

In 1911 Hinne was appointed police commissioner (*commissaris*), with the special title of deputy chief commissioner (*adjunct-hoofdcommissaris*). But he never attained the highest rank of all, namely chief commissioner (*hoofdcommissaris*), a title created in 1911. His age may have played a role, but so may his mixed-race background and his lack of technical expertise. Hinne could console himself, however, with the thought that in addition to his regular salary he had earned more than 25,000 guilders in reward

Illus. 10 Wayang golek puppet representing 'Schout' Hinne. (Private collection Max Rijkschroeff)

money over the course of his career for the bandits and thieves whom he had brought to justice. He always generously shared these rewards with his men, throwing big parties at his home.[25]

His career on the force came to a sad end, however. One day he asked one of his men to clean his pistol. When the gun was returned to him, he pulled the trigger, thinking it was not loaded, and shot a police officer dead. This event brought on a nervous breakdown. Hinne retired that same year, after receiving his second knighthood, and died not long after.

Soon after Hinne's death, F. Wiggers published a Malay-language detective novel called *Fatima*, about the mysteries surrounding a woman of that name. The book presents Hinne not only as a brave, honest, and virtuous man, but also as a detective on the case. Fatima is a beautiful, successful jewel dealer. Soon after she was born, it was predicted that she would have a good life and accomplish a great deal, until the age of about 50, when she would meet with a terrible fate. The prophecy comes true: around that age she is brutally murdered. The police investigation turns up few leads. To readers used to the Sherlock Holmes variety of detective novel, the climax of the story comes as something of a surprise. Hinne's method of uncovering the truth and identifying the killer is to have eyes and ears — police spies, that is — in the right places.[26]

The novel implies that Hinne used this method to solve many of Batavia's most puzzling cases. He is also said to have unmasked the notorious bandits Sakam, Pitung, and Gangtang. As far as Pitung goes, this is true, but research in newspapers and other sources does not suggest that Hinne played an important role in arresting Sakam and Gangtang and their followers.[27] Malay-language books like *Fatima* are always somewhat socially engaged and educational in intent. For instance, *Fatima* ends by holding up Hinne as a shining example for all police officers.

The mythologizing of Hinne reached its pinnacle between 1930 and 1940. Europeans perceived Indonesian society as a chaos in which only a few insiders could manoeuvre successfully. This perspective was shared by ordinary European colonists and the authorities in Batavia. In the 1933 story 'De Tentoonstelling' (The Exhibition) by journalist Victor Ido, Hinne helps the Resident of Batavia out of a perilous situation. In a story that should be read symbolically, the Resident is trapped in a garden maze set up for the Batavia Exposition of 1893:

> In the distance, he saw Sheriff Hinne, that plucky, still-unforgotten policeman, who had saved the lives of so many of Batavia's citizens. Hinne ran towards him, and was surprised to see the Resident, who cupped his hands into a little megaphone and called out with all his might, 'Hinne, have some of these *paggers* [bamboo enclosures — MvT] chopped down. I'm trapped here.'
>
> 'Understood, Resident,' came the reassuring reply. In the twinkling of an eye, Hinne had set to work ten coolies armed with machetes, who cleared a direct path to the centre of the maze.
>
> 'Thank you, Hinne, you have done me a great service,' the Resident said with relief.[28]

This passage shows how much importance was attached to intermediaries like Hinne when there were problems to be solved.

The Indo detective's greatest triumph

Hinne was a legendary figure, and it is difficult to separate the man from the myth. The figure of the indispensable intermediary appears frequently in popular fiction from the Dutch East Indies. The title of this section — 'The Indo Detective's Greatest Triumph' — comes from that of a detective novel published in 1924, *De schoonste triomf van de Indo-detective*. In fact, this title reveals the essence of the book's plot: an ordinary Indo boy proves himself smarter than the police, using his ingenuity to track down a gang of bandits. This novel, written by Ucee (a pen name of the Indo official Ulrich Coldenhoff), was reprinted in 1986 in a limited edition with a foreword by the Indo author Tjalie Robinson.[29] This foreword describes the elements of the book: the ethnic mixing bowl of Batavia, humour, suspense, mystery, and descriptions of scenes that were familiar to the readers, such as a hunt in Pesing or a masked ball in the Batavia Zoo.

De schoonste triomf van de Indo-detective was a runaway success. This undoubtedly encouraged Ucee to write more books of the kind, such as *De rode gerbera* (The Red Gerbera) and *Het spookhuis in Tanjoeng Priok* (The Haunted House in Tanjoeng Priok). The power of these stories lies in their use of local colour. The main character in *De schoonste triomf van de Indo-detective* is Leo, an Indo who is just as home among Europeans as he is in a kampong. He is best friend with the chief police commissioner and rubs shoulders with the Batavian elite, but he also travels incognito to the Ommelanden by third-class train, venturing into a rural kampong on foot. After numerous accounts of hunting, fights between *jago*s, and jaunts on mopeds, motorcycles, and other vehicles described in painstaking detail, the novel reveals that the head of the gang is an Indo who turned to crime after his trust was betrayed by his boss at the trading company where he worked.

The striking thing is that Leo, like Hinne, is an Indo protagonist who aids the colonial regime, the ultimate European bulwark, in its fight against crime. The status of the Indo in the Dutch East Indies is comparable to that of other Eurasian (part-European, part-Asian) groups in Asia at that time. Members of these mixed-race groups were in a position to cross social borders within their respective colonies, changing not only their clothes but also their conduct and circles of friends. Anne McClintock calls this phenomenon 'colonial passing',[30] giving the example of Kim, the main character of the novel of the same name by the British author Rudyard Kipling.

Kim lives in British India, where — like Hinne and Leo in the Dutch East Indies — he occupies the borderlands between the European and Asian communities. Because Kim's father was an Irish sergeant, he is 'racially' closer to the Indian community than he would have been if his father had been a full-blooded Englishman. Kim is an orphan, raised in the old city of Lahore by a mixed-blood woman who keeps him out of the hands of the missionaries by passing as white. Kim loves disguises, and can fit into many different social and ethnic environments. Europeans see him as diving effortlessly 'into the happy Asiatic disorder'.[31] As a spy, he is a great asset to the colonial leaders.

The similarities to Hinne's story are plentiful. Hinne also claimed to have been adopted, and his many false identities are mentioned in Jan

Illus. 11 Investigators in training, probably 1928. (Collection Arie Hoorweg, IFA)

Fabricius' book *Tempo doeloe* (1949). He is said to have wandered the Residence of Krawang disguised as a Javanese cripple in order to capture a *rampok* leader. While shadowing criminals, he might wear the uniform of a soft drink salesman, a coachman, or any number of other occupations. He also spoke four or five local languages.[32]

According to McClintock, lives such as Kim's suggest that Eurasians did not have a divided or torn identity imposed on them by the colonial authorities, and were not engaged in systematic anti-colonial resistance. The same point could be made about the Indo detectives discussed above. Kim's powers of imitation blur the boundary between the colonizers and the colonized, suggesting a new, reformed variety of colonial control in which the ambiguous nature of individuals such as Kim is harnessed to strengthen colonial authority.

Intermediaries such as Hinne, the Indo writers Ucee and Wiggers, and Raden Prawoto — who gave the authorities in the Dutch East Indies the idea of compiling a book of criminals — played an important part in shaping the public image of bandits. It was in these intermediaries' interest to make people believe that the world of banditry was difficult to fathom, because that belief made them indispensable.[33]

CHAPTER 8

The Bandit Si Pitung and Popular History

Around the mid-twentieth century, Batavian banditry started to disappear from popular Dutch historiography. Two books were published just after the Second World War: the memoirs of I.H. Misset, Batavia's chief of police, and a book by Jan Fabricius entitled *Tempo doeloe*, one entire chapter of which is devoted to Hinne and Si Pitung. The name Hinne also cropped up occasionally in the magazine *Moesson*, produced for a Dutch readership with roots in the Dutch East Indies.[1] Hinne's truncheon still lies in an attic in Oldemarkt, in northern Overijssel. Unfortunately, his letters were recently thrown away by a great-grandson.

The Indonesian collective memory is in a somewhat better state, and the memory of the bandit Si Pitung is still alive and kicking. He is the popular hero of the *Betawi*, the 'real' native Jakartans. According to oral tradition, Si Pitung lived at the end of the nineteenth century and was a thorn in the side of the colonial authorities, as one of the many outlaws who prowled around Batavia and the Ommelanden. But legend has it that Si Pitung was more than just a bandit; he possessed supernatural gifts that enabled him to outwit the authorities time and again. It is interesting to see what his story has to teach us about banditry in the Dutch East Indies.

We shall see in the following pages that there is nothing new about today's interest in documenting the popular history of Batavia/Jakarta. Writing popular local history has long been part of the city's culture, and it was influenced by the ideas of the people who lived in Batavia around 1900. The resulting stories were shaped by oral tradition, the press, the theatre and later the cinema. In this chapter I shall try to shed some light on this process by studying the stories of the legendary *jago* Si Pitung. We shall look at the interaction between newspaper articles, films and indigenous literary art forms such as *lenong* and *rancak*,[2] before turning to consider the value of the story of Si Pitung as a historical source.

The colonial sources

The folkloristic figure of Si Pitung can be traced back to a historical person of that name who lived at the end of the nineteenth century. The first items about him appear in the Malay daily newspaper *Hindia Olanda* in the summer of 1892. That he was not well known at that time is clear from the different spellings of his name: sources refer to him variously as 'a certain Bitoeng' or 'Pitang', but after a few months his name is spelt consistently as 'Si Pitoeng'.[3]

It is immediately apparent from the earliest newspaper reports that he was a colourful figure. On 18 June 1892, *Hindia Olanda* reported that the sheriff of Tanah Abang had searched the house of one Bitoeng in the Sukabumi kampong in Kebayoran, south of Batavia. He found stolen goods including a black coat, a sheriff's cap and the uniforms used by the bandit and his accomplices when entering kampongs, dressed as police officers, to rob houses.[4] A month later, during another search, a hiding-place was discovered under the house, containing 125 guilders and the proceeds from two big recent robberies targeting the homes of Nonya de C. and Hadji Sapiudin, the latter being a Buginese man from Marunda.[5] Si Pitung had forced his way into this *haji*'s home with five accomplices (Abdul Rachman, Moedjeran, Merais, Dji-ih and Gering) in the night of 30–31 July 1892, armed with pistols. One of the bandits threatened the owner with a firearm while his comrades fired warning shots to keep the neighbours at bay.[6]

In August 1892, Si Pitung and some of his companions were arrested after the police was tipped off by the village chief, Kebayoran, who received 50 ringgit in return for the tip.[7] In the spring of 1893, Si Pitung and his friend Dji-ih staged a mysterious escape from the prison of the village Meester Cornelis. An internal investigation of this escape yielded little useful information. The four prison guards fell under suspicion but all denied any involvement in the escape. One fellow-convict admitted having given Si Pitung a pick-axe. It further transpired that the fugitives had negotiated a roof-gutter before climbing over the wall to freedom.[8]

So Si Pitung was at large once again. Numerous rumours about his comings and goings circulated in Batavia. According to one, he had been seen wearing women's clothes aboard a French packet boat. Two plain-clothes police officers were despatched to the ship forthwith, but they could not find their quarry among the crowds of passengers.[9] The bounty on the heads of Si Pitung and Dji-ih gradually rose to 400 guilders.[10] Their escape presented the governor-general of the Dutch East Indies with a dilemma. Si Pitung and his gang had been sentenced to death for the robbery of Hadji Sapiudin. They had submitted a collective plea for a reprieve that the court had been inclined to grant, but then just before the commutation of their sentences was to be announced, two of the convicts escaped. So what should be done with the pleas now, especially since the two escaped convicts were reported to have immediately resumed their old profession? The case spawned lengthy legal debates in Buitenzorg about the nature of pardons and the seriousness of the crimes committed by Si Pitung and Dji-ih. From Si Pitung's plea for clemency we learn that his real name was Salihoen and that he was illiterate, since he signed the document with a cross.[11]

Illus. 12 The house of Hadji Sapiudin, currently the Pitung Museum in Marunda. Along the coast well-to-do Buginese lived in such houses. (Private collection Ron Habiboe)

After his escape, Si Pitung focused on settling his accounts with his enemies; at least, this is the impression created by the large robberies he and his gang committed, in which ample use was made of pistols. In one instance he set off with Dji-ih and shot Djeram Latip, a known police informer.[12] His violent robbery of the indigenous woman Mie yielded a remarkable booty including a knife and a pinfire revolver.[13] Pitung and other robbers' gangs did not flinch from choosing women as their victims; Nonya de C. has already been mentioned, and on another occasion Pitung stole sarongs worth hundreds of guilders from the proa of a woman merchant.[14]

Dji-ih was re-arrested. Having fallen ill, he had been compelled to leave the safety of the forest and go to the kampong to be nursed back to health. He moved in with an old acquaintance in Kebayoran. A *juragan* (supervisor) heard of his arrival and reported it to the *demang*, who descended on the house in question with a group of armed attendants. Although Dji-ih had two revolvers virtually within hand's reach, he was unable to defend himself.[15] He decided to surrender and was taken away amid a great show of official muscle:

> It was the demang of Kebajoran who arrested Dji-ih [Dji-ie],[16] after which the sheriff of Meester Cornelis was sent to help transport the man to prison. This transfer was effected with an escort of kampong chiefs, while the demang and the sheriff walked ahead, their sabres drawn. The procession drew crowds of onlookers.[17]

The newspapers concluded that Dji-ih had received help from people in the kampong, and that the same must apply to Si Pitung. One Dutch-language paper carried an item suggesting a certain internationalization of crime: 'Dji-ih had escaped to Singapore once before'.[18]

The official who had provided the information leading to Dji-ih's re-arrest had little time to enjoy his success. He found himself face to face with Pitung in a quiet, remote place, and though he aimed his weapon at the bandit, 'Si Pitung drew his own revolver at lightning speed and shot the official, who died on the spot.'[19]

Sheriff Hinne determined to track Si Pitung down, as did the *jaksa* (local public prosecutor) Moedjimi, later known as the 'demang Bekasi'. Both turn up frequently in the oral tradition as the antagonists of Si Pitung. In the turbulent month of August 1893, Si Pitung and his gang tried to get rid of a Chinese spy who was working for Moedjimi.[20]

Not long after this, in October 1893, Si Pitung was finally put out of action. Sheriff Hinne heard from a police informer that the bandit was in

Kampong Bambu, between Tanjung Priok and Meester Cornelis. But on his way there, another spy told him that Si Pitung had gone to a graveyard in Tanah Abang. A Dutch newspaper reported that the criminal had been lured away from Meester Cornelis by another local informer working for Hinne. The sheriff and his assistants surrounded the graveyard, making it impossible for Si Pitung to escape. Hinne's two assistants saw Si Pitung among the graves, wearing shorts and a revolver-belt full of cartridges. In the ensuing gun battle, Si Pitung fled in the direction of Hinne, who lay ready to ambush him. But when the sheriff saw a man running towards him he did not immediately recognize him and asked the neighbourhood officer close by who it was:

> 'Anak ketjil' [= a small child], replied the officer. But when the figure turned around, stood still and asked the sheriff to approach, the latter instantly complied, at which the tot fired a shot from his revolver. The sheriff immediately responded in kind. Both shots missed their targets. The next bullet hit Si Pitung in the arm. He stayed standing and continued to return fire, but without success. A third shot pierced the criminal's chest and knocked him to the ground. At this, the sheriff approached him, but when he was close to the wounded man, the latter rose and aimed another bullet at his pursuer, who nimbly sprang aside and avoided it. At the same moment, constables who had heard the loud cracks of gunfire came running, and one of them shot Si Pitung again; the bullet entered his lower back and went through his body, emerging from his belly. That shot put him out of action. He was immediately taken to the local infirmary. Si Pitung responded to the insults of the constables who accompanied the transport by occasionally singing a merry song. Not long afterwards, he died of his injuries.[21]

As he lay dying, Si Pitung asked for a glass of *towak sama ijs* (sake with ice), which a Dutch newspaper stated that he was given,[22] but the Malay newspaper *Hindia Olanda* stated that he was not.[23] The man's relatives came to claim the body, which request was initially turned down. On Sunday, at 5 p.m., Si Pitung's body was taken to the graveyard of Kampong Baru.

The Malay newspaper also reported that Si Pitung had been seen that Sunday morning in Pasar Senen, where his hair had been cut.[24] This isolated observation may be related to the popular superstition that is still encountered today in some versions of the Si Pitung story, according to which the haircut supposedly robbed him of his strength.[25]

Sheriff Hinne was showered with praise for his actions. The medal he received as 'Brother' in the Order of the Netherlands Lion was richly deserved, according to the *Hindia Olanda*.[26] The *Locomotief* added the following comments:

> Mr Hinne's conduct in this case cannot be praised highly enough. For nights on end he lay concealed in the shrubbery to arrest the scoundrel, to no avail. The police was kept busy with that fellow for over six months. Everyone was afraid of him, and trembled at the mere mention of his name, and the people gave him whatever he asked for.[27]

When Hinne was promoted from deputy sheriff in the Tanah Abang district of Batavia to sheriff of the city and suburban districts of Batavia/ Weltevreden one year later, Si Pitung's arrest was still fresh in his superiors' minds: it was 'something that no other police officer had been able to achieve'.[28]

But Si Pitung was not forgotten either. In fact there was some danger that his grave might become a place of pilgrimage. The authorities stationed four soldiers around it to prevent this happening.[29]

Si Pitung for Dutch readers

The Dutch writer Jan Fabricius has also written about Si Pitung. Jan Fabricius (the father of the more famous Johan Fabricius, whose works include the children's classic *De scheepsjongens van Bontekoe*) was a journalist, besides which he produced plays and history books. Father and son were adepts of a genre that was very popular both in the Netherlands and in the colony. The short story collection *Tempo doeloe* (published in 1949) includes a piece entitled 'Hinne', but the title 'Pitung' (as Jan Fabricius himself remarks) would have been just as apt. It tells the story of Hinne's arrest of the notorious bandit Pitung. In this story, Pitung is a bandit who terrorizes the population of Batavia in the nineteenth century, committing murder and rape, arson and plunder. He frequently operates alone, but holds the villagers under his spell with an insidious mix of charm and intimidation. No one who betrays him can escape his avenging hand. Pitung is also invulnerable on account of a *jimat* shaped like a cock's feather that he wears in his headscarf. This *jimat* was given to him by a *dukun* and can make Pitung invisible if he touches it.

The version of Pitung who appears in Fabricius' story, however, has a fatal flaw: a weakness for women. Although his attentions are not unrequited, the women's admiration is admixed with a large dose of fear. It is an indigenous woman who brings Si Pitung down after he rapes her; seeking revenge, she informs Hinne of Pitung's movements. Hinne, a master of disguise, dresses up as a sado cab-driver and manages to take up a strategic position: Pitung unsuspectingly gets in as a passenger and is overpowered after a long struggle. Fabricius has Pitung die on the gallows in Batavia's old city square. The writer describes the outlaw smoking a cigar as he is driven to his death.

This version of the Pitung story diverges from others: not only is Pitung's death changed, but so too is the arrest by Hinne, which in this case occurs when the sheriff is disguised as a sado cab-driver. Interestingly, this episode occurs in stories about a different bandit, Gantang. All in all, we see that stories targeting the Netherlands are crafted differently from those written for the colony.[30]

Fabricius' story, written 50 years after the event, contains few of the elements we have noted in the news reports. The function of the story is the same as that of the crime stories in the previous chapter: to provide reassurance to Indo-European citizens in a changing world beset by ill-defined foes.

Oral tradition

After decolonization, little more was written in the Netherlands about banditry in the Dutch East Indies. But quite the opposite applied in the newly independent Indonesia: Si Pitung became a popular hero. A few years ago, when I visited the eighteenth-century country estate of Cilincing, just beyond Tanjung Priok, the local population assumed that I was looking for Si Pitung's house, now a museum, in the nearby village of Marunda. This is a good example of the way in which the descendants of colonizing and colonized peoples may find themselves talking utterly at cross purposes, on the basis of their respective historiographies.

The adventures of Si Pitung are part of the standard repertoire of *Betawi* story-tellers. Palupi Damardini, a student at the University of Indonesia, has catalogued the stories of Si Pitung and analyzed them in accordance with literary rules.[31] A great many variations exist on the story of Si Pitung, but the following tale of his life can be broadly distilled from them.

Si Pitung was born in the *desa* of Pengumben in Rawabelong, close to the present-day station of Palmerah in Jakarta. His parents were *Bung* Piung and *Mbak* Pinah. In his youth, Si Pitung was sent to study at an Islamic boarding-school or *pesantren* run by Hadji Naipin. At the same time he had to trade in goats to provide for himself. One day he was robbed of the money he had received for the sale of his father's goats at market. It was this incident that prompted him to become a thief. According to some versions of the story, he started down this path to repay his debts. And some emphasize that he established his reputation as a *jago* in the ensuing struggle to recover his money from the bandits.

Si Pitung formed a gang with Dji-ih, Rais and Jebul, and together they planned to rob the house of Hadji Sapiudin, a wealthy land-owner in Marunda (today the premises of the Si Pitung Museum). According to popular tradition, the gang devised the following trick. They gave the *haji* a letter stating that he had been accused of counterfeiting and instructing him to have all his money checked at the office of the *demang* of Bekasi (the local chief administrative official). When he appeared, they took his money and made off with it.

The colonial authorities obviously puzzled their heads over a response to this and other robberies. Hinne, sheriff of Batavia,[32] resolved to catch Pitung and his accomplices. At one point he actually managed to arrest them, but the villains staged a successful escape from the prison of Meester Cornelis, supposedly by invoking supernatural powers. Hinne subsequently forced Si Pitung's mentor, Hadji Naipin, to reveal Si Pitung's *jimat*, so as to neutralize its hidden force (other versions state that Si Pitung's accomplices, with the exception of Dji-ih, turned police informers). Si Pitung was then deprived of his talisman and his knife, and eventually killed with a gold bullet. In other stories, Si Pitung's powers were lost when his hair was cut, or — in one more banal version — when someone pelted him with a rotten egg.

Si Pitung's grave was placed under guard by the Batavian authorities since a rumour was circulating among the local population that he would rise from the dead. The following lines are taken from an English version of the ballad *Rancak Si Pitung*:[33]

> Si Pitung is dead; and his relatives have been told.
> His bier was carried from Krekot; he was buried in Penjaringan.
> I know someone in the hospital who spread the story
> That his guts were preserved in spirit.

At his funeral the police provided an escort.
The grave of champion Pitung was guarded;
Those keeping watch on Pitung's grave through the night
Were forbidden to leave until their reliefs had arrived.
For the night guard
Had told the story that Pitung had come to life again in his grave.
The convicts in chains who had to dig him up said it was very hard,
Even though picks and shovels had been provided.
They had to dig him up because the commissioner was suspicious.
Looking into the grave with a telescope they saw that it was still Pitung's corpse.
You could see clearly that it was Pitung's body.
It was printed by the newspaper, of the news agency,
That his ribs were shattered where the bullets had struck.
When Pitung died, Mr Hinne ordered a feast at Tomang,
To which hordes of people came,
And where all kinds of games were permitted.
The feast was permitted to go on for seven days and nights.
The aim of the feast was to catch Pitung's band of men,
It was planned to capture Pitung's band.

The nature of Si Pitung's robberies varies from one story to the next. Some narrators describe him as a hero who stole from the rich to give to the poor, while others take a more cynical view.[34] An elderly resident of Jakarta explains the current adulation of the bandit in terms of the film industry. Si Pitung was the ideal hero for the *merdeka* Zeitgeist that until recently guaranteed full houses at Indonesian cinemas.[35]

The Robin Hood image of Si Pitung appears to derive primarily from the Jakartan author Lukman Karmani,[36] whose version of the bandit's story, published in the late 1960s, highlighted the socio-ethnic aspects of his life. He also wrote a number of successful screenplays for the Si Pitung films of the 1970s, based on stories told by ageing Jakartans.[37]

Finally, that Pitung's memory is alive and well among 'real' Jakartans (the Betawi people) and can be invoked for many purposes is shown by the 2002 slogan, 'menjaga warisan Si Pitung' ('watch over Si Pitung's heritage'). This catchphrase was adopted by a movement headed by Sabeni Jr, a popular local leader, in which the indigenous Betawi people joined forces to oppose the criminal gangs threatening Jakarta from the east of the archipelago.[38]

Pramoedya Ananta Toer

In the book *House of Glass* by Indonesia's most celebrated writer, Pramoedya Ananta Toer, Pitung plays a leading role as the embodiment of the initial 'primitive' resistance to colonial rule. *House of Glass* (published in 1988) is the final volume in Pramoedya's Buru Quartet, four novels about the early days of Indonesian nationalism. In the first three books, the first-person narrator and protagonist is Raden mas Minke, and the story begins at the time of his birth in the late nineteenth century. Minke gradually becomes aware of the existence of colonial oppression. He found a popular liberation movement (similar to *Sarekat Islam*) and takes a job as a journalist for a Malay-language newspaper. At one point the authorities expel him to the Moluccas.

The fourth book, *House of Glass,* is narrated by Pangemann, Minke's adversary, who had served as chief of police before becoming an official of the Internal Affairs department of the General Secretariat of the colonial government. Pangemann is of indigenous extraction and is plagued by divided loyalties: an ambitious man who wants to be loyal to the authorities he serves, he nonetheless finds himself increasingly in sympathy with the Indonesian protest movement. This inner conflict provides the backdrop for Pangemann's view of the colonial authorities.

House of Glass is a novel about colonial paranoia. The colony is the glass house — that is, the place in which nothing escapes the attention of the security service and his spies. But Pangemann in turn feels cornered. His conscience torments him, especially his memories of Pitung, the man he has long since disposed of:

> My superior officer, the chief of police Van Dam tot Dam, a man who boasted that he was a full-blooded Dutchman, without any English or Jewish blood, gave me an odd assignment one day: to destroy the remains of Si Pitung's gang, who were still active around Cibinong, Cibarusa and Cileungsi, and in the area surrounding Batavia and Buitenzorg.
>
> From the desk in the crime department I set off into the field. At the time, the police was responsible for maintaining internal security. The army was not involved unless specifically asked to join in. The establishment of a permanent police force was a consequence of all the wars, great and small, that were being fought beyond Java. I had been part of it from the outset. So I had set off with a regiment of military police, a force of some sixty men from Batavia and Buitenzorg.

> In the district where the remains of Si Pitung's gang still held sway, there was no law or administrative authority, and the place was ruled by terror and anxiety, murder and manslaughter, abductions and physical abuse. I divided the district up into small areas, which I transformed, in rapid, harsh and merciless actions, into miniature battlefields. The British, Dutch and Chinese owners of the estates had already moved their families to places of safety in Batavia or Buitenzorg.
>
> ... [The gang] used sawn-off rifles that were easy to carry unobtrusively. They had already destroyed the landlords' own security services, and that did not make our operation any easier. Services of that kind greatly alleviate the task of the police, even though they too are essentially violent gangs concerned to defend the landlords' interests.[39]

Pangemann studied meticulously the case files he had on Si Pitung, besides which he spoke to a journalist who was writing an article about the bandit. He combined all the information from these sources to form a picture of Si Pitung:

> He was depicted as a cruel, unpredictable, uncivilized man who invaded villages with his gang, murdering, plundering and committing arson, and subjecting tax collectors to sadistic ill-treatment as if they were his personal enemies. He killed people who were doing the government's bidding, regardless of their ethnic origin. And all his actions were poorly mimicked by the remnants of his gang.... But not one of the gang members could explain the reasons for his resistance ... since they were unable to express their emotions. Even so, I gradually began to form a better picture of this Si Pitung. A small moustache and a thin beard, thick-set and not very tall. According to the papers, he wore a white robe and a turban for every robbery, flanked by servants carrying his sirih box and his rifle.[40]

Pangemann goes on to dub Minke the modern Pitung, in other words someone who *could* express his grievances verbally. It must be added that both Minke and Pangemann come to a sorry end: Minke dies disillusioned and alone, while Pangemann ends up as a hopeless alcoholic. Still, it is clear how Pramoedya wishes to present Pitung as the first resistance fighter in the struggle against colonial rule, and as a social bandit *pur sang*.

Pitung in popular history ...

Why tales of outlaws such as that of Pitung were created, and with what readership in mind, has frequently exercised the minds of historians. In 1960, the celebrated ballad of Robin Hood was subjected to scholarly research in an attempt to identify its origins and readership. A key issue in the ensuing debate was whether the epic had been written for commoners or for the landed nobility.[41] More recently, the historian John T. Sidel studied twentieth-century bandits in the Philippines, a country not far from Indonesia. He analyzed the public that enjoyed films and comics about the mafia leader or social bandit Putik (1920–70). Sidel discovered that Putik's real admirers were to be found not so much in his own local community as among wealthy Philippine businessmen and politicians.[42]

Although Eric Hobsbawm briefly discusses the creators of — and the market for — books, plays and films about social bandits, in *Primitive Rebels* (1959) and *Bandits* (1969), it is hard to avoid concluding that this issue is rather neglected in his work. Were we to find that the stories of bandits were written and appreciated by the middle classes and not the poor peasants, his theory of banditry as a form of pre-capitalist peasant rebellion would be fairly untenable. For picaresque novels supplied Hobsbawm with his primary source material. According to one leading critic of Hobsbawm, Anton Blok, bandits were to a large extent idealized by the urban middle classes. Nonetheless, Blok continued to maintain that the idea of the social bandit originated from the small peasants, which may of course have been true of the areas he studied, such as the island of Sicily.[43]

A good reconstruction is given of the recent genesis of a bandit's legend in the book *God Protect Me from My Friends*, about the bandit Giuliano Salvatore (1923–50). The author, Gavin Maxwell, was fortunate enough to be able to do his research for the project just after Salvatore's death. This made it possible to study myth formation while the truth was still accessible. His work reveals the overriding influence of the press and the vanity of the bandit, who modified his life-style to fulfil the expectations of the press and the general public.

Past research on the sources of stories about robbers and 'social bandits' is relevant to this study, since it can be used to expose any bias that might exist in that source material. This in turn can help to devise a more objective approach to 'the bandit and his surroundings'.

Initially, the story of Si Pitung was probably based on rumours. It was structured by indigenous and Eurasian journalists, who based themselves on the plethora of European robbers' tales that appeared in the nineteenth century, in the local and European press. Soon afterwards, the stories were adopted by other media. It was probably the Chinese managers of *bangsawan* and *lenong* (types of Indonesian theatre) and the readers of newspapers published in Dutch and Malay who introduced the illiterate Indonesian public to the bandits' stories. Along the way, the stories absorbed a certain influence from Chinese culture. It appears that the Indo-European and Chinese urban middle classes played just as large a part in the stories' evolution as the Indonesian urban population.

... and in Hobsbawm

The relationship between oral tradition and the written versions of stories is not easy to define. This leads to the whole question of the adoption of one social group's culture by a different group. Mutual influences between oral tradition and 'high' culture is a central concept in *Popular Culture in Europe 1500–1800* by Peter Burke. But he adds Dwight Macdonald's notion of the existence of a middle class of society that mediates between the culture of the lower classes and that of the upper class, transmitting them in both directions. For the dissemination of robbers' tales in the Dutch East Indies, too, this is a plausible viewpoint.

Some locals may well have fed information to journalists when the robbers' tales were taking shape in the late nineteenth and early twentieth centuries. After that, the stories attracted the attention of primarily Chinese writers and were published in chap-books. This was how Si Pitung's story was disseminated, and much the same happened with the tales of other notorious bandits such as Si Ronda and Si Tjonat.[44] These heroes also turned up in the dramatic plays known collectively as *stamboel.* Poems about these bandits were even made into gramophone records,[45] and appeared in films.[46]

One question that arises is why Si Pitung in particular should have become so famous, rather than Tjonat or one of the many later bandits, some of whom were far better known during their lifetime. Burke does not believe that this is a question of mere chance. It is easier to modify a person to correspond to an existing story than to create a new story about someone. Possibly Pitung had the characteristics of a noble outlaw. Or perhaps other factors, such as the introduction of revolvers in this period, may have played an important part.

Another question concerns the revival of interest in Si Pitung in the 1960s, this time with the paraphernalia associated with the social bandit.

Was this a matter of chance? The book and films about Si Pitung had been written by Indonesian intellectuals. It would appear quite possible — although it remains pure speculation — that Hobsbawm's work may have reached them by then. After all, *Primitive Rebels* appeared in 1959 and *Bandits* in 1969.

The same had happened in the late nineteenth century, when readers all over the world were inundated with stories about bandits, prompting journalists in the Dutch East Indies to create their own version of Rinaldo Rinaldini (a notorious Italian bandit). Other well-known novels about outlaws included *Schinderhannes van het Rijnland* ('Schinderhannes of the Rhineland') and *The Robbers of Calabria*. Stories of this kind had generally found their way to a growing readership in cheaply-produced books in the nineteenth century. When we consider the influence of tales of foreign outlaws on those about Batavian bandits, we are also struck by the similarity between the story of Si Pitung's disguises and the robbery carried out by Wilhelm Voigt while dressed up as a Prussian army officer (see Chapter 5).

Clearly then, the bandit stories have been influenced by diverse groups in Batavia over the past century, from Indo journalists to popular theatre

Illus. 13 A scene from one of the Si Pitung movies from the beginning of the seventies. Si Pitung, acted by Dicky Zulkarnaen, in the house of a Batavian *haji*. (Sinematek Indonesia, Pusat Perfilman H. Usmar Ismail, Jakarta)

troupes, *lenong* actors, *rancak* narrators and Chinese film producers. And all this raises the question of whether the following comment by Hobsbawm can withstand critical scrutiny:

> Social banditism of this kind is one of the most universal social phenomena known to history, and one of the most amazingly uniform. Practically all cases belong to two or three clearly related types, and the variations within these are relatively superficial. What is more, this uniformity is not the consequence of cultural diffusion, but the reflection of similar situations within peasant societies, whether in China, Peru, Sicily, the Ukraine, or Indonesia.[47]

As far as Indonesia is concerned, we can conclude that there was indeed a certain cultural influence at work in the creation of legends about banditry, social or otherwise. Perhaps the basis consisted not of uniform social conditions, but of a uniform discourse.[48]

While studying the sources, we must bear in mind that two influential narratives helped to shape the stories of outlaws in and around Batavia. Both had their origins in the urban middle classes. One dates from the 1960s, and describes the bandit as a popular hero. The other one is older, dating from the late nineteenth century, and is based on the city-dweller's subjective view of colonial order versus the chaos of the countryside.[49] As noted in Chapter 6, the latter is characterized by the projection of sex and violence onto Batavia's rural surroundings, and by the recurrent sense of confusion concerning the identity of these stories' protagonists.

Nonetheless, it is perfectly clear in popular culture which people loomed large in the perceptions of ordinary people. For the *rancak* 'Si Pitung' is not only about the hero Si Pitung. Within this story, a good *rancak* player also takes his audience down as many side-paths as possible, to depict the experiences of ordinary people and their conflicts with the surrounding world. Figures long forgotten in the official historiography are given special attention in the epic tradition — junior civil servants, for instance, people with whom the kampong-dwellers had direct dealings.

Looking at the written colonial sources, it is clear that these officials attracted local attention in their own day through their specific behaviour and character traits. Two examples are the *demang* of Bekasi and sheriff Hinne. The former was conspicuous for the many corruption scandals in which he was involved, and the latter for his cleverness and courage. The prominent place that these two men occupy in the oral tradition was one of the reasons for devoting attention to them in this book.

Elements of various other stories of indigenous bandits dating from around 1900 were incorporated into the Pitung legend. The tale told today of Si Pitung, in present-day Indonesia, should be seen as a blend of divergent accounts of Batavian society around 1900, incorporating aspects of tales of foreign outlaws. Some parts of this Pitung story can traced not to historical sources relating to Pitung himself, but to newspaper articles about other events in Batavia in the late nineteenth and early twentieth centuries. We also find descriptions of festivities, the introduction of modern innovations — from hospitals to firearms and films — to the kampongs, and an impression of how ordinary indigenous people would have experienced prison life. The story of Si Pitung therefore serves as an important vehicle — and that is what makes it so interesting — of the social history of Indonesia.

THE STATE

CHAPTER 9

The Fight Against Crime

Notwithstanding the long history of banditry in the Dutch East Indies, the story of the concerted effort to stamp it out does not start until 1903. Voices had been raised earlier in favour of forming a more modern police force, but it was the protests that erupted in response to the plague of robberies in 1902–3 that finally compelled the colonial authorities to take action.

Even Si Pitung's *annus mirabilis* of 1893 had yielded a score of only 15 robberies, and in the following few years the numbers had dwindled further. But in 1902 Batavia and the surrounding area was beset by a dizzying 122 incidents of *rampok*. The rest of the archipelago witnessed a similar rise in this kind of crime, albeit to a lesser extent. One difference between the robberies that took place around 1902–3 and those in other periods was the degree to which the European élite now suddenly found itself the target of the bandits. Europeans are also found among the perpetrators; in some cases they masterminded operations and supplied firearms.[1] The Malay press attributed the failure of the police to achieve any results to European involvement in the gangs.[2]

Europeans and indigenous people alike were in a state of alarm. Du Perron recalls this period in *Het land van herkomst*:

> As a child I had a vague fear that the robbers might suddenly burst forth from the river, in spite of the ravine. The *tongtong* (a hollowed-out wooden trunk that was struck to sound the alarm) was heard

> almost every evening those days; there was the amok *tongtong*: the manslaughter *tongtong*, and the fire *tongtong*: the servants heard the difference immediately, but I didn't; in my mind it was always about the bandits. Especially on the Buitenzorg side, there was one robbery after another.[3]

The realization that anyone might fall victim to *rampok*, even Europeans, made the robberies of 1902 to 1904 front page news. In later years, around 1918, the number of robberies would actually increase in absolute terms, but they attracted far less coverage because very few of the victims were European.

The 1902 wave of banditry even prompted questions in Parliament. Two different solutions were proposed: changes to the system of private estates and the reorganization of the police force.

Rampok in the press: Gentis and Gantang

The autumn of 1902 witnessed the biggest robbery in the history of the archipelago, a case that was even reported in the international press.[4] Two Europeans, Herman and Cornelis Gentis, together with their indigenous accomplice Natadisastra, committed an armed robbery of the Javasche Bank in the middle of Batavia. The incident had many features of an ordinary case of *rampok*, including the use of force and firearms, but was remarkable partly because the two main perpetrators were European and partly because of the enormous sum of money involved: an astonishing 110,000 guilders was stolen, a real fortune for the time. The event inspired an 1,800-line poem in Malay.[5] This spectacular crime may have encouraged others, such as the armed bandits who attracted attention with their theatrical violence the following year.[6]

One Gantang injected a more frivolous note into the topic of robbery, providing Batavia's newspaper readers with months of entertainment. His story is also significant in that it demonstrates the powerful effect of continuing rumours. Gantang's image was to some extent created by the press, and the pressure for an arrest steadily mounted. In consequence, a previously unknown Javanese man alleged to be Gantang was apprehended, on rather questionable grounds.

A Malay-language newspaper reported in 1902 that a robber leader called Gantang, who hated the rich and was generous to the poor, was active in the vicinity of Buitenzorg. The Malay press reported that he gave all his spoils away, that he was a ladies' man, and that he possessed arcane secrets.[7]

After a lull in crime, the number of robberies suddenly soared in the autumn of 1903, prompting a journalist from the newspaper the *Locomotief* to go to the Ommelanden to investigate.[8] In something of a journalistic cliché, the treacherous journey was described in the form of impassable roads, overgrown backwoods, intractable *sado* cab-drivers and equally intractable horses. In the end, the anonymous reporter arrived at the estate of a European who was willing to discuss the local situation.

The landowner told him that the robbers' leaders liked to call themselves *raja utan* ('kings of the forest'). To earn this title, you first had to join a gang as an apprentice and receive instruction in burglary, the martial arts, and magic. The latter would not work unless you were a devout Muslim. At length, the aspiring robbers would purchase the thieves' almanac, which would enable them to calculate the most favourable times and places for committing a robbery.

The discussion finally settled on Gantang, who held sway over the Ommelanden as *raja utan akbar* — 'the greatest king of the forest'. The story went that he had been born in a shabby little hovel on the estate of Villa Nova and had gravitated to a life of crime at an early age. He rose to become the right-hand man of Si Pitung. After the latter's death, Gantang's career flourished. He established the base of his operations in the wilderness near Buitenzorg, known as Utang Pejangan.

In a series of editorials about 'Our Mafia', the *Bataviaasch Nieuwsblad* held Gantang single-handedly responsible for the soaring crime rate.[9] These articles demonstrated the skill of journalists in the Dutch East Indies, in this case under the editorial oversight of Karel Zaalberg, in presenting implicit criticism of the government in the guise of sensational stories.

According to the 'Our Mafia' editorials, Si Gantang was an escaped prisoner who had spent six years in prison after being condemned to death. Like Pitung before him, he was sensational news, above all because of his successful mockery of 'the impotent authorities'. In public he unfailingly sported an Assistant Resident's hat, while his followers were dressed in the uniforms of colonial police officers.

When the Dutch authorities decided to apprehend Gantang, and sent the military police to track him down, he gave a fresh display of bravura. According to eye-witness accounts, he expressed delight to be finally facing worthy opponents instead of the useless indigenous police. Still, he went on, it was unfortunate that the military police had exhausted their ammunition so quickly, but he was willing to lend them some of his own.[10]

Some accounts relate that besides going about in the guise of a colonial official, Gantang also organized his own regime, collecting his own taxes and calling on the local population to perform certain regular duties. According to press reports, locals could choose whether to give him money or cattle. The services he required of them included compulsory participation in robberies. While these services were being performed, members of Gantang's gang would be stationed in strategic locations to prevent any outside interference. Besides robbing the locals, Gantang's gang also plundered the country houses of the Chinese and Europeans. The only way landowners could prevent attacks on their property, wrote the journalists, was to pay Gantang for safety and protection.

Gantang's success evidently inspired other bandits to exploit his name and fame. Just as in the case of Pitung, these enhanced his status and heightened the confusion regarding his whereabouts and true identity. The press saw in Gantang's actions an analogy with Rinaldo Rinaldini, the protagonist of an Italian crime novel that was extremely popular among Batavia's youth:

> … many-tongued rumour, with imagination as its guide, had concocted a fascinating story, something resembling a chapter from the picaresque novel *Rinaldo Rinaldini*, embellished, modified and expanded for the benefit of *couleur locale*.…[11]

Gantang was also dubbed 'Our Batavian Schinderhannes'.[12]

The story of Rinaldo Rinaldini and the careers of Pitung, Gantang — and Sakam — all display certain similarities: the many disguises, people's inability to recognize them, betrayal by close friends, frequent escapes from the prison, and the road ending at the gallows. The mix of Italian mafia stories and rumours about local bandits suggests that the population and press in Batavia liked to romanticize the bandits. And these bandits in their turn may well have been quite happy to oblige public opinion by living up to the image projected by the press.[13]

According to the *Bataviaasch Nieuwsblad*, Gantang had his headquarters in the kampong Pondok Gedé, about 15 kilometres to the south of Batavia. Yet despite the kampong's proximity to the centre of the colonial state, police seldom went there. Another newspaper, the *Java-bode*, wrote that Gantang had abandoned crime and was now living among retired colonial officials in the cool mountains of the Preanger.[14]

Eventually, Gantang — or someone believed to be Gantang — was arrested in a village near the little town of Kendal on the northern coast of Central Java, after a Batavian who had moved to Kendal happened to recognize him. Since a large police operation descending on the village would have attracted too much attention, the officers went disguised as huntsmen. As this party advanced, the village chief received a request from the police to assemble the entire local male population under the pretext of registration for taxes. The bogus huntsmen then arrested one Si Oenoes, whom they identified as Gantang. The identification was greatly impeded by facial injuries inflicted by one of the constables during the arrest. Even so, the suspect certainly looked the part: at 6 feet he was unusually tall, and he had an impressive moustache and a body that bore witness to a turbulent past, including traces of venereal disease and scars on the face and back attesting to prison beatings.[15]

The trial of Si Gantang/Si Oenoes generated little publicity. The reports may have been kept low-key quite deliberately, because Si Gantang knew too much about certain junior administrative officials. Strangely, the accused was not sentenced to death, even though this sentence had been passed on Si Gantang two years before. In any case, he continued to arouse the emotions of onlookers right up to the last moment; throughout the train journey to the forced labour site, he leered brazenly at European ladies.

But was this man really Si Gantang? Officials from the time of Gantang's earlier conviction were openly sceptical.[16] Members of the van der Capelle family — a European family that had been robbed by the bandit — also failed to recognize him.[17] A journalist from the *Java-bode* commented drily that if the *bertillonage* identification system had been introduced a few years earlier, when Gantang was still in prison, they would not be facing this problem.[18] In the end, the prisoner admitted to being Gantang, but denied any involvement in the *rampok* incidents in the Ommelanden. He maintained that he had deliberately stayed away from the Ommelanden because of some matter involving women.[19] The inconsistencies in the testimony led many to conclude that this Gantang was no longer the main culprit in the crime wave.[20] The prisoner even aroused public sympathy, with people complaining that he had been locked up in a hot cell for too long, since the court had taken so long to pronounce judgment.[21]

The convict was sent to Merauke. But just two years later, this 'dangerous criminal' was permitted to return to Batavia. What conclusion should be drawn?[22] Had the police simply arrested a different criminal to bolster its public image? Perhaps the authorities rather liked to create the impression that the mayhem in the Ommelanden, which they could not control, could all be blamed on a single bandit.

Bandits and government revisited: The *demang* of Bekasi

Gantang generated a huge number of reports in the press, and yet in government documents from the period 1903–4 he is hardly mentioned. The authorities evidently believed that the causes and possible solutions to the problem of banditry related only in part to the figure of Gantang. The Resident of Batavia saw Gantang's popular image as 'a mysterious, omnipresent individual' as a journalistic ploy to appeal to the public's sensibilities.[23] He was irritated — as were no doubt many officials at the Department of Internal Administration — by the unrelenting press coverage. In a letter to the Governor-General, the Resident commented, in reference to 'exaggerated' reports in the newspaper, that while a highly undesirable state of affairs existed in the Ommelanden, this was no recent development. The area surrounding Batavia had long been a safe haven for miscreants, even back in the days of the VOC, he maintained.[24]

But the local authorities were feeling the pressure. The newspapers and their readers not only wanted Gantang arrested, but they were also clamouring for harsh general measures against banditry; there were even calls for kampongs to be burned to the ground. In the Netherlands too, members of Parliament were demanding a solution. That the existing police force was not up to the task was clear to all. Some influential landowners therefore asked permission to set up their own private police army. This request was granted, and the deployment of this force, which was largely made up of former police and army officers, proved reasonably successful.[25] But it also led to more generalized vigilante actions, and while several bandits were arrested, some were killed during arrest. With the limited police resources at their disposal, the authorities tried to stop as many gaps as possible. One measure consisted of setting up a cordon of guards around Batavia, manned by indigenous police officers, to seal off the city from the chaos beyond. Some wanted the army brought in, but this was a tall order given the ongoing military commitments in Aceh and other parts of the Outer Islands. Instead, it was decided to deploy the military police when needed.

The authorities tried to improve their control of the Ommelanden by taking on more staff in the various Residencies and purging the administrative apparatus of unreliable elements. Attention soon focused on Moedjimi, the *demang* of Bekasi. In 1903, Moedjimi had over 20 years of public service behind him. He had started out as an unsalaried student in Tangerang, later becoming deputy public prosecutor and public prosecutor before being appointed *demang* of Bekasi.[26] A *demang* had the same rank as a *wedana*.[27] In the Ommelanden, the *demang* was accountable directly to the Assistant Resident. This made him a powerful intermediary between the local people and the colonial administration.[28]

A *demang*'s salary was 250 guilders, but in addition he was given a house free of rent and permission to generate up to 2,000 guilders in extra earnings, for instance by imposing his own local taxes. When Moedjimi was arrested in December 1903, prompting rumours that he was also the leader of a gang of robbers, the *Java-bode* commented cynically that there were many safer ways for a *demang* to make his fortune.[29] A *demang* ruled his territory like a king, with no more than weekly supervision by the Assistant Resident, who came to dispense justice as a local magistrate. Since the *demang* provided all the information on which the Dutchman's judgments were based, he was the single most influential figure in the justice system. The *demang* was the official with whom ordinary indigenous people had direct dealings, and the *demang* of Bekasi features prominently in the oral tradition of the people of Jakarta. We have already encountered him in Chapter 8, as Si Pitung's adversary. In films released in the 1970s, Moedjimi's near-mythical status is reflected in the suppression of his name: he is simply '*Demang* Bekasi'. It may be recalled that it had been the future *demang*, Moedjimi, who had tried to catch Si Pitung around 1892, when he was still a deputy public prosecutor.[30]

Veiled complaints about the *demang* of Bekasi had appeared in the Malay press as far back as in 1901.[31] Stories were told of the days when European sheriffs ruled Bekasi, until the recent replacement of this position by a *demang*. One article continues, 'This demang was most industrious and capable, but regrettably he was greatly influenced by the *prokureurs-bamboe*.'

These *prokureurs-bamboe* or *prokols* (a position not unlike the Italian *consigliere*) were counsellors who advised the people of the Dutch East Indies in the absence of qualified lawyers. Only six of the colony's cities boasted a law firm. The existence of *prokols* was universally seen as a necessary evil.[32] Their knowledge of the law was minimal, although the European *prokols* had a better reputation in this regard than the indigenous ones. European *prokols* were frequently men who had fallen on hard times and were obliged to eke out an existence in a kampong. The other kampong-dwellers called them *belanda kesasar*, 'stray Dutchmen'. Serving as *prokol* was only one option; these Europeans might take on other roles within the kampong, such as practising usury or running a brothel. European and indigenous *prokols* alike charged exorbitant fees, sometimes cannily increasing them by deliberately prolonging legal proceedings.[33]

Europeans living in the Ommelanden were also well aware of the shady practices associated with the *demang* of Bekasi. Du Perron describes an incident in *Het land van herkomst* in which the *demang*'s activities provoke a family row. The Assistant Resident J.R. Couperus was about to become the brother-in-law of Du Perron's father, and had accordingly invited the latter to stay. Du Perron Senior described Couperus as a grandiose autocrat and the protector of a *demang* 'who was in league with the bandits and received a large share of the booty, according to my father's private intelligence service'.[34] A fierce row erupted before the soup course was over, and the Assistant Resident stormed off and did not return to the table. This family row is all the more interesting because Du Perron's indictment of the internal administration, as a private individual, makes a sharp contrast with the many government documents in which Assistant Residents and Residents eagerly blamed all the trouble in the Ommelanden on private individuals. Interestingly, one Malay-language newspaper claimed that Assistant Resident J.R. Couperus had been instrumental in the appointment of the *demang* Moedjimi.[35]

In a newspaper interview three years later, Du Perron Senior looked back on the situation in Bekasi in the years just prior to 1903. At the time, he had been the superintendent of a number of Chinese estates, a position which gave him insight into the working methods of the *demang* Moedjimi. Du Perron had filed a complaint with Assistant Resident Couperus, but there was no response. He then had a notary draw up an official report of all the complaints that Du Perron had collected from indigenous people. But these local witnesses generally let Du Perron down when it mattered most, withdrawing their complaints when an official investigation was launched. Nevertheless, Du Perron eventually managed to submit three well-documented complaints to the Resident. But when the investigating judge (*Rechter-Commissaris*) finally began preparing for Moedjimi's trial, it was discovered that the documents had disappeared from the Resident's archives, even though there were records confirming their receipt. Again, this shows the extent of Moedjimi's influence.[36]

It was not until the autumn of 1903 that the authorities became suspicious of the *demang* of Bekasi. Believing him to be in league with bandits, the authorities and the police set a trap. They enlisted the services of one of the *demang*'s juniors, telling him to approach a relative of an arrested bandit with the information that the *demang* was willing to secure his release, for a fee. They gave their new agent a pile of marked notes, with which he purchased a water buffalo from the family, so that they would have some ready cash. Then the family was advised to approach a second official, who was not in the plot, to take the money to the *demang*. As soon as the latter had visited the *demang*, the *controleur* and the deputy public prosecutor made their way to Bekasi to search the *demang*'s house. There they found the marked money, furnishing the evidence they needed.[37]

The *demang* was sent to Telok Betong in the Lampoengs, southern Sumatra. The European public was incredulous that of all officials, this particular *demang*, with his frank gaze and polite manners, had proved capable of such abuses.[38] But it was only after his departure that the extent of his misconduct started to emerge. The *demang* was said to have entertained Gantang as a house-guest. According to another story, many robbers who were arrested in the days immediately following the *demang*'s downfall, unaware of the latter's arrest, asked if they might 'speak to the *demang* for a moment'. Kampong-dwellers also described the terror spread by one Abdoelah, the *demang*'s right-hand man and pupil, his *magang*.[39] This Abdoelah was a deserter from the Dutch army whose real name was Heynis. Rumours had circulated in the past that the former cashier of Batavia's proa ferry-service, described in a Malay newspaper as a European who had converted to Islam and in the *Bataviaasch Nieuwsblad* as a man who had 'gone native',[40] planned to enter the city and commit a robbery.[41] The police wanted to make a clean sweep, and a wave of arrests ensued all round Batavia. Suspect individuals without identity papers were discovered to be living in all parts of the city. A number of neighbourhood officers too were arrested.[42]

Rumours continued to fly that Europeans were involved in the robbers' networks.[43] The *Java-bode* called them the 'silent European partners of the firm of Gantang & Co.'[44] At the time of his arrest, the *demang* was in his house, talking to a European 'of ill repute'. Both were startled when the officials came in.[45] The daily newspaper the *Locomotief*, a paper that traditionally stood up for the indigenous population, complained about the involvement of Europeans and Eurasians in the robbers' gangs.[46] If they were indeed involved, they certainly kept out of harm's way. The *demang* and Gantang disappeared from the scene at roughly the same time, so their relationship, if any, has remained a matter of speculation down to the present day.

Focus on private estates

Inspired by the Netherlands' new 'ethical policy', the government's investigation of the causes underlying the *rampok* incidents took economic and social factors into consideration for the first time. While in 1893 the entire discourse had revolved around the lone figure of Si Pitung, with little information emerging about the world in which he lived, in 1903 crime was blamed largely on the poor social conditions on Batavia's estates and the ineffectiveness of the police service.

The year 1903 also witnessed the visit to the colony of the well-known socialist parliamentarian H. van Kol (1852–1925). On his return to the Netherlands he was full of horror stories about the conditions on private estates. To illustrate the seriousness of conditions in the Batavia region, van Kol wrote that *sado* cab-drivers no longer dared to go as far as Cikini, just a few kilometres to the south of the city centre, without European travellers (whom the robbers generally left in peace, for fear of repercussions). Van Kol described the situation in the estate of Pekayon, where 30 robbers wearing white headdresses and armed with revolvers, machetes and klewangs had tied up the Chinese owner and robbed him. It was thought particularly shocking that the robbers had performed a defiant *tandaks*, a kind of ritual war dance, in front of their victim. Van Kol also reported the horrifying story of a robbery during which one of the perpetrators had murdered a baby.

Van Kol's travel journal *Uit onze koloniën* gave a detailed account of his day trip through the Ommelanden.[47] He did not get far, as it was raining, and the roads were so muddy that the wheels of his carriage got stuck. His brief excursion barely graced the outskirts of Kuningan, about five kilometres south of the city centre. He described the poorly maintained farmland: large expanses of grassland, useless for the population but lucrative for the landowner, who could sell the grass in Batavia as fodder for coach-horses. The fruit trees were neglected and no new trees had been planted, so that the area displayed considerable deforestation. From other accounts, however, we know that there was still plenty of woodland further to the south, around Buitenzorg, near the foothills of the mountains. This area was frequently used as a refuge by bandits.

Van Kol also commented on social conditions in what he called 'these feudal lands':

> In each castle or fortress known as the *Gedong* resides a *Toewan Tanah*, as he is popularly known. Some hoist their own flag, while others place artillery on either side of the gate as a threat.[48] The submissiveness and servitude of the inhabitants, and indeed their serfdom — there are even bands of robbers — all completes this picture of the Middle Ages.
>
> The primary occupation of the rulers is collecting rent for slum dwellings, miserable-looking yards, and land that they do not sell but lease out in little patches.[49]

Unlike many other observers, van Kol describes the local people in largely positive terms, as patient, submissive and solicitous. He reports a near-absence of prostitution, opium addiction, and thievery. These virtues went hand-in-hand with a stable family life, in which the men went out to work and their wives stayed at home.

To protect the people from the combined impact of exploitation, crime and economic decline, van Kol proposed that the private estates be repurchased or appropriated. Previous centuries had largely witnessed the reverse procedure, with the government selling off estates to private individuals. When Jan Pieterszoon Coen sold estates to private landowners in the seventeenth century, he did so with the aim of improving security around Batavia. Later on, land was sold to solve financial problems. But the practice had never been without its critics. In addition, by the end of the nineteenth century, more and more land threatened to come into the hands of foreign commercial companies. The estates of Nanggung, Jasinga and the lands of Pamanukan and Ciasem (if they were not Chinese-owned) were English, for instance, and Cibodas was French. The influence of other colonial powers was seen as undesirable.[50]

In 1903 the Government embarked in earnest on a policy of repurchasing land. It started by trying to buy the estate of Nanggung, to the west of Buitenzorg. This transaction eventually fell through, since the huge expense — 260,000 guilders — was vetoed by the Parliament in The Hague. The Minister of Colonies had more success in 1911, when Parliament approved a plan to buy back West Indramayu and Kandanghauer. With a surface area of 1,274 km^2 and a population of 84,000, Kandanghauer was the most productive rice-growing area in the Dutch East Indies, and cost 3.5 million guilders.

Later still, the 'IJzerman resolution' made repurchasing easier, since it scrapped the need for Parliamentary approval.[51] Even so, each purchase was a daunting financial enterprise. It was estimated that repurchasing the private estates would cost a total of 400 million guilders. On average, each estate cost between 500,000 and a million guilders: Cibodas was priced at 204,000, Bolang 500,000 and Leuwiliang 1,940,000![52]

Nonetheless, the wheels were gradually set in motion. Since the government always had to wait until a particular estate was offered for sale, the area surrounding Batavia gradually became a patchwork of privately-owned and government estates. This meant that the robbers were still able to take refuge in a few mismanaged estates, just as they had done before.

It was not unknown for government estates to be mismanaged, prompting indigenous people to abandon them in favour of 'old-fashioned' private estates.[53] Government estates were quite often located on hilly, wooded terrain that provided an ideal habitat for bandits. In retrospect, the government's campaign to repurchase private estates appears to have been largely driven by those who were intent on implementing the new 'ethical' policy, and who sought to expunge the feudalism of the Ommelanden as an archaic excess. But they were too convinced that repurchasing the land would solve the security problem. This belief proved to be mistaken.

The opponents of the repurchasing project, including A. van Houten and C.J. van Motman, each of whom wrote a pamphlet on the subject,[54] also rightly commented that the entire colonial system, not just landlordism, was archaic. The system of indirect rule, as it operated in other parts of the Dutch East Indies, was not an edifying sight. These authors argued that the people of the Ommelanden at least had an opportunity and the courage to express their grievances. Van Motman observed that someone living on a private estate would think nothing of bypassing the head of his *desa*, the chief of police and the district head to present his grievance directly to the Assistant Resident, something that was unheard of in the rest of Java.[55] In those regions, tales of abuses were kept private. Since the Ommelanden were close to Batavia, their problems tended to become public knowledge.[56] Finally, the opponents of the repurchasing project pointed out that the unrest did not affect the entire Batavia region, but was confined to the area around Meester Cornelis.[57]

Many believed that the effective way to suppress banditry was to have a well-organized police force, not by carrying out expensive repurchasing plans. Until then, indigenous police chiefs (*camats*) had been appointed by the local landowner (see Appendix I). They were badly paid and consequently often incompetent. Although the government could theoretically demand the dismissal of any police chief who was performing badly, it never did so in practice. Advocates of police reform wanted this regulation properly enforced, and proposed a standardization of the police force throughout the Ommelanden. In other words, they felt that the government should once more assume full responsibility for policing.

The judicial system too was in a sorry state. The quality of the system imposed by the colonial authorities was partly to blame. In addition, many of the local public prosecutors (*jaksa*) had too little legal training, and bandits often exploited procedural errors to secure their release. Another problem was the expense involved in going to court to testify. Witnesses often had to travel long distances to the city, and the travel and accommodation allowance they received was so meagre that having to testify was sometimes almost as bad as standing trial.

Illus. 14 The country estate of Tjimanggis (Cimanggis), as it looked during the 1990s (photograph by Roel van der Veen). It was built between 1775 and 1787 and is located to the South of Jakarta on the road to Bogor. At the time the picture was taken, several families lived in it. Of the dozens of country estates only about five remain. (Heuken, *Historical Sights of Jakarta*, p. 224; Van Diessen, *Jakarta/Batavia*, pp. 290–1)

The police until 1908

'Toean baljuw tidoer' — 'the officer is asleep'. According to a journalist of the *Soerabajaasch Handelsblad* writing in 1881, this was the response you might expect to hear — from a 'caretaker' — if you went in search of a European police officer during siesta time.[58] He wrote that the European sheriffs or *schouten* (a title that survived into the twentieth century in the Dutch East Indies) largely served as personal attendants of the respective Assistant Residents, which meant that they were expected to parade at his side in full regalia. Early in the morning the sheriff had to appear in uniform as a guard of honour in front of the Assistant Resident's house. The sheriff would attend festive occasions and official gatherings of the European community, and could not go home until the senior administrative officials had left.

The real task of a sheriff, however, was to bring criminals to justice. Sheriffs were only appointed in the larger cities of the Dutch East Indies, since those were the only places with a substantial European population. Within the indigenous community, law enforcement was in the hands of the kampong chiefs, aided by voluntary assistants. While the colonial authorities regarded this form of law enforcement as largely ineffective, they did not see it as a matter of priority.[59]

The most senior figures in the colonial administration had little interest in tackling the problems systematically. Only in 1872, the governor-general had declared that newspaper reports alleging a lack of security in the archipelago were greatly exaggerated and that there was no need to change the organizational structure of the police. This exponent of the highest authority in the colony went on to say that given the limited available funds, any such reorganization was in any case bound to prove a disappointment. Instead, the police were urged to perform their duties more energetically within the existing framework.[60] A committee set up to study the problem, chaired by C.N. Bosscher, reached the same conclusion.[61]

> The days are gone in which a man may brag and curse with vigour, and pour a quantity of Dutch gin into his body, seeking thus to give himself the air of a bold police officer. I know some men whose silver stripes on their caps have gone black from the alcohol fumes rising from their heads.[62]

But as the 'ethical policy' movement gathered pace, public pressure to modernize the police force increased. Such was the sense of insecurity in 1902–3 that journalists and politicians openly questioned the usefulness of improving the prosperity of the Javanese people if they were constantly being robbed. In The Hague, the Dutch parliamentarians H. van Kol and D. Fock questioned the minister about the state of security on Java, especially in the Ommelanden, where conditions were consistently described as 'medieval'.[63]

Until then, only piecemeal efforts had been made to improve the police, for instance by hiring an extra officer here or there, frequently on a temporary basis. Not until 1904 did the colony receive the go-ahead from the Netherlands for a real reorganization, and the resources to carry it out. At the request of the director of the internal administration department, Assistant Resident L.R. Priester submitted proposals for a reorganization of the police in the three largest cities of the Dutch East Indies — Batavia, Semarang and Surabaya. His report was published that same year. Priester identified the primary problems within the police force as unreliability and corruption, and cited poor wages and the lack of opportunities for promotion as contributory factors. These conditions, combined with a poor level of education, meant that the European employees in particular, naturally gravitated to 'sections of society that could not possibly enhance their standards of morality'.[64]

Not until 1911 did the Minister of Colonies finally approve reorganization on the basis of these reports. Parliament still balked at the notion of a central command structure, but voted in favour of reorganizing the European and indigenous police in Batavia (including Meester Cornelis), Semarang and Surabaya. A decision on similar measures in the rest of the colony was deferred. The three major cities acquired chief commissioners (*hoofdcommissarissen*), with the archaic positions of *schouten*, *piekeniers* and *nachtwakers* being abolished. A new rank of European senior police officer was introduced, while lower ranks were expanded and given higher wages.[65]

These measures were soon found to be insufficient. In 1914 a stronger central command was created to boost effectiveness. The three chief commissioners were given wider powers and mandated to operate with greater autonomy. Other plans in this round of improvements included a police training school and a fingerprint identification system. In addition, new training and police barracks were to be introduced to boost discipline.[66] The number of European police officers in Batavia rapidly expanded. Until 1910 there were only 7, by 1915 there were 19 and by 1920 the number had grown to 37.[67] Slowly but surely the major cities acquired a relatively large European group of senior officers, with a larger contingent of local policemen serving under them.

In addition, the year 1921 saw the operationalization of the rural police (*veldpolitie*), which operated in the Ommelanden in groups of 20

Illus. 15 Guardhouse at the entrance of a kampong. (Collection Arie Hoorweg, IFA)

or 30 and were stationed in barracks. Broadly speaking, they were the successors to the indigenous mounted police (*pradjurits*) and the later armed police force.[68]

The slow pace of reform

In effecting these reforms, Batavia was following an international trend. In the nineteenth century, police forces were professionalizing and acquiring an official apparatus and uniforms in all parts of the world. The British authorities had embarked on this process around 1830, in response to social unrest. Other countries followed suit, and the Netherlands finally went ahead with similar changes at the end of the nineteenth century. Thus, the insistence on a more professional law enforcement apparatus was relatively late in the Netherlands, a country that was also late in the process of industrialization. With the exception of the rebellious peat colonies of the northern Netherlands, where the military police were deployed, traditional village policemen (*veldwachters*) long sufficed to keep the peace. While it is true that Amsterdam's police force was reorganized in 1878, this was not so much a response to social unrest as a general reaction to the city's expansion. The people of Batavia may well have felt a more urgent need for a well-organized police force than townspeople in the Netherlands. The capital of the Dutch East Indies was one of the largest cities in the Kingdom of the Netherlands, and one where prosperous citizens felt more threatened by social unrest than those living in the mother country. Those involved in restructuring the police in the Dutch East Indies seldom looked to the Netherlands for their examples. Instead, they tended to model their plans on police forces in Singapore or London.[69]

Perhaps the machinations of the internal administration department were to blame for the slow pace of police reform. In the nineteenth century, Residents and Assistant Residents had ruled their territories as true autocrats. Their scant financial resources had compelled them to do so by indirect administration, by relying on local institutions and individuals, whose resources were equally inadequate. The authorities achieved peace and order largely through the exercise of tact and decorum, and by closing their eyes to violence that did not pose a direct threat to the colonial state.[70]

With the introduction of the ethical policy, however, a host of experts — in irrigation and agriculture for instance — descended on the archipelago.[71] The new police officers may be viewed in the same light. Accustomed as they were to autonomy in their field of action, the leaders

Illus. 16 Street scene, Tjikini. (Collection Arie Hoorweg, IFA)

of the internal administration department had no wish to see others taking over many of their responsibilities.[72] The Assistant Residents must have fumed to find skilled police commissioners working alongside them. Numerous complaints appeared in the *Nederlands-Indische Politiegids* in this period that the administrative authorities were restricting the police's scope for vigorous action. Some wanted the police to be made accountable to the judiciary, for instance, as a way of escaping from the internal administration's oppressive sphere of influence.[73]

In the second decade of the twentieth century, the security situation in the Ommelanden suffered from the friction between the modern police force and the internal administration. When there were peaks in bandit activity, the military police reinforced the regular police force; in other words, the army was also involved in law enforcement.

The three instruments of state power — the military police, the regular police, and the department of internal administration with its network of informers — constantly thwarted each other, for instance by destroying evidence or negating the effect of each other's decisions. One example was the poor cooperation between sheriff Hinne and *controleur* Johan in the Fatima affair, as described in Chapter 7.

If we follow a number of protagonists of internal administration and the police in the sources, we can build up a picture of the mutual grievances that existed, and of the way in which the many parties involved — indigenous people, administrative officials, agents, and local chiefs — found ways of turning the government conflicts to their own advantage. In his 1922 memorandum on leaving office, Resident J.D. Hunger of Batavia (representing the internal administration department) had harsh words of criticism for the new police system.[74] He claimed that the rural police or *veldpolitie* was unprofessional and completely dysfunctional. He also believed that the police lacked the subtlety needed to deal effectively with local leaders. He went so far as to blame the robberies in the Batavia region on demoralization within the indigenous local authorities, which he attributed to the influence of the modern police. He argued that the rising police force had deprived the *demangs* and *wedanas* of much of their influence in the period 1910–20. Similar criticism had been expressed some years before by former Resident Rijfsnijder.[75] He too had warned that the capital's police officers were ignorant of local customs and the local language. Some members of the internal administration longed to return to the *tempo doeloe*, the old days, with their omniscient officials.

The internal administration department certainly worked differently from the police. While the latter sought to be modern and rational, with all the machinery of officialdom, the internal administration department relied heavily on its network of indigenous informers, and all too frequently followed the principle of setting one lawbreaker to catch another. The *Sair Tjerita Rampok Si Ronda* gives the following account of the procedure whereby a man is appointed as a lower-ranking indigenous police officer.

Si Ronda has just been shot by his partner in crime Si Oedji, with whom he had undertaken numerous successful raids. The text continues:

> Three bullets in his chest
> Noted the demang, well satisfied.
> Nor did he suspect Oedji at all,
> But gave him 150 guilders' reward.
>
> The demang said to Oedji,
> You're a sturdy fellow who can follow orders,
> And you handle a rifle well.
> You're promoted to armed policeman.[76]

Illus. 17 Police station, Batavia, probably 1928. (Collection Arie Hoorweg, IFA)

The Resident tried to control kampong life by deploying the district criminal investigation department, which functioned largely as a network of informers. The aim was to employ investigators who were not too European, not too modern, not too bureaucratic, and not too demanding. For these spies were expected at times to immerse themselves completely in the life of a kampong, living on rice and fish.[77]

The friction between internal administration and the police generated a wealth of intrigues surrounding the first chief commissioners of Batavia. A case in point was C.J. Boon. Appointed chief commissioner in 1915, he was urged to give high priority to eradicating corruption in the system of sheriffs or *schouten*. Boon had called Batavia 'the most corrupt city in the whole Dutch East Indies, not only in the area of police, but in every area, and it is therefore also the most backward'.[78] He maintained that the Assistant Resident undermined his work from the moment of his arrival. Hunger accused him of actually boosting the incidence of robberies by his ill-chosen tactics. One of Boon's supporters presented a different interpretation: he claimed that Boon's antagonists had staged the *rampok* incidents themselves to discredit him.

At the heart of the conflict between the different bodies involved in fighting crime was a lack of clarity concerning the hierarchical relationships between them. Formally speaking, the Assistant Resident was the head of police. At the same time, however, there was a desire to invest the new position of chief commissioner of police with as much autonomy as possible. Another problem was that the rural police was not yet functioning properly, so that the military police was constantly being called in to suppress banditry. But the military police did not possess any power to arrest suspects; their presence was merely intended to intimidate. They were deployed against robbers' gangs in almost military-style operations. Their large-scale patrols were all too visible in the kampongs. Gangs soon spread the word and decided to strike elsewhere.

In conclusion, it may be noted that neither of the policy measures — the repurchasing of private estates and the reorganization of the police force — was fully implemented in the period studied here. Private estates were repurchased only when there was enough money. While new legislation entered into force in 1911 that enabled the authorities to appropriate land (at less expense), it was seldom invoked. In the early 1930s, two-thirds of the estates in the Ommelanden were in the colonial government's hands. After that, repurchasing operations were halted because of a lack of money. In the matter of police reform, the government also held back after 1903,

Illus. 18 Police barracks, Meester Cornelis, probably 1928. (Collection Arie Hoorweg, IFA)

again because of the costs involved. Twenty more years were to pass before the many plans, reports and analyses finally led to the suppression of *rampok*. Not until the 1920s was there a police force with a central command structure, accountable to the procurator-general.[79]

Theoretically, in any case, the risk of all kinds of people engaging in acts of violence and offering 'protection' only increased; many authors have noted that the gap between feudalism and democracy produces ideal conditions for would-be *mafiosi*. In the feudal era, landowners had control over men of violence, but their control evaporated with the disintegration of this system. Many more people and groups could employ violence; one might say that there was a market for it. Until the state actually imposed its own monopoly on the use of force, the vacuum was filled by diverse exponents of violence — from individuals to large organizations — either on their own initiative or at others' behest.[80] In the areas surrounding Batavia, where modernization stagnated for decades as a result of half-hearted attempts at reform, plenty of scope was left for those who could impose order and hence fulfil the people's need for a sense of security. As we saw in the introduction, one inhabitant of the Ommelanden listed a large number of self-appointed 'protectors' of the people living in the kampong, including the *preman*, *jago*, tax collectors and religious leaders.

Illus. 19 Rural police ready to go on patrol, probably 1928. (Collection Arie Hoorweg, IFA)

After 1903, the Ommelanden around Batavia continued to be afflicted by banditry for years, with peaks in 1908–9 and 1918–20. Whether these criminal activities could have been suppressed if the police had been reorganized more rapidly after 1903 is debatable.

Rampok in the Great Depression

In several respects, however, the modernized police force was more effective in suppressing *rampok*. New modes of transport, together with improvements in the roads and other infrastructure greatly accelerated pursuits. In addition, the indigenous police officers now received better training. It was they (aside from the European sheriff Hinne) who had done most to track down and arrest bandits.

Robberies were now confined to the peripheral districts of Batavia. In the preceding decades, outlaws had ventured into neighbourhoods close to the city centre; with the police now posing a greater threat, they focused on the areas along the borders with Karawang and Serang. In the course of the 1930s, the *Bataviaasch Nieuwsblad* focused more and more on world events. Amid these international reports, the Ommelanden once more seemed quite remote.

In this period, bandits often had to content themselves with a booty of less than a hundred guilders. People had little money in their homes, partly because of the poverty of the Depression years, and partly, perhaps, because of the growing popularity of bank and postal giro accounts. Since the turn of the century, the government had promoted savings schemes and the credit system. Officials claimed that the pattern of spending reflected a desire to move money out of the house as soon as possible because of the lack of security. People invested in property or in ploughing oxen, or spent their money at parties. Some used it for the *hajj*, the pilgrimage to Mecca.

There was no local tradition of saving money, and early attempts to encourage formal banking among the indigenous population were unsuccessful. People were reluctant to go through all sorts of formalities to get at their cash, they were afraid to enter the bank, they did not have adequate collateral to take out loans, and for these and other reasons, formal savings plans initially failed to catch on. The change came in the second decade of the twentieth century, with the advent of various Chinese and indigenous banking cooperatives that had greater appeal to the target groups. At the same time, there was a clampdown on usury.

These measures combined to boost payment by bank transfer, especially among Chinese merchants and *toko* shopkeepers. As a result, people had less need for ready cash in their homes.

It cannot be a coincidence that in this same period we find the bandits changing the way they chose their victims. They started targeting people who possessed cash only incidentally, like labourers working under contract who had just returned from Deli, or kampong-dwellers who had received payment for land they were forced to sell to the government for public works.[81]

When the bandits made off with their meagre pickings, they now ran a considerable risk of being arrested that same evening or a few days later. The year 1933 witnessed just four cases of *rampok*, in three of which the robbers were arrested. In 1934, the perpetrators were arrested in 11 out of a total of 15 *rampok* incidents.[82] This period has no individual success stories, such as the earlier tales of Pitung, Gantang, Lias and Oesoep. The risk of arrest was probably too great to allow for spectacular escapes and repeat offending, so there was no breeding-ground in which legends could flourish.

Changes within the police apparatus were also significant. Intermediaries such as police spies and indigenous officials no longer counted for much in the *rampok* business. In the years between 1920 and 1940, with the modernization of the police finally completed, the indigenous link between the police and administrative authorities on the one hand, and the perpetrators of *rampok* on the other, was eliminated. This severed one of the robbers' main lifelines.

At the end of the colonial era, it seemed as though the 'evil of *rampok*' had been brought under control. The evidence suggests that there was far less trouble than in the past, certainly in the Batavia region. Where robberies occurred, they tended to take place in the peripheral districts of the Residency of Batavia. So we find few reports of *rampok* in the newspapers, and the colonial statistics too displayed reassuring statistics.

1937

For all these reasons, the wave of terror that swept through Cibarusa in 1937 was an extraordinary aberration. Conditions had been peaceful for years, and the police's new approach appeared to be bearing fruit, until in 1937 the violence suddenly flared up with a vengeance. The gangs that appeared at this time were very different from those of the past, which

Illus. 20 Gang member, just arrested, who had been participating in the wave of crime in 1937 in Cibarusa. (*Nieuws van den Dag voor Nederlandsch-Indië*, 5 April 1937)

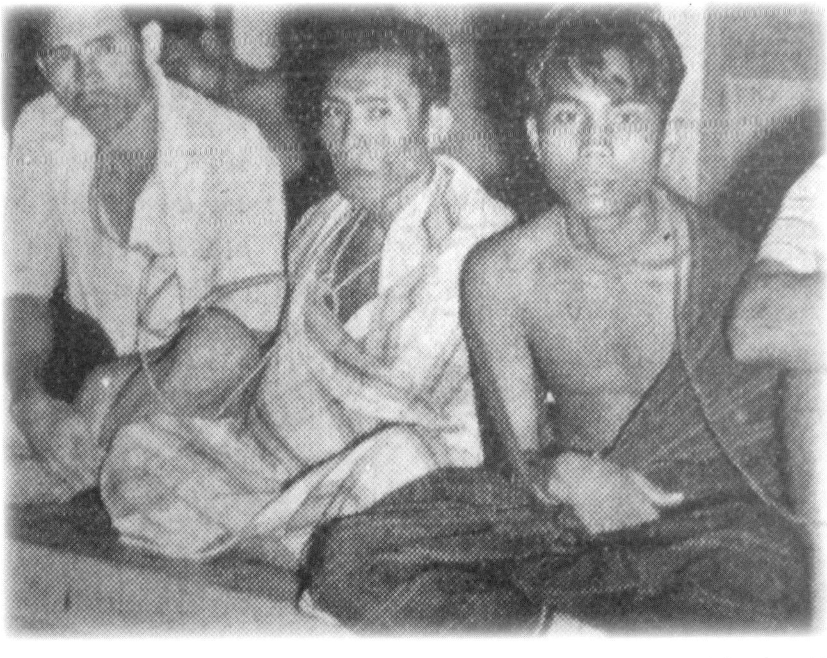

Illus. 21 Gang members. (*Nieuws van den Dag voor Nederlandsch-Indië*, 5 April 1937)

had sometimes had an almost humorous side to them. The *rampok* terror of 1937 was very far from amusing. Murders of *desa* leaders and other local officials, and of anyone suspected of being a police informer, were suddenly regular occurrences. In the Batavia region alone, 50 constables were murdered in the space of six months. Besides *rampok*, the gangs also committed crimes such as extortion and street robberies. While the robbers of the past had sometimes been able to count on a measure of sympathy within the community, this was now out of the question. The trial of Pa-I, Komin and Pandji attracted a crowd of hundreds of people, who cheered when the men were convicted. The bandit Toweh was lynched by the local population.[83] Pramoedya Ananta Toer's description of the *rampok* attacks in Cibarusa, in his *House of Glass* (see Chapter 8), probably refers to the gangs that were active in 1937. But they did not confine their activities to Cibarusa. They appeared to be slowly advancing in the direction of Meester Cornelis and Batavia.

The unrest also attracted the attention of the People's Council (*Volksraad*). Some representatives, including Raden Prawoto, who had displayed his expertise in law enforcement before (see Chapter 7), asked incisive questions. They demanded how it was possible that acts could be committed so close to Buitenzorg that 'made a mockery of all notions of peace, order and public security'. The proposed solutions included tackling poverty and better remuneration for police informers.[84]

The governor of Western Java, L.G.C.A. van der Hoek, in an interview with the press about the resurgence of *rampok* crime, put forward the following hypothesis:

> Over the centuries, a guild of thieves has grown out of the ragbag native community in the Ommelanden of Batavia, which is now causing trouble for the people and the government with renewed vigour. The remnants of the native armies of the rulers who were repelled from the area of the first settlements on Java in the days of the VOC lingered in the area, and this rabble attracted a following among escaped slaves and absconded sailors who preferred idling to work and who found robbery — *rampok* — an easy way to earn a living.[85]

He added that private estates, with their poor management and impassable roads, were also partly to blame. He cited the case of Kebayoran, recently repurchased by the government, which had been afflicted by *rampok* in the past but that was now peaceful. In short, his comments repeat much of the popular rhetoric about banditry that we have encountered several times in this book. The only difference was his lack of faith in the military police, which had been considered such an effective instrument against the robbers in the past, since it had too little contact with the local people. Instead he favoured the revival of the rural police, which had been decimated by budgetary cuts in the 1930s.

In the end, it was the assistant *wedana* of Cileungsi who arrested the first gang members and in the wake of this success came a flurry of other arrests. So in the end, in spite of all the reorganizations, the authorities had to place their reliance in a low-ranking indigenous official to halt the robberies.

Sometimes bandits were halted without any arrest being necessary, since the gangs often descended into ruthless internecine conflict. This is clear from the career of the bandit Komin. It bears little similarity to the lives of the robbers who were active in previous decades. Komin started out as a station porter at Senen in Batavia's city centre. He was caught thieving, and joined Kiami, Boin and Sabam, in a gang that was active in the Cisalak area to the west of Buitenzorg. Posing as timber merchants, they terrorized the population with robberies and extortion and killed or mutilated suspected police informers. The *Bataviaasch Nieuwsblad* reported at one point that the local people were so terrified that they had taken to sleeping in trees.

After the leader Kiami was arrested, there was turmoil in the gang. Tensions mounted further when it transpired that Kiami had promised a village girl to Komin, while other gang members had been eyeing her. The gang boycotted Komin's wedding to this girl. Then, when Sabam's brother held a marriage feast for his daughter, he was killed by Komin in the midst of the festivities. More acts of reciprocal vengeance followed. Boin and Sabam were also killed, and Komin emerged the winner. Two rival gangs then clashed, each with small armies some 80 men strong. They tossed their dead into the river. These battles eventually attracted attention when 'official figures' became involved and were taken to hospital, wounded. Komin was eventually betrayed to the authorities.[86]

From *rampok* to *bersiap*

The question arises of the connection between the pre-war robbers and the 'gangsters' who took up the role of freedom fighters during the Indonesian revolt or *bersiap*. While Cribb reviews the 1930s on the basis of interviews and documents about post-war gangsters, I shall take documents dating from the 1930s as my point of departure in looking at the way in which the careers of *jagos*, robbers and gangsters developed in later years.

There was a lull in robberies between 1920 and the Second World War. Misset observes in his memoirs that after the actions of the bandit Lias, who was shot dead in 1918, *rampok* activities were suspended.[87]

Many social and ecological changes had made robbery a far less profitable proposition. Yet some writers posit a linear connection between the robberies by bandits (whom they call *jagos*) and the plunder and acts of violence committed during the freedom struggle of 1945–8. A salient case in point is Professor P.M. van Wulfften Palthe of Batavia University, whose book *Over het bendewezen op Java* was published in 1949. This study of Javanese banditry is still cited as an authoritative study to this day, and was one of Hobsbawm's main sources of information about Javanese bandits. Sartono Kartodirdjo and Robert Cribb also drew extensively on van Wulfften Palthe's work. In 1997, Frances Gouda published an article

Illus. 22 Mohammed Hassan, who participated in many arrests of bandits. (*Nieuws van den Dag voor Nederlandsch-Indië*, 5 April 1937)

entitled 'Language of Gender and Neurosis'. In it, she analyzes not only van Wulfften Palthe's approach to the subject of robbers' gangs, but also, and more notably, his views regarding Indonesians' emotions during their struggle for independence. Gouda shows that the author projected specific pathological emotions onto the Indonesian freedom fighters, claiming that after the horrors of the Japanese occupation they were disappointed in their Dutch 'father' and consequently turned instead to Ibu Pertiwi ('mother Indonesia').[88]

Besides proposing this psychological theory, van Wulfften Palthe also claimed that the Javanese countryside served as a breeding-ground for mysticism and millenarianism. The history of Java had witnessed countless revolts with prospects of salvation, inspired by ideas of a utopia. But it had also bred the institution of the *jago* bandit, a leader who controlled fellow-villagers with his mysterious powers, attracting a band of followers with whom to commit robberies. It should be noted, however that van Wulfften Palthe did distinguish between the leaders of the millenarian movements and the leaders of *rampok* gangs.[89]

Robert Cribb's *Gangsters and Revolutionaries* (published in 1991) discusses the *rampok* leaders from before the war and the freedom fighters of the *bersiap* as part of a single continuum. He maintains that 'we should bear in mind ways in which the revolution drew upon older styles of rebellion' and 'the national struggle in the Jakarta countryside drew on very much the same kinds of social organization which underlay these earlier risings'.[90] In contrast to van Wulfften Palthe, however, Cribb holds specific people — *jagos*, or as he calls them, gangsters — responsible for both criminal activities and rebellion.

> The Jakarta underworld challenged Dutch authority not simply by its criminal activity. The gangsters were a major element in the Jakarta region's tradition of rural unrest and rebellion. Rebellions of varying seriousness peppered the decades of the nineteenth century in the area. From early in the twentieth century, moreover, this traditional unrest became linked with growing nationalist agitation against the Dutch.[91]

Given the findings of my own research, the relationship postulated here is questionable.

Robbers and people's militias

My study of the sources reveals that few if any pre-war bandits were actively involved in the freedom struggle of 1945–9. The sole exception I could find was Pandji, who had been active as a bandit before the Japanese occupation. The Dutch had imprisoned him for these crimes, but in the Japanese period he had escaped. He joined forces with Hadji Darip, a 'gentleman burglar' who was very popular in the local community. After the Japanese forces left, Hadji Darip established his own territory near Klender. Pandji made up his mind to take over Darip's position of power, and eventually ousted him. The gang was gradually transformed into a 'people's militia' (*laskar rakyat*). Pandji held sway over Bekasi and the surrounding area for several months, but in May 1947 he surrendered, along with many of his followers.[92] Of the other figures named in Cribb's book, not one can be linked to any of the robbers who were active in the 1930s.

It will have become clear in the course of this book that the nature of the violence committed during robberies differed enormously from the violence of the revolution. Before 1940, *rampok* violence was largely a matter of show, and with the exception of the brutal acts of 1937, it claimed a strikingly small number of casualties. After 1942, and certainly after 1945, things were very different. William Frederick describes the pattern of *rampok* raids in this period in his article 'Shadows of an unseen hand'. The attacks were often accompanied by arson, murder and acts of sadism. As far as East Java is concerned, Frederick believes that those involved were not traditional gangs of robbers but ordinary villagers.[93]

In the same article, Frederick explains the mechanism whereby the excessive violence used by Indonesians against Dutch and Chinese

Illus. 23 Pa-I. The text with this photo read: The magic circle of crime has been broken. With his pulses in chains Paih is being photographed, with Satian joining enthusiastically. (*Nieuws van den Dag voor Nederlandsch-Indië*, 5 April 1937)

inhabitants as well as fellow Indonesians has remained largely unknown. The first reason is that these acts of brutality were initially condemned by the Dutch. Since the Dutch were the moral losers of the war, their voices were disregarded. The second reason is that the Indonesian army itself was far from blameless, since it had frequently resorted to tactical violence. The army had a stake in promoting an idealized picture of the revolution. Like many other revolutions, the Indonesian uprising became a perfect narrative in which to invest feelings of romanticism and nostalgia.

In a different article, Frederick discusses the myth of the resistance fighter as a romantic libertine.[94] He exposes the misconception that the revolution was engineered by long-haired, flamboyant *pemuda*. Other authors conclude from this that the *pemuda* drew their inspiration from pre-war *jagos*, who had the same characteristics, including self-confidence and a certain appearance and style of clothing. It was an image spun by the fondness of middle-class Javanese boys and girls for having themselves photographed in this romantic style during the revolution. Another — banal — factor that contributed to the unkempt appearance of many was a simple shortage of fabric.

Gradually, then, an idealized image of revolutionary fighters was forged, as *jago*-like figures who violated social norms but had hearts of gold. This discourse forged a continuum between the earlier robbers' gangs and the revolution. Acts of brutality that were in fact hard to explain were attributed to a long tradition of violence. In reality, those responsible for the violence were not the traditional robbers at all. The context of revolution, as Frederick observes, may be conducive to types of extreme violence.

It would therefore appear that violence as perpetrated in the colony by Indonesians was not uniform over time. In the case of *rampok*, in any case, there was a definite sea-change just before 1942. In other words, the violence documented during the revolution, including the brutality that attended *rampok*, was essentially a new phenomenon.

Concluding Remarks

The variegated world of Indonesian crime

The temptation to write a book that would focus on the sensational exploits of a few bandit chiefs was something I was determined to resist. Not because no such figures existed in the Dutch East Indies, but precisely because these striking figures have tended to produce a romanticized image of robbers' lives.

The banditry of the early twentieth century was a lucrative business that received plenty of attention in the press. The bandits' success stemmed in part from two developments in the Dutch East Indies: the replacement of the feudal government of the archipelago by a rule-bound bureaucracy, and the growth of a money-based economy. The legendary image that grew up around them was to a large extent determined by the demographic changes made possible by the opening of the Suez Canal. All three factors played a key role in Batavia and the surrounding area.

The phenomenon of *rampok* or armed robbery attracted growing public interest in the Dutch East Indies from 1900 onwards. The media — the indigenous and Chinese as well as the European press — started to project European ideas about robbers onto the perpetrators of *rampok*. These ideas derived in part from the literature of Italian hoodlums and the mafia. Social Darwinism, most notably Lombroso's theory of the inferior physiological features that distinguished criminals, was also highly influential. Romanticization subsequently coloured theories of crime in the Dutch East Indies, by creating a certain distance to the historical reality. Nineteenth-century city-dwellers, in particular, harboured fears of the countryside that spawned a view of indigenous robbers as wild forces working against the modern age and undermining the colony's emerging modernity. The bandits were seen as the embodiment of barbarous violence, primitive sexuality and superstition.

After 1910, variations on this theme appeared. Anthropologists started taking an interest in *rampok*, as did the new police sciences, although the latter adopted a largely technological perspective. There was a change in tone from the fairly businesslike approach that had marked internal administration officials' discussions of *rampok*. Researchers and police alike happily used local people and Indo administrative officials as informants. But it is debatable whether such sources produced a sounder understanding of the indigenous bandits' world. One consequence, in any case, was a still more elaborate mythologization of these activities, revolving around the robbers' supposed use of supernatural powers. It was these mythologized bandits who became the basis for influential studies by authors such as P.M. van Wulfften Palthe and D.H. Meijer. These articles served in turn as important sources for later historians and social scientists.

From this point onwards, many researchers started using the term *jago* in studies of crime or violence in the archipelago. One disadvantage of the emphasis on *jagos* was that it produced an undifferentiated picture of crime in the Dutch East Indies. What is more, in its crude form, this approach was decidedly ahistorical. There is a tendency to regard violence as a constant factor in the precolonial, colonial and postcolonial society of the archipelago. Thus in *Gangsters and Revolutionaries* (1991), Robert Cribb takes it for granted, in discussing the relationship between *bersiap* and banditry, that the men of violence in the revolutionary period had the same attitude to violence as the perpetrators of *rampok*. But this is highly questionable. After all, professional bandits have to control and channel the use of violence, since it is 'merely' a means to an end: violence in a robbery was designed to intimidate, to create chaos and to quell any thoughts of retaliation.

The bandits' world did not generally extend into political life, even after 1920, with the rise of Indonesian nationalism. The link that Robert Cribb posits between the Batavian underworld and the revolutionary Indonesian fighters simply did not apply to bandits. Although there may well have been bandits who threw themselves into the revolutionary cause, for whatever reason, I have not found any evidence of a more systematic association. It is here that the flaws in Cribb's undifferentiated picture of illegal activity in the colony become painfully apparent. His tendency to consider all members of the underworld under one common denominator obscures the diversity of approaches to violence.

The proposition that the Batavian bandits' world possessed mafia-style structures — which was sometimes suggested by contemporaries[1] — proves similarly unfounded. The mafia is in essence worlds apart from bands of robbers. Mafia members deal in protection, while robbers deal in violent armed attacks. While the research undertaken for this book did not specifically extend to mafia-type practices, it nonetheless yielded enough information to question the existence of a mafia in the Ommelanden. In terms of organizational structure and management, the mafia is much like a regular commercial company. The same social and cultural factors that made it so hard for local entrepreneurs to develop and sustain viable large-scale companies in the colonial period also impeded potential local *mafiosi* in this period;[2] the criminals were not able to build up organizations of any substantial size or endurance. The severe lack of security in the Ommelanden also points to the absence of a well-organized mafia, which would have imposed a certain order on society.

Bandits and the authorities

In the period 1890–1942, the colony's government acquired an altogether more technocratic and bureaucratic apparatus. East Indies officials were better trained and easier to transfer from one position to another. The new trend was for duties to be assigned to specialists, in this context within the police force. It is worth asking whether the bandits' success bears any relation to this development. In other words, did they exploit gaps that arose in the transition from the old to the new system? Conversely, did the existence of banditry accelerate the introduction of a modern police force?

These questions bring us to the issue of the bandits' dependency on contacts within the colonial government. Henk Schulte Nordholt and Onghokham concluded that the bandits who were active in the Javanese hinterland frequently operated in the shadow of the authorities. In their view, this dependency was mutual. While the bandits needed the authorities to turn something of a blind eye to their activities, the authorities relied on informal armed units to maintain order in society. This study has not yielded any evidence that bandits played a significant role as intermediaries, however. A great many were arrested, and plenty of voices were raised in criticism of supposed connections between criminals and European as well as indigenous officials. We have seen several examples in these pages of official and police involvement in crime. Even so, had such cooperation been widespread, one might have expected the research to unearth far more disreputable networks.

My study of the Ommelanden has turned up a few cases of bandits being recruited from the lowest ranks of officialdom, those of village chiefs and neighbourhood officers — cases that, it should be added, were always pounced on eagerly by the press. The chapter on firearms also discussed the evidence that this level of internal administration was a source of firearms for illicit use.

These findings do not suffice to justify a conclusion that administrative officials were dependent on bandits. But it is true that for some officials, robbery was simply one of the many economic activities in their district generating a profit of which they happily accepted a share. In a few cases, known administrative corruption as accompanied by an increase in the number of robberies. Chapter 8 discussed one example of this, in the relationship between the *demang* of Bekasi and the activities of Gantang. Any such links between bandits and officials were obviously cloaked in secrecy and only indirect evidence can be found for them.

Indigenous bandits were unable to penetrate the police apparatus, which was becoming increasingly Europeanized. As time went on, they also found it harder to establish useful contacts with local administrative officials, who adopted far more rational, modern working methods around 1930. The scope for relying on corrupt government officials gradually shrank. Those who believed that the best way to fight crime was to learn more about the way local people lived and by immersing themselves in this local society — a popular view among internal administration officials — were therefore wrong. The modern, European police force, which was far removed from indigenous bandits, was probably better at combating this form of crime.

Banditry flourished most conspicuously in the relative power vacuum that existed between the end of the forced cultivation system (*Cultuurstelsel*) in 1870 and the formation of specialized police units and other government agencies in the 1920s. The authorities' actions had a major impact on bandit gangs and their crimes. The period 1906–22 is particularly striking in this regard. These were turbulent years, in which responsibility for fighting crime was shifted from the department of internal administration to a professional police force, precipitating a wave of conflicts between the two bodies. Bandits took advantage of the resulting disarray, and were particularly active in this period.

Banditry and the economy

Banditry was only profitable if a substantial amount of money was found in the victim's home. Consequently, we can trace a link between banditry and flows of money into indigenous villages and urban districts. After a slow beginning, these flows accelerated in the mid-nineteenth century with the advent of the forced cultivation system. Technological innovations in firearms were another major factor.

There is a certain correlation between the ups and downs of banditry and the general economic climate in the colony, and more especially in the area studied in this book. We find peaks in the number of robberies committed in Batavia in the years 1880, 1892, 1903, 1909–11, 1918, 1920 and 1934. Most of these years correlate closely with economic crises in the Javanese countryside that affected basic subsistence levels. The exception is the period 1909–11. The peak at this time may have been attributable to the upsurge in robbers' access to firearms; it took time for the authorities to develop an appropriate response. The period of the 1930s depression was also somewhat anomalous: there was far less banditry in this period than one would expect, if *rampok* were assumed to be linked directly to economic crisis. Peter Boomgaard rightly observes that the 1930s depression was the first crisis in Java that did not lead to widespread food shortages.[3] In fact Batavian banditry flourished most notably in the three decades of relative prosperity on the island.

Viewed as a branch of economic activity, banditry was certainly quite lucrative. In Batavia and the Ommelanden, the proceeds of a robbery generally exceeded the amount that an average Javanese man could earn in a year. Gang members were rarely involved in any other kind of economic activity; at most they perhaps worked a little land, using their money, if they did not distribute it to others, for rice-fields, cattle, women and pilgrimages to Mecca. I have not found a single case of a bandit who pursued a successful career in any other kind of activity, criminal or otherwise.

It is fair to ask whether the growth of large-scale banditry was an inevitability in the Ommelanden around Batavia, as a 'peripheral' region according to the theory of Thomas Gallant (based on the work of Wallerstein). In fact Gallant's theory does not apply here; banditry did not develop in the Ommelanden along the lines he describes. Gallant maintains that in areas incorporated into the world economic system as 'peripheral' regions, estates were created when small farmers were thrown off their land.[4] But this did not happen in the Ommelanden, which were very sparsely populated before 1850. Most of their later population had been born on an estate or had migrated there, rather than being dispossessed former smallholders. Furthermore, the specific kind of banditry that Gallant's theory would lead one to expect — robberies targeting export products being transported to the coast for international trade — did not develop in the area around Batavia. It must be said, however, that the period I have studied in this book certainly corresponds to the economic development model of incipient modernization generated by mass exports of produce from country estates in the hinterland to overseas markets. We also find other typical features of this model, such as the introduction of a money-based economy, the modernization of firearms (and the absence of controls on them) and the growth of a colonial society with a more prominent European component.

The bandits' activities prompted the urban population to demand a more effective approach to tackling crime, which was achieved with the large-scale reorganization of the police. The state gradually gained more control of regions and areas of society that had been all but invisible in the past. In this sense, the banditry in and around Batavia did much to precipitate an expansion of modern state authority in what had formerly been a frontier territory.

Appendices

Appendix I

The organization of security

This diagram shows both the official and the informal organization of public order and safety in Batavia and the Ommelanden in the colonial period, from the perspective of a few older residents of Jakarta and its environs. It is based on interviews that took place around 1980, reported in Junus Melalatoa and Rivai Abu (eds.), *Sistem kesatuan hidup setempat daerah dki Jakarta*, and J. Rogier Nieuwenhuys, 'De Tjiomas-zaak', p. 28.

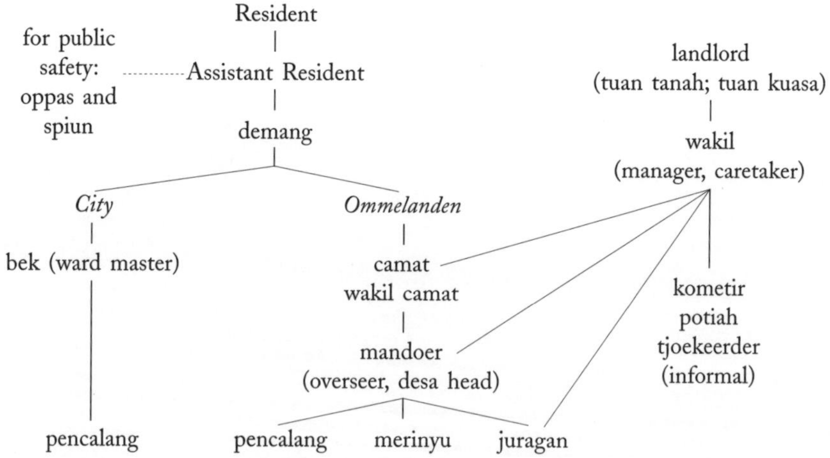

Ranks in the city police force after 1911:[1]

- *hoofdcommissaris*; chief commissioner
- *adjunct-hoofdcommissaris*; deputy chief commissioner
- *commissaris van politie en wedana van politie*; police commissioner and police wedana
- *commissaris van politie 2de klasse*; police commissioner, 2nd class
- *hoofdpolitie opziener*; chief police inspector
- *adspirant commissaris van politie en assistent wedana van politie*; deputy police commissioner and assistant police *wedana*
- *politie opziener der 1ste klasse*; police inspector, 1st class
- *politie opziener der 2de klasse*; police inspector, 2nd class
- *adspirant politie opziener*; deputy police inspector
- *mantri politie*; police *mantri*
- *hoofdagent en hoofdrechercheur*; senior officer and senior investigator
- *posthuis commandant der 1ste klasse*; station commander, 1st class
- *posthuis commandant der 2de klasse*; station commander, 2nd class
- *politieagent der 1ste klasse*; police officer, 1st class
- *politieagent der 2de klasse*; police officer, 2nd class
- *rekruut*; recruit

Appendix II

Robberies between 1890 and 1920

(accompanying Chapter 2, 'The Economics of Banditry')

This diagram shows the number of robberies per year in the research area, as calculated by the author on the basis of the *Koloniale Verslagen* (Colonial Reports).

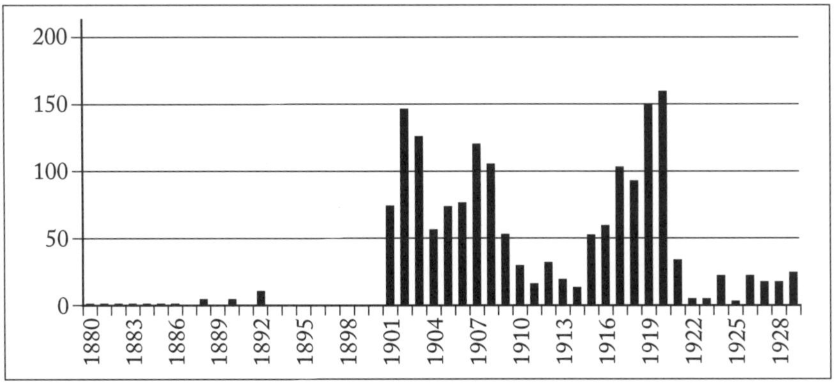

Appendix III

The calculation and planning of robberies

(accompanying Chapter 5, '*Jagos, jimats,* and *dukuns*') [Source: W.G. Vergouw, 'Animisme in de Javaansche dievenwereld' (1929), pp. 92–5.]

Thieves of this kind [*ketjoes* — MvT] are generally counted among the most dangerous. They almost always band together to commit their crimes, and their thefts are usually accompanied by life-threatening assaults on their victims or members of their victims' household. Accordingly, *ketjoes* must always be prepared to offer resistance. This is therefore the primary purpose of their superstitious calculations.

One of the principal calculation methods of the *ketjoes* is known as the Radjamoekah. The derivation should, I believe, be sought in the following sources:

Radja = nobleman, distinguished person (sometimes in unfavourable sense, hence: a Master Thief).

Moekah = verbal form of po(e)kah = tear apart violently.

In other words, the Radjamoekah protects a thief from being torn apart violently.

Its main purpose is to offer resistance. Those who come across a radjamoekah by chance do not know what to make of it. It is a piece of wood inscribed with all sorts of peculiar drawings and hieroglyphs.

After some investigation, I was finally able to determine the meaning of all these figures. The drawing below gives an impression of the Radjamoekah:

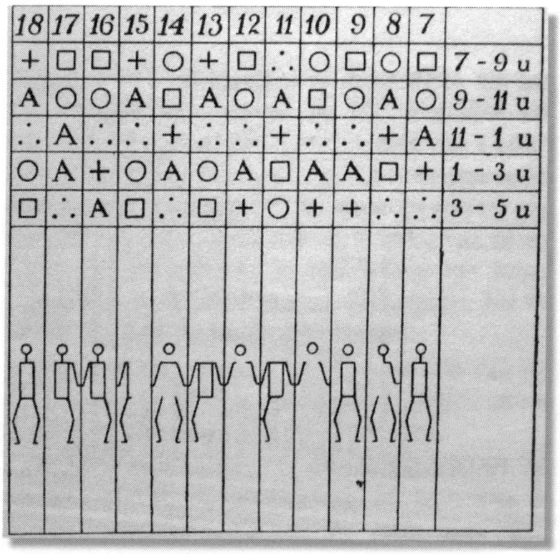

Illus. 24
Radjamoekah 1

This drawing can be interpreted as follows:

The uppermost row of numbers indicates the combined value of the ordinary weekday and the pasar day.[1] The smallest number must therefore be 7 (Tuesday, Wagé) and the greatest 18 (Saturday, Pahing). All other combinations of weekday and pasar day lie between these two. One can therefore see that it is based on the values of the different days.

The numbers in the boxes on the far right indicate the hours of night at which the *ketjoes* will strike.

The hieroglyphs at the bottom denote the criminal himself. The body parts missing from the human figure are at risk of being injured during the venture and should thus be well protected in advance.

Finally, the peculiar signs in the middle indicate whether the venture has a chance of succeeding.

Their meanings are:

+ = Sri = very easy prey
? = Gigis = a sure thing
? = Kalamomor = dubious (momor = unite)
? = Kalasembodjo, patjak wezi = impossible
? = Loenggoeh, Danjang pengantenan = almost assured

Let us now take a number. Suppose the *ketjoes* wish to strike on Wednesday, Pon, between 11 and 1 o'clock. Will they be successful?

Wednesday = 7, Pon = 7; 14 in total. We look in the column headed by the number 14 and the row with '11-1 u' at right [u. stands for *uren*, hours – trans.]. At their intersection we find +. This means easy prey. In other words, the *ketjoes* are very likely to succeed. The vulnerable parts of their bodies are the neck and torso. They should take good care of these parts of their bodies in advance, e.g. by putting on a coat of mail or some other kind of armour. They will be able to use their arms and legs without fear of injury.

The Radjamoekah is usually made of sembodjo wood or from a gnarl of the *djati*, *tjendono*, or *kelor* tree. Before the *ketjoes* are permitted to consult the Radjamoekah, however, they are supposed to fast.

Sometimes a different kind of Radjamoekah is used:

This figure is much simpler and serves simply to indicate whether a person engaged in such a venture will or will not be vulnerable at a certain time. The innermost segments of I to VIII each represent 1/8 of the time period of the night; the missing body parts again correspond to the parts of the human body actually at risk, but with *this* difference from the first

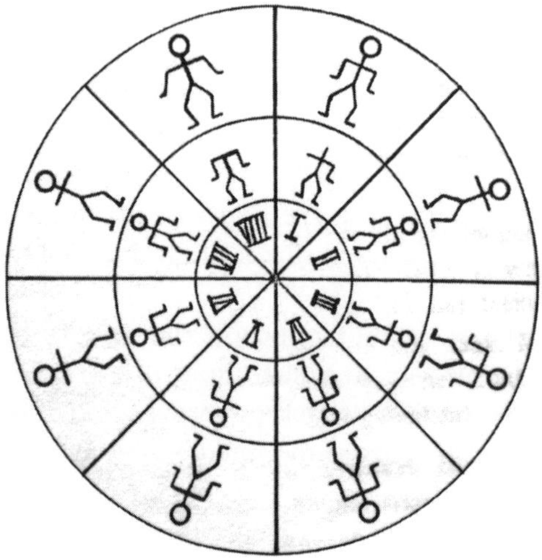

Illus. 25 Radjamoekah 2

Radjamoekah: here, the outermost drawings represent the bodies of the robbers and drawings in the inner circle represent the bodies of the victims or police officers.

This may be why people speak of *roesak djero* (inside) when the proprietors meet with an accident and *roesak djawi* (outside) when the *ketjoes* are injured.

Appendix IV

Robberies in four peak years, namely 1902, 1907, 1908, and 1920

[as described in the *Bataviaasch Nieuwsblad* (abbreviated to *BN*). The place names are given in the original spelling.]

The abbreviation *f* stands for guilders, the Dutch currency used in the colony at the time. To put the sums of money into context: Peter Boomgaard's *Children of the Colonial State* gives the typical annual incomes of indigenous people in several occupations in nineteenth-century Java (pp. 126 and 135). A farmer's annual income was generally between 125 and 150 guilders. Batavian artisans and labourers sometimes received wages of 300 guilders a year. This makes it clear that the proceeds of the robberies listed below sometimes greatly exceeded the annual income of an indigenous inhabitant of Java.

1902

5 January, time unknown
Location: Rawa Belong
Victim: an indigenous person
Number of robbers: many
Proceeds: unknown
Special features: a great deal of revolver fire; the victim was injured
Source: *BN*, 6 January 1902

6 January, time unknown
Location: Kebajoran, Kebon Djeroek
Victim: an indigenous hadji
Number of robbers: a gang
Proceeds: unknown
Special features: revolver fire; victim killed when he tried to defend himself
Source: *BN*, 7 January 1902

7 January, time unknown
Location: Gang Aboe
Victim: Amin (indigenous)
Number of robbers: unknown
Proceeds: a chest of clothes
Special features: incident took place during *puasa* (a fasting period)
Source: *BN*, 8 January 1902

19 January, time unknown
Location: Kebajoran
Victim: Hadji Naidi
Number of robbers: 1
Proceeds: none
Special features: revolver fire; the robbery failed
Source: *BN*, 20 January 1902

Mid-January, time unknown
Location: Meester Cornelis, Tandjoeng Jiang Baroe
Victim: Bango (indigenous)
Number of robbers: more than 2
Proceeds: goods
Special features: two of the robbers were later arrested
Source: *BN*, 21 January 1902

20 January, time unknown
Location: Tanah Tingi
Victim: Boerhan
Number of robbers: probably 4
Proceeds: goods worth *f*60
Special features: none
Source: *BN*, 21 January 1902

9 January, time unknown
Location: Karet, Kampong Lima
Victim: Gouw Gok Lim (Chinese)
Number of robbers: 6
Proceeds: *f*35, two watches, and some other goods
Special features: bystanders were kept at a distance with revolver fire
Source: *BN*, 10 February 1902

8 March, evening
Location: Meester Cornelis, Tanah Commandant
Victim: a Chinese shopkeeper
Number of robbers: 5
Proceeds: *f*12 plus goods of unknown value
Special features: revolver fire; the robbers were chased away by a police *oppasser*
Source: *BN*, 10 March 1902

5 May, time unknown
Location: Gang Traté
Victim: the Chinese woman Oeij Song Nio
Number of robbers: 3
Proceeds: unknown
Special features: the robbers, armed with three revolvers, fled because of the victim's cries
Source: *BN*, 6 May 1902

7 May, evening
Location: Meester Cornelis, Pondok Labu
Victim: Kah Bing (Chinese)
Number of robbers: 3
Proceeds: *f*300 worth of money and goods
Special features: the robbers were armed with revolvers
Source: *BN*, 9 May 1902

15 May, time unknown
Location: Tanah Sereal
Victim: the indigenous shopkeeper Djasim
Number of robbers: 5
Proceeds: *f*10
Special features: the victim was shot in the side; the robbers fled when help arrived from nearby. Three of the robbers, who came from Rawah and Kebon Djeroek (in Kebajoran) were arrested on 16 May. On 24 and 25 June, the last two perpetrators were apprehended in Kedoyo Kebajoran; one of them was recognized by the bite in his hand, inflicted by his victim.
Source: *BN*, 15 & 16 May, as well as 24 & 26 June 1902

5 June, 2 a.m.
Location: Tanah Sereal
Victim: Doel (indigenous)
Number of robbers: 6
Proceeds: jewellery (including two gold bracelets and brooches) and goods
Special features: revolver fire
Source: *BN*, 5 June 1902

5 August, at night
Location: Kebajoran
Victim: the indigenous Hadji Hamid
Number of robbers: 'a gang'
Proceeds: none
Special features: the hadji was injured by a shot from a revolver after he resisted. Neighbours then came to his assistance and chased away the robbers.
Source: *BN*, 6 August 1902

9 August, 2 or 3 a.m.
Location: Doeri (near Tangerang)
Victim: Nasirin (indigenous)
Number of robbers: 3
Proceeds: 'not much': *f*10, silver jewellery, and mortgage bonds
Special features: Nasirin was injured in the thighbone by a shot from a revolver. During the pursuit, the robbers discarded the proceeds, which were later found.
Source: *BN*, 9 and 12 August 1902

5 September, 7:30 p.m.
Location: Jacatraweg in Mangga Doea
Victim: the European widow W.
Number of robbers: 10
Proceeds: *f*9 plus weapons (the wrong cupboard was opened)
Special features: a great deal of revolver fire (but no injuries). The perpetrators/suspects include a former domestic servant and a gravedigger at the Mangga Doea cemetery; Europeans were also involved.
Source: *BN*, 6 and 11 September 1902

6 September, 11 p.m.
Location: Moeara Karang (Fluit)
Victim: the indigenous wife of the ward master, who had been killed in 1901
Number of robbers: 6
Proceeds: goods
Special features: vengeance killing, because the woman had reported her husband's killers to the police. One of the perpetrators was later arrested in Kebajoran; the goods were recovered.
Source: *BN*, 8 and 18 September 1902

20 September, at night
Location: the servants' quarters of the girls' school in Gang Riemer
Victims: a married indigenous couple
Number of robbers: 4
Proceeds: *f*150 and goods
Special features: none
Source: *BN*, 22 September 1902

23 May, time unknown
Location: Kebon Djoe
Victim: the indigenous woman Assem
Number of robbers: 3
Proceeds: clothing and *f*15
Special features: threatened with a *golok*; the perpetrators were known to the victim
Source: *BN*, 24 September 1902

24 September, at night
Location: Tjeliuntjing
Victim: an indigenous person
Number of robbers: unknown
Proceeds: unknown
Special features: the victim put up a fight and was shot in the side
Source: *BN*, 25 September 1902

8 October, time unknown
Location: Meester Cornelis, Kampong Melajoe
Victim: a Chinese person
Number of robbers: multiple
Proceeds: unknown
Special features: the ward master came to the assistance of the victim, but his revolver would not fire and he was shot dead by the robbers.
Source: *BN*, 9 October 1902

22 November, time unknown
Location: Nieuwpoortstraat
Victim: the Javasche Bank
Number of robbers: 3 (2 European and 1 indigenous)
Proceeds: unknown
Special features: see Appendix 7
Source: *BN*, 24 November 1902

4 November, time unknown
Location: Tandjoeng Priok
Victim: unknown
Number of robbers: 'a few'
Proceeds: unknown
Special features: a *pentjalang* (low-ranking indigenous official) intervened and was shot in the leg. One of the robbers was taken captive but quickly escaped. Blackened face.
Source: *BN*, 5 December 1902

12 December, time unknown
Location: Meester Cornelis, Karet
Victim: a wealthy indigenous person
Number of robbers: 20
Proceeds: a large amount of jewellery and clothing
Special features: threats of revolver fire. The *demang* arrested several robbers.
Source: *BN*, 17 December 1902

1907

23 January, 2 a.m.
Location: Kemajoran, Bedoengan
Victim: a Chinese overseer
Number of robbers: unknown
Proceeds: *f*2,000 and goods
Special features: battery
Source: *BN*, 23 January 1907

4 March, time unknown
Location: Bekasi, Tjakoeng (railway stop)
Victim: an indigenous station master
Number of robbers: 9
Proceeds: none.
Special features: the robbery failed because the station master used his revolver.
Source: *BN*, 4 March 1907

9–10 March, at night
Location: Kampong Gede
Victim: Kan Tia Te (Chinese)
Number of robbers: 18
Proceeds: *f*10,000, *f*2,000 in silver coins, and *f*4,600 worth of jewellery
Special features: revolver fire by robbers; Kan Tia Te was shot in the arm and his wife was shot through the mouth; neither one was at risk of dying.
Source: *BN*, 12 March 1907

10–11 March, time unknown
Location: Tjiomas, Kampong Nabo
Victim: unknown
Number of robbers: unknown
Proceeds: unknown
Special features: fighting between robbers and occupants
Source: *BN*, 19 March 1907

16–17 March, at night
Location: Kampong Karet
Victim: unknown
Number of robbers: 10
Proceeds: none
Special features: the indigenous guards (*gardoes*) took action, and one of them was shot dead by the robbers.
Source: *BN*, 19 March 1907

16–17 March, at night
Location: Kramat, Tjililitan
Victim: a hadji
Number of robbers: unknown
Proceeds: meagre
Special features: the proceeds were disappointing to the robbers, who had expected the hadji to have a great deal of money in his home in connection with the sale of a house. The buyer had asked to pay later, however. The hadji was tied up.
Source: *BN*, 19 March 1907

17–18 March, at night
Location: Krawang, Gempol
Victim: unknown
Number of robbers: unknown
Proceeds: unknown
Special features: occupant injured
Source: *BN*, 20 March 1907

18 March, time unknown
Location: Kramat, Tjililtan
Victim: an administrator
Number of robbers: unknown
Proceeds: none
Special features: robbers caught and beaten by locals

9–10 March, 7 p.m.
Location: Meester Cornelis, Tjipinang
Victim: a Chinese person
Number of robbers: more than 3
Proceeds: unknown
Special features: none
Source: *BN*, 10 April 1907

7 April, time unknown
Location: Mauk, Tandjung Kait
Victim: Hadji Liang
Number of robbers: 6
Proceeds: *f*137
Special features: the robbers had blackened their faces
Source: *BN*, 11 April 1907

16–17 May, time unknown
Location: Buitenzorg, Kebon Pedis (a five-minute walk from the Palace in Buitenzorg)
Victim: the merchant and money-lender Kam Lim Nio, widow of Horninge
Number of robbers: 25
Proceeds: *f*5,000 worth of goods
Special features: the gang was led by a European. The paper asked ironically how long it would take before the robbers visited the palace and the Governor-General's insignia of office ended up in a pawnshop.
Source: *BN*, 18 May 1907

19 June, at night
Location: Kampong Baroe
Victim: the shopkeeper Lau Bo Tjeng
Number of robbers: unknown
Proceeds: *f*826
Special features: none
Source: *BN*, 21 June 1907

17 July, at night
Location: Tjililitan, Kampong Melajoe
Victim: unknown
Number of robbers: 4 men from Bojong Gedeh
Proceeds: *f*20 and goods
Special features: none
Source: *BN*, 18 July 1907

Around the same date
Location: East Tandjoeng.
Victim: unknown.
Number of robbers: unknown.
Proceeds: unknown.
Special features: none.
Source: *BN*, 18 July 1907

19 July, at night
Location: Tangerang, Tjipandai.
Victim: the agent in charge of the country estate, Oei Giok Koen.
Number of robbers: 15.
Proceeds: *f*600 and a revolver.
Special features: the robbers were heavily armed.
Source: *BN*, 22 July 1907

12 September, time unknown
Location: Tangerang, Goenoeng Batoe.
Victim: The Tian Hok.
Number of robbers: 5.
Proceeds: *f*86
Special features: the robbers were armed with revolvers
Source: *BN*, 13 September 1907

Around 15 September, time unknown
Location: Sawah
Victim: an indigenous merchant
Number of robbers: unknown
Proceeds: unknown
Special features: none
Source: *BN*, 18 October 1907

September, time unknown
Location: Tjiboeaja
Victims: a group of indigenous fishermen
Number of robbers: 8
Proceeds: unknown
Special features: the robbers were armed with revolvers
Source: *BN*, 18 October 1907

Around 1 October
Location: Tjilamaja
Victim: unknown
Number of robbers: a few
Proceeds: unknown
Special features: two robbers were shot dead
Source: *BN*, 18 October 1907

Around 2 October ('last week')
Location: East and West Tandjoeng (two separate robberies)
Victims: indigenous people

Number of robbers: unknown
Proceeds: unknown
Special features: one of the victims was killed; a few people were injured
Source: *BN*, 9 October 1907

13 October, time unknown
Location: Rengas Dengklok
Victims: unknown
Number of robbers: unknown
Proceeds: *f*160 plus jewellery
Special features: none
Source: *BN*, 18 October 1907

15 October, time unknown
Location: Angoeng, near Buitenzorg
Victim: Nariem (indigenous)
Number of robbers: 8
Proceeds: *f*1104
Special features: the victim killed one robber with his revolver and injured another
Source: *BN*, 22 October 1907

30 October, time unknown
Location: Meester Cornelis, Kampoeng Ramboetan
Victims: a married indigenous couple
Number of robbers: unknown
Proceeds: unknown
Special features: the victims put up a fight and were severely injured
Source: *BN*, 31 October 1907

30 October, time unknown
Location: Meester Cornelis, Poeloe Gadoeng
Victim: an indigenous person
Number of robbers: unknown
Proceeds: household effects
Special features: the owner put up a fight and was severely injured
Source: *BN*, 31 October 1907

30 October, time unknown
Location: Meester Cornelis, Kebon Klappa
Victim: an indigenous person
Number of robbers: unknown
Proceeds: unknown
Special features: the victim put up a fight and later died from his injuries
Source: *BN*, 1 November 1907

4 November, 9 p.m.
Location: Meester Cornelis, Kampong Melajoe
Victim: a Chinese shopkeeper
Number of robbers: 6
Proceeds: jewellery worth *f*160 and other goods worth *f*140
Special features: the robbers fired revolvers as they fled
Source: *BN*, 5 November 1907

7 December, at night
Location: Tanah Abang
Victim: a hadji
Number of robbers: more than 5
Proceeds: unknown
Special features: the area was closed off; one of the robbers came from Kebajoran
Source: *BN*, 9 and 28 December 1907

8 December, at night
Location: Kebajoran, Kebon Djeroek
Victim: unknown
Number of robbers: unknown
Proceeds: unknown
Special features: none
Source: *BN*, 19 December 1907

1908

17 March, time unknown
Location: Meester Cornelis, Tanah Kerbo
Victim: unknown
Number of robbers: unknown
Proceeds: unknown
Special features: none
Source: *BN*, 17 March 1908

31 March, 8 p.m.
Location: Rawa Bangke, Pisangan
Victim: a Chinese person
Number of robbers: unknown
Proceeds: goods
Special features: victim died from his injuries
Source: *BN*, 1 April 1908

7 April, 7:30 p.m.
Location: Pasar Minggoe
Victim: Toen Amat
Number of robbers: 6
Proceeds: *f*800 in goods and *f*65 in cash
Special features: the robbers were armed with revolvers
Source: *BN*, 8 April 1908

7 July, time unknown
Location: Pegansaan
Victim: a Chinese person
Number of robbers: unknown
Proceeds: *f*600
Special features: the Chinese victim was tied up; his house was across the street from that of a police inspector
Source: *BN*, 8 July 1908

15 August, at night
Location: Tjimanggis
Victim: an unknown Chinese man
Number of robbers: unknown
Proceeds: *f*78
Special features: none
Source: *BN*, 16 August 1908

15 August, at night
Location: Cibaroesa
Victim: Bapa Kaidan
Number of robbers: unknown
Proceeds: *f*686
Special features: none
Source: *BN*, 16 August 1908

August, time unknown
Location: Kebajoran
Victim: an unknown indigenous person
Number of robbers: unknown
Proceeds: *f*75
Special features: the victim was shot and injured during the incident
Source: *BN*, 25 August 1908

3 September, time unknown
Location: Kemajoran
Victim: a hadji

Number of robbers: more than 3; 1 robber came from Meester Cornelis
Proceeds: *f*55
Special features: victim tied up; the house was targeted because one of the members of the family had been an indentured labourer in Deli
Source: *BN*, 4 & 8 September 1908

24 September, time unknown
Location: Kebajoran, Pondok Betoeng
Victim: a Chinese man
Number of robbers: 20
Proceeds: portable household effects and *f*130
Special features: the victim's wife was injured
Source: *BN*, 25 September 1908

24 September, time unknown
Location: Serpong, Babakan
Victim: a Chinese man
Number of robbers: 15
Proceeds: *f*300 and *f*600 worth of jewellery
Special features: the victim sustained a head injury
Source: *BN*, 25 September 1908

24 September, time unknown
Location: Kwitang
Victim: Sapan (indigenous)
Number of robbers: unknown
Proceeds: 'substantial'
Special features: none
Source: *BN*, 25 September 1908

15 October, 7 p.m.
Location: Gedong Pandjang
Victim: Teng Tjong Soei
Number of robbers: 4
Proceeds: *f*100
Special features: the robbers included a former forced labourer and a former police *oppasser*
Source: *BN*, 16 October 1908

18 October, 9 p.m.
Location: Tanah Abang
Victim: The Soen Hoei
Number of robbers: unknown
Proceeds: unknown
Special features: attempt failed
Source: *BN*, 19 October 1908

19 October, 10 p.m.
Location: Boekit Doeri
Victim: a Chinese shopkeeper
Number of robbers: unknown
Proceeds: clothing
Special features: none
Source: *BN*, 20 October 1908

19 October, 7 p.m.
Location: Gang Tomas
Victim: a bamboo seller
Number of robbers: unknown
Proceeds: goods
Special features: none
Source: *BN*, 20 October 1908

25 October, midnight
Location: Kampong Boegis
Victims: two indigenous women
Number of robbers: 5
Proceeds: *f*90

Special features: the robbers were naked and had blackened faces; one of the women recognized a former neighbour; the robbers were armed with revolvers.
Source: *BN*, 26 October 1908

Around 20 October, time unknown
Location: Tjililitan
Victim: a Chinese person
Number of robbers: unknown
Proceeds: *f*1,000
Special features: none
Source: *BN*, 26 October 1908

1 November, 2 a.m.
Location: Moeara Karang/Moeara Angke
Victim: a fishpond guard
Number of robbers: 7
Proceeds: *f*100
Special features: one of the robbers was the junior ward master in a neighbouring village
Source: *BN*, 2 November 1908

November, 3 a.m.
Location: Tanah Abang
Victims: an elderly indigenous woman and her daughter and son-in-law
Number of robbers: 5
Proceeds: *f*200
Special features: none
Source: *BN*, 3 November 1908

18 November, time unknown
Location: Kebajoran
Victim: an indigenous person
Number of robbers: unknown
Proceeds: unknown
Special features: the victims died from the injuries inflicted on them by the robbers
Source: *BN*, 20 November 1908

17 December, time unknown
Location: Pedjankoran (in Bekasi)
Victim: a Chinese person
Number of robbers: 5
Proceeds: unknown
Special features: a robber named Sian was shot down by the Chinese victim; Sian's wife was later arrested because Sian had said shortly before his death that the robbery had been planned at her house.
Source: *BN*, 18 and 19 December 1908

1920

1 January, 9 p.m.
Location: Balistraat
Victim: an elderly European housekeeper
Number of robbers: 2
Proceeds: *f*20
Special features: the robbers impersonated police officers; once they were inside the house, they knocked down the woman and tied her up
Source: *BN*, 2 January 1920

5 January, early evening
Location: Meester Cornelis, Pisangan Baroe

Victim: a shopkeeper
Number of robbers: 5
Proceeds: *f*40 plus jewellery
Special features: the robbers were armed with revolvers. The shopkeeper defended himself and sustained a head injury in the fight. Two robbers, who came from Menteng, were arrested on the spot. One of them later turned out to be a deserter from the military.
Source: *BN*, 6 and 14 January 1920

23 January, 3 a.m.
Location: Gang Sampi, Goenoeng Sahari
Victim: a Chinese shopkeeper
Number of robbers: 3
Proceeds: *f*210
Special features: the victim was tied up. The robbers fired into the air as they left ('as a greeting'). They victim recognized one of the robbers as an acquaintance.
Source: *BN*, 23 January 1920

26 January, evening
Location: Gang Kelapang
Victim: a Chinese shopkeeper
Number of robbers: 6
Proceeds: *f*50
Special features: the victim was injured by a shot from a revolver
Source: *BN*, 27 January 1920

18 February, evening
Location: Gang Kober
Victim: an indigenous person
Number of robbers: 4
Proceeds: *f*400 plus *f*106 worth of jewellery and clothing
Special features: two robbers were on lookout outside, one kept a revolver pointed at the victim, and the fourth did the stealing. The victim recognized two of the robbers as acquaintances.
Source: *BN*, 19 February 1920

19 March, at night
Location: Meester Cornelis, Tjipinang
Victim: an indigenous woman
Number of robbers: 3
Proceeds: two gold bracelets and personal effects
Special features: the robbers dug a tunnel into the house and threatened the victim with a knife
Source: *BN*, 20 March 1920

15 April, time unknown
Location: Gang Solitude
Victim: unknown
Number of robbers: unknown
Proceeds: unknown
Special features: one of the robbers came from Tjakoeng
Source: *BN*, 29 April 1920

21 April, evening
Location: Kampong Gaboes, Bekasi
Victim: a Chinese shopkeeper
Number of robbers: 15
Proceeds: *f*500 and goods worth *f*700
Special features: the shopkeeper's wife was hit; her young daughter had petroleum poured in her hair, but she knocked the lamp out of the robbers' hands
Source: *BN*, 22 April 1920

Probably 18 May, time unknown
Location: Kedoeng Alang, Buitenzorg
Victim: unknown
Number of robbers: unknown
Proceeds: unknown
Special features: two robbers were arrested; one came from Kampong Mampang, and the other from Pasar Minggoe
Source: *BN*, 19 May 1920

30 May, time unknown
Location: Molenvliet, Central Batavia
Victim: a Chinese hotel-keeper
Number of robbers: 4
Proceeds: *f*20.
Special features: the four robbers were European. In addition to the robbery, vandalism took place.
Source: *BN*, 1 June 1920

June, time unknown
Location: Kampong Baroe
Victim: a Chinese person
Number of robbers: 6
Proceeds: *f*50
Special features: four perpetrators were arrested in Pendjaringan
Source: *BN*, 10 June 1920

21 June, at night
Location: Manggaray
Victim: an indigenous shopkeeper
Number of robbers: 5
Proceeds: undergarments and valuables worth *f*259
Special features: three of the robbers were armed with revolvers
Source: *BN*, 22 June 1920

24 June, 4 a.m.
Location: Salemba Besar
Victim: an indigenous woman
Number of robbers: 4
Proceeds: jewellery and undergarments worth *f*300
Special features: none
Source: *BN*, 24 June 1920

19 July, evening
Location: Pasar Peté (Senen)
Victim: a Chinese shop
Number of robbers: 4
Proceeds: *f*80
Special features: a woman was stabbed with a knife
Source: *BN*, 20 July 1920

Probably 30 August, time unknown
Location: a hotel in Batavia
Victim: the Chinese family that owned the hotel
Number of robbers: 6
Proceeds: none
Special features: the robbers were Europeans. They threatened the man and woman who owned the hotel with three revolvers.
Source: *BN*, 1 September 1920

6 September, 8 p.m.
Location: Meester Cornelis, Gang Ambon
Victim: an indigenous hadji
Number of robbers: about 20
Proceeds: a wallet with money in it
Special features: the robbers, who had two revolvers, were chased away by people who lived in the neighbourhood
Source: *BN*, 7 September 1920

15 September, evening
Location: Djembattan Merak
Victim: a European
Number of robbers: 12
Proceeds: jewellery worth *f*900, 4 rifles, and 1 revolver
Special features: the robbers were armed with machetes. One of them was later caught in Bekasi.
Source: *BN*, 16 & 21 September 1920

18 or 19 September, time unknown
Location: Goenoeng Sahari, Gang Jenne
Victim: an indigenous person
Number of robbers: 8
Proceeds: none
Special features: the robbery failed because the police were tipped off by spies. A robber from Kebajoran was arrested, and a shoot-out followed.
Source: *BN*, 20 September 1920

22 September, before dawn
Location: Soengei Bamboe (harbour)
Victim: an indigenous person
Number of robbers: 8
Proceeds: jewellery worth *f*85
Special features: the robbers were armed with revolvers and had blackened their faces
Source: *BN*, 23 September 1920

21 October, 1 a.m.
Location: Salemba Tegalan
Victim: an indigenous person
Number of robbers: unknown
Proceeds: *f*400
Special features: the owner of the house was injured
Source: *BN*, 22 October 1920

26 October, around 3 a.m.
Location: Sawah Besar
Victim: an indigenous person
Number of robbers: 7
Proceeds: clothing

Special features: the robbers were armed with revolvers and chopping knives. Police spies had learned of the robbery in advance. During the encounter, the robber Saoemoen from Kampong Djawa Batavia was shot dead.
Source: *BN*, 26 October 1920

November, evening
Location: Kebon Baroe (on the border of Meester Cornelis and Kebajoran)
Victim: an indigenous person
Number of robbers: 5
Proceeds: jewellery worth *f*86
Special features: the victim was shot in the legs with a revolver. The robbery was said to have been motivated by vengeance. One of the criminals, Nawi, had previously been sentenced to 12 years in prison for killing an Arab on the basis of eyewitness testimony by the occupants of the house that was robbed, but in 1920 he managed to escape.
Source: *BN*, 4 November 1920

12 November, 2 a.m.
Location: Gang Baroe
Victim: an indigenous person
Number of robbers: unknown
Proceeds: *f*1,300
Special features: robbers entered by digging a tunnel. A great deal of revolver fire, but the robbers missed their targets.
Source: *BN*, 13 November 1920

13 November, 8 p.m.
Location: Djamboelaan
Victim: a Chinese ice house
Number of robbers: 10
Proceeds: *f*225 and *f*45 worth of goods
Special features: the weapons used were sticks, but the robbers were also in possession of revolvers and knives
Source: *BN*, 15 November 1920

6 December, time unknown
Location: Salemba
Victim: an indigenous person
Number of robbers: 2
Proceeds: unknown
Special features: the victim was shot with a pistol by the robbers
Source: *BN*, 7 December 1920

11 December, evening
Location: Kali Pasir
Victim: an indigenous person
Number of robbers: 5
Proceeds: *f*1825 in goods and cash
Special features: the robbers tunnelled their way into the building; the occupant put up a fight and was hit on the head
Source: *BN*, 3 December 1920

30 December, time unknown
Location: Soengei Bamboe (near Tandjoeng Priok)
Victims: indigenous people
Number of robbers: 4
Proceeds: *f*40
Special features: a shoot-out took place. Both the occupants and a robber were shot dead.
Source: *BN*, 31 December 1920

Notes

Introduction

1. 'Zoo is gisteravond om 9 uur in de kom der gemeente weer gerampokt. Het was bij een chineeschen waronghouder in den chineeschen kamp bij de brug van Kampong Melajoe. Zes rampokkers drongen het huis binnen en roofden voor 160 gulden aan sieraden en 140 gulden aan andere goederen. Terwijl zij met hun buit aftrokken, losten zij revolverschoten om zich de achtervolgers van het lijf te houden.' *Bataviaasch Nieuwsblad*, 5 November 1907.
2. A few general remarks are called for about the spelling of Malay words. In the 1970s, Indonesia adopted a new spelling system: 'oe' became 'u', 'dj' became 'j', 'tj' became 'c', 'j' became 'y', and so forth. Except for the name of the legendary bandit Pitoeng, now written as Pitung, the names of people from the period studied are written as they originally were — that is, in the old spelling. It should be added that names are often written in more than one way; in such cases, I have opted for the most frequent spelling. In quotes, I have of course retained the original spelling. The prefix 'Si' was used with the names of some bandits. Place names and other Malay words are spelled in accordance with the new system, so that they are easily recognizable, but the old spelling has also been supplied where relevant. At the back of this book are an explanatory glossary, an index of personal names, and an index of place names.
3. This is how banditry or *rampok* was defined in the jargon of the colonial administration in the late nineteenth and early twentieth centuries. See for

example Arsip Nasional Republik Indonesia (ANRI), Archives of the General Secretariat, Besluit 17-10-1893, no. 14, rekest Maoen, Rimoen en Marip.

4. Terms for the indigenous people of the archipelago are an especially difficult issue. Nineteenth-century words such as *inboorling*, *inheemse*, and *inlandse* (rough equivalents of the English 'native') are now seen as derogatory, whether or not that was originally the case. The Dutch version of this study uses the terms *Indonesiër* and *Indonesisch*, the equivalents of 'Indonesian'. The advantage of these terms is that they have their origins in the Malay Archipelago, but the disadvantage is that they are anachronistic for most of the period studied, because the name 'Indonesia' did not come into widespread use until the twentieth century. This English version of the study generally uses the term 'indigenous', which has no exact Dutch equivalent in common use.
5. Pannekoek, 'De viering van het 250-jarig bestaan van Batavia in 1869'.
6. In Heyman (ed.), *States and Illegal Practices*, pp. 25–62.
7. Wallerstein, *The Modern World-System*.
8. See also Wesseling, 'Van Europese geschiedenis naar wereldgeschiedenis', pp. 266–9.
9. Shannon, *An Introduction to the World-System Perspective*, p. 59.
10. Arnold, 'Dacoity and Rural Crime in Madras', pp. 142–3; Ahmad, 'Thugs, Dacoits, and the Modern World-System in Nineteenth Century India'.
11. Examples include Chandler, *The Bandit King: Lampião of Brazil*; Lewin, 'The Oligarchical Limitations of Social Banditry in Brazil'; Brunk, 'The Sad Situation of Civilians and Soldiers' (about Mexico); and Katz, *Riot, Rebellion, and Revolution: Rural Social Conflict in Mexico*.
12. Koliopoulis, 'Brigands with a Cause'.
13. Brown, 'Brigands and State Building: The Invention of Banditry in Modern Egypt'.
14. Gallant, 'Brigandage, Piracy, Capitalism and State-Formation', p. 30.
15. Pandey, 'In Defense of the Fragment', pp. 18–9; as quoted in Purdey, 'Describing Kekerasan', pp. 196–7.
16. In the Javanese Vorstenlanden, robbery or *rampok* was also known as *ketjoe*.
17. 'Leest men uit andere streken het bericht dat ergens geroofd of geketjoed is, of bij een Europeaan van enig aanzien een diefstal gepleegd, dan bevat dit bericht de eenvoudige meededeling van het feit, maar te Batavia voegt men daaraan breede beschouwingen toe, of met de boosaardige strekking het Europees bestuur in ongunstig daglicht te stellen, of gedreven door een zwakken moed, waardoor men in elken inlander een Gantang ziet.' Remark inserted by the author, Margreet van Till.

18. National Archives (NA), The Hague, Archives of the Ministry of Colonies, 2.10.36.04, inv. no. 282, Vb. 15 December 1904, no. 64, letter from the Resident of Batavia, Bakhuizen van den Brink, to the director of the internal administration, Batavia, 29 June 1904.
19. The ANRI in Jakarta also hold many legal documents, but most of these are highly partisan, and they are not always easily accessible. For example, the many trial document in the archives for the Tangerang Residency were disorganized and in poor condition. The documents that were legible dealt primarily with cattle theft.
20. Schulte Nordholt, 'De jago in de schaduw', p. 665.
21. The Dutch and the Chinese were not faced with large-scale *rampok* until the Japanese occupation, when large groups of looters seized their possessions.
22. Boomgaard, *Frontiers of Fear: Tigers and People in the Malay World, 1600–1950*, pp. 146–66.
23. Fasseur, *De indologen*.
24. Boeka, *Uit Java's binnenland: Pah Troeno* en *Uit Java's binnenland: Beschaving* (2 vols.); and Bloembergen, 'Een koffieopziener in de desa. P.C.C. Hansen en zijn beeld van Java's binnenland'.
25. Adas, 'From Avoidance to Confrontation'.
26. Schulte Nordholt, 'De jago in de schaduw', p. 674.
27. Schulte Nordholt, 'De jago in de schaduw'; and Schulte Nordholt with Van Till, 'Colonial Criminals in Java, 1870–1910'.
28. In late nineteenth-century Malay-language newspapers (such as the 9 April 1872 issue of *Bintang Barat* and the 13 April 1886 issue of *Pemberita Betawi*), the citizen militias were called *barisan preman* or *soldadoe preman*, perhaps because Europeans often hired Asians to replace them. In this case, the word *preman* is used in the context of the city of Batavia and is associated with the free citizens belonging to the militias. I conclude that the word *preman* referred to the free Asian, Eurasian, and European citizens of the city of Batavia. The term was used in the seventeenth, eighteenth, and nineteenth centuries to distinguish this group from members of the Asian population who were slaves. For an overview of demographic groups in the population of Batavia, see Niemeijer, 'The Free Asian Christian Community and Poverty in Pre-Modern Batavia', pp. 78–83.
29. *Bataviaasch Nieuwsblad*, 11 February 1923.
30. *Pemberita Betawi*, 8 December 1903. Based on the author's Dutch translation from the Malay: 'Apa sebab afdeeling Mr. Cornelis djadi terganggoe kasenangannja, pendoedoek kampoeng terantjam eleh kawan prampok, jalah ada behrapa sebabnja: pertama lantaran di pidjit oleh kapala kampoeng, kadoewa

di paras oleh toewan tanah preman, katiga teramtjam pikoel oewang padjak negri dan ka ampat di ganggoe kabimbangan hatinja aleh goeroe-goeroe sakti dan kalima di ganggoe oleh kapala-kapala djago.'

31. On p. 668 Schulte Nordholt describes the criminal activities of the *jagos*, and on p. 669 he explains that *jagos* maintained public order within their own *desas*.
32. Gambetta, *The Sicilian Mafia: The Business of Private Protection*; and *Trust: Making and Breaking Cooperative Relations*.

Chapter 1

1. This story is based on a detailed account written by G.H. Pannekoek at the time, published under the title 'De viering van het 250-jarig bestaan van Batavia in 1869', *Tijdschrift voor Nederlandsch Indië* 18, no. 2 (1889): 161–205. See also ANRI, Jakarta, Batavia Archives, inv. no. 18, Politiek Verslag der Residentie Batavia over 1869.
2. Pannekoek, 'De viering', p. 169.
3. Van Delden, *De particuliere landerijen op Java*; Niemeijer, *Batavia, een koloniale samenleving in de 17de eeuw*, pp. 140–1.
4. Pannekoek, 'De viering', p. 178; 'toen allerwege cavalerie piketten met de karabijn in de vuist Batavia en voorsteden doorkruisten; toen het gerucht zich verspreidde, dat de troepen, die het feest tot opluistering bijwoonden, met scherpe patronen bewapend waren, dat de munitie kisten van de veldbatterijen, die de feestschoten zouden laten donderen, behoorlijk van kartetsen voorzien waren, gereed om dood en verderf te zaaien, toen kromp ieders hart ineen en viel het feest deerlijk in het water.'
5. Pannekoek, 'De viering', p. 181; 'menig cavalier moest om de jonge dames gerust te stellen haar beloven op het feest niet ongewapend te zullen verschijnen; en van verschillende kanten hoorde men later de verzekering, dat menig costuum een revolver in zijne plooien verborgen hield en dat, wanneer op het bal in de Harmonie ieder eens had moeten uitpakken, er zelfs bij de jonge dames enkele dolken zouden zijn te voorschijn gekomen.'
6. Pannekoek, 'De viering', p. 202; 'Zoo zielvol, zoo verrukt; 't klinkt weer: "ontzet! ontzet!/Een vlag, een vloot in 't zicht! Coen komt! Wij zijn gered!"/(...)/En valt ons, thans nog, na twee honderd vijftig jaar,/Die kreet niet op het hart, alsof 't nog gistren waar?'
7. 'De vloekzang' was written in 1859 by S.E.W. Roorda van Eysinga. He was advised not to publish it, but the poem became well known by oral transmission. See also Reitsma, *S.E.W. Roorda van Eysinga, de dichter van Sentot's vloekzang*, pp. 18–21; and Roorda van Eysinga, *Mijne verbanning en mijn vloekzang*.

8. Du Perron, *Het land van herkomst*, 1989 edition, for example pp. 109–12.
9. Raben, 'Round about Batavia: Ethnicity and Authority in the Ommelanden, 1650–1800'; Nagtegaal and Nas, 'Jakarta Greenery: An Essay on Urban Natural Environment', p. 265.
10. Jellinek, *The Urban Cycle*, p. 6.
11. *Java-bode*, 15 September 1871, quoted in Van Ballegoijen de Jong, *Spoorwegstations op Java*, pp. 78–9.
12. Preanger (now Priangan) is the mountainous area to the south and southeast of the Batavian Ommelanden.
13. A *bouw* was a unit of area used on Java: 1 *bouw* = 7,096 m^2. The word is derived from *bahoeen*, which originally meant 'as much farmland as one man and his family can cultivate'.
14. Van Kol, *Uit onze koloniën*, p. 813.
15. Du Perron, *Het land van herkomst*, p. 70.
16. Raben, *Batavia and Colombo*, pp. 62–3.
17. Nas, *Jakarta, stad vol symbolen*, p. 16.
18. Bloembergen, 'Koloniale staat, politiestaat?'
19. Du Perron, *Het land van herkomst*, p. 68; 'Mijn vader was gewaarschuwd voor een van de djoeragans die met roofbenden in betrekking stond. Toen hij de "rol" overnam, dat wil zeggen de opgezetenen van de Chinees liet aantreden om hem persoonlijk te leren kennen, stuitte hij op de naam Ali-Biman. De man die zo heette, een stevige brede Maleier, stond op uit zijn hurkende houding, kwam vlak naast mijn vader staan, die nog met de rol voor zich aan de schrijftafel zat, rekte zich uit en zei op hem neerkijkend, met de verachtelijke stem van de inlander die zich sterk waant, en woord voor woord: "Ik ben Ali-Biman".' and 'Het bleek later dat hij inderdaad met roof uitstaande had. Mijn vader stelde hem vooraf verantwoordelijk voor iedere roofpartij die op zijn landerijen plaats zou hebben: "Ik ben niet van de politie en heb met andere landen niets te maken, maar als hier wat gebeurt weet ik jou te vinden, Ali-Biman." Er gebeurde nooit iets....' Translation from English edition: *Country of Origin*, pp. 50–1. For more about this episode see Snoek, *E. du Perron*, p. 37.
20. ANRI, Jakarta, Batavia Archives, inv. no. 357.3, correspondence between the Assistant Resident of Buitenzorg and the Assistant Resident of Tangerang, letter of 5 November 1882.
21. De Jong, *De waaier van het fortuin*, pp. 93–107.
22. Nagtegaal, *Riding the Dutch Tiger*, pp. 52–4. For the term 'contest state', see Adas, 'From avoidance to confrontation', pp. 217–8 and 247; and Schulte Nordholt, 'De jago in de schaduw', p. 665.

23. These facts about Surapati (whose name is also written 'Suropati') are taken from De Graaf, *Geschiedenis van Indonesië*, pp. 233–44; Blussé, *Bitters bruid*, p. 60; Ricklefs, *A History of Modern Indonesia*, pp. 79–80; Kumar, *Surapati: Man and Legend*; and *Babad Tanah Djawi*, pp. 214–20.
24. De Haan, *Priangan*, vol. IV, p. 737.
25. Sartono Kartodirdjo based his information about Djakaria on the memoirs of colonial administrators (E. Francis, P.P. Roorda van Eysinga, and Resident Bruijn) and government archives. I also use information from the newspaper *Javaansche Courant* and the Banten Residency Archives in the ANRI, in Jakarta.
26. Sartono Kartodirdjo, *The Peasants' Revolt of Banten*, p. 177.
27. Ibid., p. 135.
28. ANRI, Jakarta, Banten Residency Archives, inv. no. 181, Resident of Banten to the Governor-General of Batavia, 29 November 1827.
29. Schulte Nordholt, 'A Genealogy of Violence', p. 38; on this incident, see also Nieuwenhuys, 'De Tjiomas-zaak. Een Indische "cause célèbre" uit 1886'.
30. Adas, 'From Avoidance to Confrontation', p. 229. The Javanese, it might be added, often intended to negotiate; large 'demonstrations' of this type were meant to place pressure on the authorities.
31. See also Sartono Kartodirdjo, *The Peasants' Revolt of Banten*, p. 111; and *Laporan-laporan tenang gerakan protes di Jawa pada abad xx*, which contain illustrations of how seriously the colonial authorities took such investigations.
32. Bosma, *Karel Zaalberg. Journalist en strijder voor de Indo*, p. 23.
33. Bosma and Raben, *De oude Indische wereld*, p. 98.
34. Riesz, *De particuliere landerijen van Westelijk-Java*, vol. 1, p. 98.
35. Gallant applied Wallerstein's theory of the modern world system to the subject of banditry (see the Introduction); 'Brigandage, Piracy, Capitalism and State-Formation', p. 30.
36. Riesz, *De particuliere landerijen van Westelijk-Java*, vol. 1, p. 98.
37. Bosma and Raben, *De oude Indische wereld*, p. 108; Ottow, *De oorsprong van de conservatieve richting*, p. 238.
38. Stibbe (ed.), *Encyclopaedie van Nederlandsch-Indië*, vol. 3, pp. 345–50.
39. Stibbe (ed.), *Encyclopaedie van Nederlandsch-Indië*, p. 348; Gonggryp, *Geïllustreerde encyclopaedie van Nederlandsch-Indië*, pp. 1144–5.
40. Nevertheless, there was an enduring image of estate owners as tremendously rich, mainly because they regularly threw lavish parties on special occasions. Between times, however, they had to lead increasingly frugal lives. See Nieuwenhuys, 'Tempo doeloe (1870–1920)', p. 6.

41. Van de Wall, *Oude Hollandsche buitenplaatsen van Batavia*, pp. 133–4.
42. Quoted from the letters of Mr Van der Hucht, in *Nieuwenhuis, Komen en blijven*, p. 43.
43. Bosma and Raben, *De oude Indische wereld*, p. 108.
44. Wolf and Mintz, 'Haciendas and Plantations in Middle America and the Antilles', *Social and Economic Studies* 6, no. 3 (1957): 380–412.
45. *Onderzoek naar de mindere welvaart der inlandsche bevolking op Java en Madoera.* 12 vols.
46. *Changing Economy in Indonesia*, vol. 8; *Onderzoek naar de mindere welvaart der inlandsche bevolking op Java en Madoera*, vol. VIB, p. 168, appendix VII.
47. Termorshuizen, *Journalisten en heethoofden*, pp. 91–4.
48. Termorshuizen, *Journalisten en heethoofden*, p. 158; Bosma, *Karel Zaalberg, journalist en strijder voor de Indo*, p. 68.
49. Wormser, 'De pers in Indië', p. 442.
50. Adam, *The Vernacular Press,* p. 38.
51. Ibid., p. 48.
52. After 1912, Tirtoadisoerjo founded several chapters of Muslim trade organizations in Buitenzorg and elsewhere.

Chapter 2

1. Gonggrijp, *Brieven van Opheffer*, p. 48.
2. Neijtzell de Wilde, *Een en ander omtrent den welvaartstoestand der Inlandsche bevolking*, pp. 327–9.
3. For a discussion of the terminology, see also NA, The Hague, Archives of the Ministry of Colonies, inv. no. 282, Vb. 15 December 1904, no. 64, internal fol. no. 1. Appendix to a letter from the Resident of Batavia, 20 June 1904, no. 3756a/4. Letter from Assistant Resident P.W. Hartelust of Meester Cornelis to the resident of Batavia, Meester Cornelis, 8 May 1904.
4. Included in Boomgaard and Brown (eds.), *Weathering the Storm. The Economies of Southeast Asia in the 1930s Depression.*
5. V.d. Eng, 'Halting Progress'.
6. For the absence of any correlation between robbery and poverty, see also Egmond, *Banditry in de Franse tijd* and Blok, *De Bokkerijders.*
7. Ministry of Defence, The Hague, Centraal Archieven Depot, Archives of 7 December Division, inv. no. 37, letter from the Assistant Resident of Purwakarta, D. Schermers, to the commander of the 2nd Inf. Brig. Group, 19 March 1948.

8. Gallant, 'Brigandage, Piracy, Capitalism, and State-Formation', pp. 30–1.
9. *Java-bode*, 4 June 1918.
10. Some examples of this rich tradition were the reports on the trial of the criminal Sakam in 1888, the statements made in the Ciomas affair (also in 1888) — in which numerous Javanese lives were lost when the authorities fired indiscriminately on a crowd of insurgents — and on the trial of the bandit Wangsa, who killed a European in 1892. A long account of a 1925 court case includes statements made by witnesses concerning a riot in East Tanjung, at which many claimed that dozens of rioters had been shot unnecessarily in a clash with the army; the rolls of film documenting the event had been seized and destroyed by the chief of police. The army, internal administration and police all came in for criticism (*Bataviaasch Nieuwsblad*, 18 March 1925).
11. *Bataviaasch Nieuwsblad*, 12 May 1919.
12. *De Zweep*, no. 2, 13 January 1923, p. 18.
13. *Bataviaasch Nieuwsblad*, 6 January 1923.
14. *Bataviaasch Nieuwsblad*, 27 March 1908.
15. Slatta (ed.), *Bandidos: The Varieties of Latin American Banditry*, p. 8.
16. Brown, *Brigand and State*, pp. 260–2.
17. Blok, 'The Peasant and the Brigand: Social Banditism Reconsidered'.
18. *Het politieschandaal te Batavia*, p. 11.
19. *Bataviaasch Nieuwsblad*, 12 May 1919.
20. *Het Vaderland*, 20 May 1912.
21. *Bataviaasch Nieuwsblad*, 4 March 1925.
22. NA, The Hague, Archives of the Ministry of Colonies, inv. no. 2713, Vb. 9 March 1925, no. 3, Rapport omtrent de Afdeeling en het Afdeelingsverband bij de Algemene Politie, opgesteld door de hoofdopziener Scheepmaker, f. 9.
23. NA, The Hague, Archives of the Ministry of Colonies, inv. no. 2713, Vb. 9 March 1925, no. 3, Rapport omtrent de Afdeeling en het Afdeelingsverband bij de Algemene Politie, opgesteld door de hoofdopziener Scheepmaker, f. 8. Appendix 2 to Rapport assistent-resident van Batavia J.J. van Helsdingen (Organisatie Politie op Grote Hoofdplaatsen, hoofdstuk 1 en 2).
24. *Java-bode*, 4 March 1925.
25. Van Dijk, 'The Good, the Bad and the Ugly' and Colombijn, 'Maling, Maling! The Lynching of Petty Criminals'.
26. Orig.: 'en dat op een padisnijdag'.
27. *Stamboel*=theatre; *maloe*=embarrassment. 'Vooruit, *main toneel sadja*, moedigt de voorzitter verder een getuige aan, die zal voordoen hoe Pa-I hem heeft willen kelen alvorens drie kwartjes, z'n eenige geldje, van hem los te krijgen. Getuige moet nu maar Pa-I spelen en Pa-I den beroofde. Als getuige lang

aarzelt, scheldt het volk hem [uit voor] lafaard en men uit z'n verontwaardiging door schopbewegingen te maken. Als den getuige eindelijk, krijtwit, z'n vingers liefjes om Pa-I's hals heeft gelegd, wordt luidruchtig opgemerkt, dat het "harder" moet. De voorzitter merkt telkens, fijntjes glimlachend, op: "nou, nou Pa-I, dit is toch betoel een hari-sial voor jou, terlaloe toch."' *Bataviaasch Nieuwsblad*, 20 May 1937.

28. *Bataviaasch Nieuwsblad*, 19 May 1937.
29. Blok, *De Bokkerijders*, pp. 156–8.
30. See for example the case against five or six Indonesian brigands who had robbed a Japanese shop in Kramat (*Bataviaasch Nieuwsblad*, 12, 13 and 14 February 1920).
31. The authorities were only in doubt as to the leader of the robbery, Abdoelrachman. The sources do not make clear what punishment was eventually meted out to him. ANRI, Jakarta, Archief Algemeene Sekretarie, MGS, December 1893; papieren behorend bij besluit nr. 4, 7 December 1893; reactie op gratieverzoeken Abdoelrachman c.s. (response to appeals for clemency lodged on behalf of Abdoelrachman c.s.).
32. ANRI, Jakarta, Archief Algemeene Sekretarie, Decision of 15 November 1904, inv. no. 11; de gratieverzoeken van Piah, Djoenan en Saënan (appeals for clemency lodged on behalf of Piah, Djoenan and Saënan).
33. NA, Jakarta, Archief Algemeene Sekretarie, Decision of 17 June 1904, no. 31, dossier rond gratieverzoek Piie (case file on the appeal for clemency lodged on behalf of Piie)
34. Zinoman, *The Colonial Bastille*, pp. 13–37; Zinoman, 'The History of the Modern Prison and the Case of Indo-China', pp. 164–5.
35. See the conclusions of Bruinink-Dalang's doctoral thesis, *Het penitentiair stelsel in Nederlands-Indië van 1905 tot 1940*, pp. 358–62.
36. *Bataviaasch Nieuwsblad*, 3 March 1904.
37. *Bataviaasch Nieuwsblad*, 6 February 1915.
38. A *rancak* is a poem customarily recited according to Indonesian tradition.
39. The final four verses of this *rancak*, 'Si Pitung', discuss prison life.
40. *Het politieschandaal te Batavia*, p. 14.
41. From the article 'Rampokkers' ('Perpetrators of *rampok*') by the author Paré, in the *Nederlandsch-Indische Politiegids*, December 1917, p. 10.
42. *Het politieschandaal te Batavia*, p. 13.
43. *Nederlandsch-Indische Politiegids*, December 1917, p. 100.
44. Bruinink-Darlang, *Het penitentiair stelsel in Nederlands-Indië van 1905 tot 1940*, pp. 143–7. About 3,000 men escaped from the mines each year (*Nederlandsch-Indische Politiegids*, January 1925).

45. Erwiza, *Miners, Managers and the State*, pp. 87–8 (note 29, based on information derived from *Sinar Sumatra*).
46. Erwiza, *Miners, Managers and the State*, pp. 57, 88–9.
47. This alleged state of affairs was later confirmed by interviews with those concerned; see Erwiza, *Miners, Managers and the State*, pp. 57 and 75 (statistical survey).
48. Emang jadi jago engga berguna
    Kendati dapet sejuta dua juta itu engga cukup sepagi mana
    Musuhnya militer, kompeni segala wedana
    Jangan pula kita yang bodo, si Pitung yang pinter engga urung kena.

    Dari kita jadi jago mendingan kita jadi orang tani
    Sebab kalo jadi jago musuhnya segala kumpeni
    Biar kita dekil kotor kayak begini
    Dapet seleter dua leter berkah selamet anak bini

    Source: Palupi Damardini, *Cerita Si Pitung sebagai sastra lisan*, p. 160.

Chapter 3

1. Dobbin, 'Accounting for the Failure of the Muslim Javanese Business Class'; Geertz, *The Social History of an Indonesian Town*; see also Castles, *Religion, Politics and Economic Behaviour in Java* and Henley, 'Entrepreneurship, Individualism and Trust in Indonesia'.
2. Fukuyama, *Trust: The Social Virtues and the Creation of Prosperity*. See also Gambetta (ed.), *Trust: Making and Breaking Cooperative Relations*; and the chapter 'The Ambiguity of Violence, Secrecy and Trust', in Zaitch, *Trafficking Cocaine*, esp. pp. 276–80.
3. Jewish gangs are described in Egmond, *Banditisme in de Franse Tijd*; and Blok, *The Mafia of a Sicilian Village (1860–1960)*.
4. Sartono Kartodirdjo, *Protest Movements in Rural Java*, p. 136. One exception, perhaps, is the Oah sect described by Sartono that was active in the surroundings of Cilegon (in the Residency of Banten) around 1920. This was a religious sect that carried out acts of theft, robbery and burglary.
5. Meijer, 'Over het bendewezen op Java', p. 180.
6. NA, The Hague, Ministry of Colonies, Vb. 3 July 1872, no. 30, letter from Amand of 17 April 1872.
7. Meijer, 'Over het bendewezen op Java'.
8. See for example the *rancaks* Si Pitung (chapter 2: treachery between guru and pupil) and Si Ronda (chapter 9; on treachery among robbers).

9. *Bataviaasch Nieuwsblad*, 17 March 1938.
10. *Java-bode*, 25 November 1903; Misset, *In de schaduw van de gevangenis*, p. 178.
11. Gambetta, *The Sicilian Mafia*, p. 1.
12. Gambetta, *The Sicilian Mafia*, pp. 32, 190–1; see also Maxwell, *God Protect Me From My Friends* on the strained relationship between the robber Salvatore and the mafia.
13. The *Bataviaasch Nieuwsblad* actually chose the title 'Onze maffia' (Our mafia) for a series of leading articles on the Ommelanden published in 1907 (14, 19, 21 and 30 November; 1 and 15 December 1903).
14. *Pemberita Betawi*, 30 November 1903, p. 2. See also the introduction to the present book.
15. See for example Edward Banfield, whose *The Moral Basis of a Backward Society* examines places that suffered so badly from a loss of mutual trust that society became wholly dysfunctional.
16. Eindstadter, 'The Social Organization of Armed Robbery', p. 79.
17. Cohen, *Komedie Stamboel*, p. 260.
18. *Bataviaasch Nieuwsblad*, 14 May 1919. See also the *Bataviaasch Nieuwsblad* of 12, 13 and 14 February 1920. The term 'stamboel', for a rather melodramatic kind of popular theatre, derives from the name of the city of Istanbul. *Wayang* is a kind of indigenous shadow-puppet theatre. *Krontjong* is a popular music genre, Portuguese in origin.
19. Groneman, *Een ketjoegeschiedenis*.
20. Saaba Entjak was shot dead in June 1920 during his arrest by the assistant *wedana* Mankoeningrat. He was known by a number of honorary titles, including Raden Oemar, Raden Soehana bapa Djakoeng ('Djakoeng' for short). He had connections with Oesoep (see Chapters 2 and 6) and was accused of involvement in crimes including the robbery of the overlord of Babakan (see Chapter 4). *Bataviaasch Nieuwsblad*, 15 June 1920.
21. *Bataviaasch Nieuwsblad*, 12, 13 and 14 February 1920.
22. Blok, *The Mafia of a Sicilian Village (1860–1960)*, p. 141.
23. NA, The Hague, Archives of the Ministry of Colonies, Scheepmaker, *Koloniale Verbalen* 2713.
24. Many of the robberies listed in Appendix IV took place on a Friday, Saturday or Sunday evening. See also Bosma, *Karel Zaalberg, journalist en strijder voor de Indo*, p. 23.
25. Lamster, 'De veiligheid van personen en goederen op Java en de noodzakelijkheid eener systematische politiereorganisatie', pp. 1466–7.
26. They were also referred to as *Betawi Arak* (*Bataviaasch Nieuwsblad*, 15 February 1903).

27. *Bataviaasch Nieuwsblad*, 7 December 1920.
28. *Nieuwe Rotterdamsche Courant*, 21 February 1903.
29. Bankoff, 'Bandits, Banditry and Landscapes of Crime in Nineteenth Century Philippines'.
30. For example the Pajangan woods in Cimanggis (*Nieuwe Rotterdamsche Courant*, 2 December 1903).
31. Ministry of Defence, The Hague, Centraal Archieven Depot, Archives of the 7 December Division, inv. no. 37, letter from the Assistant Resident of Purwakarta, D. Scherman, to the commander of the 2nd Inf. Brig./Group 7 December Division, 19 March 1948.
32. NA, The Hague, Archives of the Ministry of Colonies, inv. no. 282, appendix to the communication of 27 April 1904 from the Assistant Resident Van Santwyk of Buitenzorg, no. 5766/4; and appendix to the communication of 8 May 1904 from Assistant Resident Hartelust of Meester Cornelis to the Resident of Batavia, no. 2176/4. Vb. 15 December 1904, no. 64.
33. Quoted in De Veer, *Particuliere landerijen en de openbare veiligheid in de residentie Batavia*, p. 38.
34. In the Ceylon of the nineteenth and early twentieth centuries, the distance between victim and robber was generally much greater, averaging some 50 km (Rogers, *Crime, Justice and Society in Colonial Sri Lanka*, p. 219). In the case of gangs such as the 'Hollandse Bende' and 'Grote Bende', which operated in the Netherlands in the eighteenth and nineteenth centuries, the robbers also came from far further afield. Robbers who were unfamiliar with the district in which they intended to commit a crime were dependent on informants. It would appear that this extra link consisting of informants did not exist in the Dutch East Indies.
35. *Bataviaasch Nieuwsblad*, 30 May 1902.
36. ANRI, Bogor, archives of the Algemene Sekretarie, papieren bij gratieverzoeken Abdulrachman c.s., in the files MGS, 13 May 1893; MGS, 19 August 1893; MGS, 9 September 1893; MGS, 7 October 1893; *besluit* (decision) of 7 December 1893.
37. ANRI, Jakarta, archives of the Algemene Sekretarie, *besluit* (decision) of 27 October 1893, no. 14, *gratieverzoeken* (appeals for clemency) on behalf of Maoen (age 30), Rimoen (50) and Marip (36); and *besluit* of 17 June 1904, no. 31, gratieverzoek Piie (45).
38. Hobsbawm, *Bandits*, pp. 25–8. See also Blok, *The Mafia of a Sicilian Village (1860–1960)*, p. 144.
39. For a further discussion of the position of women in Javanese ideology, see Djajadiningrat-Nieuwenhuis, 'Ibuism and Priyayization', pp. 45–7.

40. One victim recognized his waylayer as a former neighbour (*Bataviaasch Nieuwsblad*, 26 October 1908). See also the *Bataviaasch Nieuwsblad* of 27 June 1902.
41. Cattle theft was relatively common in the Residency of Batavia, but 90 per cent of these thefts took place in the outlying district of Krawang. See the *Koloniale Verslagen*, appendix C to the Verslag der Handelingen van de Tweede Kamer der Staten Generaal (Proceedings of the Lower House of the States-General).
42. Rogers, *Crime, Justice and Society in Colonial Sri Lanka*, p. 115.
43. 'Daar waren een paar grote boeven. De hoofdoppasser kreeg de opdracht om een zekeren Kario, een beruchten schavuit uit de dessa Padang, te bewaken, en de gewone moest hetzelfde doen met Pawirono, een fijn merk uit de dessa Pengkol. "Jullie gaan eens stiekum al hun gangen na; ik moet precies weten wat ze uitmuizen, hoor. Ik heb vertrouwen in jullie rechercheursslimheid. Je hebt nu zóólang mij gedjaga'd [bewaakt], nu moeten jullie het eens een echten boef doen." De rechercheurs vertrokken. Ik hoorde geruimen tijd niets. Op een prachtigen maannacht was er een zekere onrust in mijn gemoed, en ik liet mijn braven Piet opzadelen en ging naar de dessa Padang. Al op een afstand klonken de lieflijke gamelangtonen mij in de ooren, en ze bleken te komen uit het huis van Kario, den boef, waar een flinke bruiloftspartij gegeven werd. Hij had blijkbaar niet veel last van de bewaking van mijn hoofdoppasser. Een aardig bruidje; maar wat drommel, wie zit daar als bruidegom? Mijn hoofdoppasser in hoogsteigen persoon! Ik kan zijn gelaatsuitdrukking niet zien, want hij buigt zich erg voorover, maar ... wie zijn die twee, die zich óók zoo diep voorover buigen? De Padoeka assistent-wedono en de Doro de mantri-politie. Om flink te djaga en Kario geen minuut uit 't oog te verliezen, had mijn hoofdoppasser maar zijn intrek genomen bij Kario, die, als flinke boef, een welgesteld man was; de vriendschap was zóó innig geworden, dat hij tot schoonzoon was gepromoveerd. Bij zoo'n notabelen boef mochten het onder-districtshoofd en de mantri niet wegblijven van de bruiloft. Kario was meestal zoo beleefd, om voor een flinke som geld een klein deel van't gestolene bij de assistent-wedono te brengen; dat geld kwam uit 's lands kas, en de mantri-politie vond die werkwijze erg leuk. Hij had bijna altijd ketragan [=opheldering], omdat Kario bijna altijd meedeed aan de inbraken en eigenlijk een goeie vent was; hij bracht de politie niet gaarne in moeilijkheden, hielp ze zelfs graag er uit. Mijn hoofdoppasser beweerde, dat alles pure slimmigheid van hem was.' Gonggrijp, *Brieven van Opheffer*, pp. 46–7.
44. *Java-bode*, 5 March 1925.
45. *De Zweep*, no. 2, 13 January 1923, p. 18.
46. *Het politieschandaal in Batavia*, p. 17.

47. Van Dijk, 'Magic and Violence', pp. 2–3.
48. Mrázek, *The United States and the Indonesian Military, 1945–1965.*
49. Anderson, *The Pemuda Revolution*, p. 208.
50. Meijer, 'Over het bendewezen op Java'.
51. Smail, *Bandung in the Early Revolution*, pp. 88–9; Van Dijk, 'Magic and Violence', p. 4.
52. Onghokham supposedly based himself on the work of the well-known Snouck Hurgronje (presumably 'Brieven van een Wedono Pensioen'), but Van Dijk has been unable to trace any passages about *jagos* in Snouck Hurgronje's writings.
53. Van Dijk himself strangely denies this, however, positing an ambivalence to the *jago* in Onghokham's work that is not found in the writings of Schulte Nordholt ('Magic and Violence', p. 6).
54. Schulte Nordholt, 'De jago in de schaduw', pp. 665 and 674.
55. Van Dijk, 'Magic and Violence', pp. 6–7.
56. Schulte Nordholt, 'Een staat van geweld', p. 12.
57. See also Mrázek, *The United States and the Indonesian Military, 1945–1965*, vol. 1, p. 20.
58. Adas, 'From Avoidance to Confrontation', p. 238.
59. Ibid., pp. 243–4.
60. For Cribb's further definition of the gangsters and their predecessors, see pp. 19, 39 and 51.
61. See for example the work of Diego Gambetta, esp. *The Sicilian Mafia: The Business of Private Protection.*

Chapter 4

1. Einstadter, 'The Social Organization of Armed Robbery', p. 77.
2. Du Perron, *Het land van herkomst*, p. 69.
3. Barker, 'Surveillance and Territoriality in Bandung', p. 96.
4. ANRI, Jakarta, Residentie archief Batavia, inv. no. 18, Politiek Verslag Residentie Batavia 1864. For this incident, see also the file in the ANRI, Jakarta, Archief Algemeene Sekretarie, Decision (*besluit*) of 7 July 1864, no. 5 (may be found in MGS, 5 August 1864, no. 1619). See also the *Java-bode*, 8 June 1864.
5. The authorities even thought it necessary to rectify certain details of the account in the Politiek Verslag: 'Many have claimed the honour of having shot the main perpetrator Mangoon bapa Arbie. Whoever may have been responsible, it was certainly not the Assistant Resident. His claim to have

done so is a fiction.' In ANRI, Jakarta, Residentie archief Batavia, inv. no. 18, Politiek Verslag Residentie Batavia 1864, fol. 11.

6. *Laporan-laporan tentang gerakan protes di Jawa pada abad-XX*, p. 74.
7. Tagliacozzo, 'Secret Trades of the Straits', p. 330.
8. Ibid., p. 335.
9. Alatas, *The Myth of the Lazy Native*, p. 36.
10. De Jonge and Van Deventer, *De opkomst van het Nederlandsch gezag in Oost-Indië*, vol. 3, p. 155; IJzerman (ed.), *De reis om de wereld door Olivier van Noort*, vol. 1, pp. 113–4.
11. Reid, 'Europe and Southeast Asia: The Military Balance', p. 1.
12. The Malay word for rifle, *senapan*, derives from the Dutch *snaphaan* (snaphaunce).
13. Boomgaard, *Frontiers of Fear*, pp. 133–5.
14. These are weapons containing a firing pin that causes an explosion that fires the bullet.
15. Lenselink, *Vuurwapens van 1840 tot heden*, pp. 14–23 and 41–3.
16. *Locomotief*, 29 October 1903.
17. Voorhoeve, *Inlandsche jagers*, pp. 28–31. A more recent example is the weaponry used by the Indonesian militias on East Timor in 1999.
18. Boomgaard, *Frontiers of Fear*, pp. 134-5.
19. *Bataviaasch Nieuwsblad*, 2 May 1893.
20. *Bataviaasch Nieuwsblad*, 9 March 1891.
21. Tagliacozzo, 'Secret Trades of the Straits', p. 338.
22. *Java-bode*, 25 November 1884.
23. *Algemeen Handelsblad*, 6 June 1903.
24. Gonggrijp, *Brieven van Opheffer*, p. 62.
25. Tagliacozzo, 'Secret Trades of the Straits', p. 339.
26. *Java-bode*, 8 April 1903; *Bataviaasch Nieuwsblad*, 14 November 1903.
27. *Algemeen Handelsblad*, 27 September 1906 (second page).
28. Sartono Kartodirdjo's study, *Protest Movements in Rural Java*, also contains few references to firearms, but many to weapons used for cudgelling and stabbing.
29. Adas, 'From Avoidance to Confrontation', p. 229.
30. For a report of this case, see Chapter 1.
31. For more information on this subject, see de Vries and Martens, *Nederlandse vuurwapens*; Lenselink, *Vuurwapens van 1840 tot heden*; and Kempers, *Antieke vuurwapens*.
32. See also van Till, 'In Search of Si Pitung'.
33. *Bataviaasch Nieuwsblad*, 26 March 1892.
34. *Bataviaasch Nieuwsblad*, 20 November 1909.

35. *Hindia Olanda*, 15 April 1890. The original text reads: 'Di Kampoeng Tjideng (Tjikini) sekarang ini banjak sekali maling, tida ada satoe malem jang orang disitoe tida ada kemalingan. Itoe maling — maling menjadi berainja, sebab Wijkmeester di itoe Kampoeng djarang berdjalan ronda dan djikaloe orang bertirak maling tida satoe orang keloewar, sebab sekarang maling-maling bajakan jang membawa sendjata api, djadi ia orang takoet.'
36. See for example the daily newspaper *Algemeen Handelsblad*, 29 May 1903; and the *Tijdschrift voor het Binnenlandsch Bestuur*, 1903, pp. 443–9.
37. *Locomotief*, 23 November 1903. 'Het politiegevecht van Djati-Militan [Cililitan]. Episode uit het Gantang bewind te Meester Cornelis'. See also ANRI, Jakarta, Archief Algemeene Sekretarie, Decision of 15 November 1904, no. 11, rekesten Piah, Djoenan en Saënan, houdende verzoek om gratie van de straf des doods (appeals for clemency lodged on behalf of Piah, Djoenan and Saënan).
38. *Bataviaasch Nieuwsblad*, 14, 19, 21 and 30 November; 1 and 15 December 1903.
39. *Koloniaal Tijdschrift*, 1938, p. 119.
40. Luckenbill, 'Generating Compliance'.
41. ANRI, Archief van de Algemene Sekretarie, decision of 15 November 1904, no. 11, gratieverzoeken Piah, Djoenan en Saënan (appeals for clemency lodged on behalf of Piah, Djoenan and Saënan).
42. *Het Vaderland*, 14 January 1904.
43. Egmond, *Banditisme in de Franse tijd*, pp. 25–6; see also Cobb, 'La bande d'orgères', pp. 198–9.
44. In this case, the newspaper rectified its earlier account of the events (*Bataviaasch Nieuwsblad*, 27 April 1937).
45. Slatta (ed.), *Bandidos*, p. 196.
46. Groneman, *Een ketjoegeschiedenis*, p. 198.
47. NA, The Hague, Ministry of Colonies 1901–53, inv. no. 282, appendix to letter from Assistant Resident Van Santwijk of Buitenzorg to the Resident of Batavia, 27 April 1904. Openbaar Vb. 15 December 1904, no. 64.
48. List of robberies in the period September 1903 to April 1904 in the district of Meester Cornelis. NA, The Hague, Ministry of Colonies 1901–53, inv. no. 282. Vb. 15 December 1904, no. 64. Appendix to letter from Assistant Resident Hartelust of Meester Cornelis to the Resident of Batavia, 8 May 1904, no. 15766/4, and appendix to letter from Assistant Resident Van Santwyk of Buitenzorg to the Resident of Batavia, 27 April 1904, no. 2176/4.

49. *Bataviaasch Nieuwsblad*, 20 October 1919.
50. 'De politie in den Bataviaschen Gemeenteraad', in *Nederlandsch-Indische Politiegids*, May 1917, no. 3.

Chapter 5

1. As far as I have been able to ascertain, the meaning of *jago* as a macho adventurer appears to have crystallized in the 1930s. This is clearest in the novel *Batavia bij nacht* (1940) by J. van der Heijden, with its descriptions of Batavia's night life. Men of diverse ethnic origin — locals, Europeans and people of mixed race — who had fallen on hard times resorted to illicit activities to secure an income. Van der Heijden uses the word 'hippies' for the female counterparts of these *jagos* (p. 7), local women who haunted the streets at night dressed in unconventional attire — in other words, women of easy virtue. This early use of the word 'hippie' may be interesting from an etymological point of view. *Jagos* often wore drab felt hats with the brim turned down, ragged open coat, a towel around their neck, loose trousers and patent leather shoes (see also p. 7).
2. *Bataviaasch Nieuwsblad*, 1 December 1903.
3. Misset, *In de schaduw van de gevangenis*, p. 182.
4. Daily newspaper *NRC*, 2 December 1903.
5. *Locomotief*, 3 December 1903.
6. Ibid.
7. NA, The Hague, archives of the Ministry of Colonies, inv. nos. 282. Openbaar Vb. Ministry of Colonies, 15 December 1904, no. 64. Letter from Assistant Resident Hartelust to the resident of Batavia, 8 May 1904.
8. *Bintang Betawi*, 3 March 1904.
9. Blok, 'Eer en de fysieke persoon'.
10. Anderson, 'The Idea of Power in Javanese Culture'; Errington, 'Recasting Sex, Gender and Power', pp. 45, 46 and 54. For a recent discussion of this theme, see Gianno, 'Women are not brave enough'.
11. Keeler, 'Speaking of Gender in Java', pp. 127–52.
12. Gonggrijp, *Geïllustreerde encyclopaedie van Nederlandsch-Indië*, p. 599.
13. Cribb, *Gangsters and Revolutionaries*, p. 19. The text reads, 'Many *jagos* were magicians (*dukun*), who could produce charms (*jimat*) which would bring the bearer strength, safety or success.'
14. *Bataviaasch Nieuwsblad*, 26 February 1930.
15. *De Indische Gids*, 1888 II, p. 1177.
16. *Bataviaasch Nieuwsblad*, 19 January 1932.

17. Gobbé and Adriaans (eds.), *Ambtelijke adviezen van Snouck Hurgronje*, vol. II, pp. 1226–30.
18. *Bataviaasch Handelsblad*, 18 August 1919.
19. Quoted in *De Indische Gids*, vol. 42, I, p. 161.
20. Appendix III on the calculation and planning of robberies, from Vergouw, 'Animisme in de Javaansche dievenwereld', pp. 92–5.
21. Raden Prawoto, 'Dievenbijgeloof op Midden-Java', p. 205.
22. In 1998, the former world champion of pencak silat, O'ong Maryono, published a comprehensive book about this sport, including its history and cultural facets: *Pencak silat: Merentang waktu.*
23. O'ong Maryono, *Pencak silat. Merentang waktu*, p. 34.
24. Ibid., pp. 60–2.
25. See Caverle, *Pencak silat*, p. 24.
26. *Bataviaasch Handelsblad*, 23 August 1913, 'Pukulan, een populair-ethnografische schets', by Rudi Veha.
27. O'ong Maryono, 'Jago, Friend or Foe', p. 7.
28. *Nieuws van den Dag voor Nederlandsch-Indië*, 20 February 1937.
29. O'ong Maryono, *Pencak silat. Merentang waktu*, pp. 62–3; see also O'ong Maryono, 'Jago, Friend or Foe', p. 11.
30. Some colonial customs migrated to the Netherlands, especially to The Hague, which had the largest contingent of former residents of the Dutch East Indies. On 19 July 2003 the *Haagsche Courant* contained an article 'Dubbelleven bekocht met de dood', which reported that two men had aroused suspicion by riding their scooter around a prosperous district, while being warmly dressed on a summer's day. When a police officer arrived on the scene, one of the men stabbed him in the leg, after which the officer shot him. It later transpired that the two men on the scooter worked for a suspect debt collection company and were on their way to a job. The man who was shot, of Eurasian origin, had evidently acted in a fit of panic, since in everyday life he was a respectable family man with a permanent job at a security company, but he was also an expert in the Indonesian martial art of *pukulan*. The article also notes that as late as the 1970s a *pencak silat* teacher in Amsterdam had once urged his students to rob banks because he needed the money.
31. Hobsbawm, *Bandits*, p. 43.
32. Hutton, *Dacoits and Thugs* (1857; edition of 1981), pp. 15 and 28–33.
33. Einstadter, 'Armed Robbery', p. 69.
34. Misset, *In de schaduw van de gevangenis*, pp. 79–80.
35. Blok, *De Bokkerijders*, pp. 138–9.
36. Ucee, *De schoonste triomf van de Indo-detective*, p. 191.

37. Groneman, *Een ketjoegeschiedenis*, p. 194.
38. Gouda, 'Language of Gender and Neurosis in the Indonesian Struggle for Independence 1945–1948'.
39. Cohen, *Komedie Stamboel*, p. 269.
40. Ibid., pp. 260–1.
41. *Bataviaasch Nieuwsblad*, 18 March 1909.
42. *Bataviaasch Nieuwsblad*, 15 May 1929, 'Vermaak en verwildering'.
43. *Bataviaasch Nieuwsblad*, 17 July 1923.
44. Misset, *In de schaduw van de gevangenis*, p. 176.
45. *Algemeen Dagblad*, 11 December 1903.
46. *Bataviaasch Nieuwsblad*, 14 December 1903. The first prize went to one of the gentlemen who came dressed as a poodle and offered the ladies bouquets from his jaws. This illustrates the sexually-charged atmosphere of such parties. See Chapter 6.
47. Verkaaik, *Inside the Citadel, Violence and Religious Nationalism in Hyderabad*, pp. 231–2.
48. Meijer, 'Twee Javaanse kapiteins van Köpenick'.

Chapter 6

1. Stepan, 'Race and Gender'.
2. McClintock, *Imperial Leather*, p. 49.
3. For a survey of this scientific development, see McCown and Kennedy, *Climbing the Family Tree: A Collection of Writings on Human Phylogenie, 1699–1971*.
4. McClintock, *Imperial Leather*, p. 50.
5. Pick, *Faces of Degeneration*, pp. 111–6.
6. Ibid., p. 122.
7. De Veer, *Particuliere landerijen*, pp. 37–8.
8. ANRI, Jakarta, Batavia Archives, 314/3 1869, political report from the Meester Cornelis division of the residence of Batavia for the year 1869.
9. ANRI, Jakarta, Batavia Archives, 314/3 1869, political report from the Meester Cornelis division of the residence of Batavia for the year 1869.
10. NA, The Hague, Ministry of Colonies (and Royal Institute for the Tropics), *memorie van overgave* (memorandum on leaving office) by the Resident of Batavia, C.R. Bakhuizen van den Brink, for the period 15 September 1901 to 9 May 1906, p. 9.
11. NA, The Hague, Ministry of Colonies (and Royal Institute for the Tropics), *memorie van overgave* (memorandum on leaving office) by the Resident of

Batavia, H. Rijfsnijder, covering the period from 28 July 1911 to 2 August 1916, p. 5; 'Een gevolg van deze vermenging van rassen is dat men hier met een zeer eigenaardige, lastige en ongehoorzame bevolking te doen heeft, eene bevolking wier leden over vele slechte, weinig goede eigenschappen de beschikking heeft.'

12. Keuchenius, *Beschrijving der Bataviasche jurisdictie en onderzoek naar de oorzaken der meerdere ongezondheid van Batavia*, p. 63; 'Daar de kinderen, in ontucht bij de slavinnen geteelt, meestal zonder zorg en zonder opvoeding in het wilde, in vrijheid, werkeloosheid, en in allerlei ondeugden en schelmerijen opgroeiën is het droevig gevolg hiervan gelijk de ondervinding leert, dat het veelal de volwassche zoonen der mandoors zijn, die de onveiligheid veroorzaaken, die de hoofden der rooversbenden uitmaken, en de misdaaden op publieke wegen, en in de kampongs plegen, en zich vervolgens in de uitgestrekte eigendommen schuilhouden.'
13. *Bataviaasch Nieuwsblad*, 11 February 1923.
14. *Bintang Barat*, 9 April 1872; *Pemberita Betawi*, 13 April 1886.
15. In *Het leven in Nederlandsch-Indië* (1900), Bas Veth describes the mixing of races as leading to degeneration, amorality, and violence. See also Bosma and Raben, *De oude Indische wereld*, p. 286; and Stoler, 'Carnal Knowledge and Imperial Power', pp. 77–9.
16. The British philosopher Herbert Spencer (1820–1903), who independently of Darwin made evolution the basis of a wide-ranging philosophical system, was exceptionally influential for many years, both in the English-speaking world and far beyond.
17. Bosma and Raben, *De oude Indische wereld*, p. 286.
18. The original text is 'dia poenja roepa terlaloe djahat, matanja menjala dan mera dan tampang moekanja seperti matjan' (2 July 1870). In his article 'Bandits, Banditry and Landscapes of Crime in the Nineteenth-Century Philippines', Greg Bankoff reports finding the same type of rhetoric about robbers in late-nineteenth-century newspapers in the Philippines (p. 324).
19. A translation (through Dutch) of: 'Sekarang ia ada poenja tjambang dan koemis matanja dalem dan toelang pipinja timboel maka orang jang dapet liat padanja misti merasa takoet. Kendati orang itoe berdjalan tjepet njata sekali ia tida poenja kakoeatan lagi. Apa pembatja kenalin ini orang. Kita sendiri poen tiada kenal dia, djika kita tida dapet liat matanja jang amat djeli. Orang ini boekan orang laen iaitoe si Tjonat jang soedah boenoeh si Bohong, dan si Gondit dan jang soeda bawa lari Njai Saipa dengen barang mas intennja senta dengen membawa lari oeangnja toean Opmeijer.' Pangemanann, *Tjerita Si Tjonat*, pp. 41–2.

20. *Bataviaasch Nieuwsblad*, 20 February 1904.
21. Two decades later, the dark blotches that formed on the skin during a prison sentence (perhaps because of too much standing in the sun) were seen as one of bandits' main physical traits. Similar-looking birthmarks had a traditional meaning according to Javan 'superstition', indicating a person with remarkable characteristics. On this subject, see Maijer, *De pigment-vlekken op het menschelijk lichaam en hare waarde en beteekenis naar het algemeen onder de Javanen heerschende bijgeloof.*
22. *Bataviaasch Nieuwsblad*, 1 December 1903; 'Het volk uit deze streken is tegenover den Europeaan terughoudend en brutaal, iets van dat ruwe *sans gêne* dat in den anders zoo gedweën inlander tegenstaat. Echte boeventronies, dus vertolkte een onzer zijn meening.'
23. Grijns, *Jakarta Malay*, p. 25.
24. Hobsbawm, *Bandits*, p. 58.
25. *Bataviaasch Nieuwsblad*, 1 December 1903; 'We zagen een behoorlijk aantal Europeanen, zelfs jonge dames, op weg naar de pasar Tjelilitan; ze wilden allen graag de Chinese winkelier zien die zich in zo'n moeilijke positie had bevonden toen hij beroofd werd; ze moesten allen de winkeldeur zien die zo zwaar was beschadigd door bijlslagen en kogels; misschien hoopten ze, en dan bedoel ik de jongedames, plotseling Gantang te zien verschijnen vanuit de bosjes langs de weg, wild schreeuwend. Tegenwoordig is het allemaal emotie waar het om draait.'
26. *Java-bode*, 19 January 1904, serial.
27. *Locomotief*, 3 November 1903: 'Kijkjes in het rooverland'.
28. Fabricius, *Tempo doeloe*, p. 126.
29. Hobsbawm, *Bandits*, p. 68.
30. Ibid., p. 53.
31. Clancy-Smith and Gouda, *Domesticating the Empire*, pp. 17–8; Hyam, *Empire and Sexuality*, pp. 204–5.
32. Lucas, 'Trouwverbod, inlandse huishoudsters en Europese vrouwen'; Pollmann, 'Bruidstraantjes. De koloniale roman, de njai en de apartheid'.
33. Stoler, 'Making Empire Respectable', pp. 58–63. This subject is also explored in depth in Stoler, 'Carnal Knowledge and Imperial Power', pp. 61–70; and Pattynama, 'Secrets and Danger'.
34. McClintock, *Imperial Leather*, p. 34.
35. This phenomenon is described in McClintock, *Imperial Leather*.
36. *Bataviaasch Nieuwsblad*, 7 December 1908.
37. *Java-bode*, 19 January 1904, and *Bintang Betawi*, 29 and 30 January; 2, 3, and 4 February 1904.

38. ANRI, Jakarta, Batavia Residency Archives, inv. no. 357.6; letter from the Assistant Resident of Tangerang to the Resident of Batavia, 21 March 1903.
39. *Bataviaasch Nieuwsblad*, 6, 7, and 8 April 1903; *Java-bode*, 6 April 1903.
40. The dates are 29 and 30 January; 2, 3, and 4 February 1904. The *Java-bode* of 19 January 1904 published more or less the same article under the title 'Uit de Indische rechtszaal: een rampokker'.
41. *Bintang Betawi*, 30 January 1904.
42. The original text is 'orang lelaki sanget takoet pada si Kesen, orang prempoean banjak jang tjinta pada ini kepala penjamoen'. *Bintang Betawi*, 3 February 1904.

Chapter 7

1. Vanvugt, *Een propagandist van het zuiverste water*.
2. De la Valetta, 'Politiekunst', p. 465.
3. Ibid., p. 473.
4. *Bataviaasch Nieuwsblad*, 11 April 1916.
5. Jellinek, *The Urban Cycle*, p. 6.
6. ANRI, Jakarta, Archives of the General Secretariat, Decision (*besluit*) of the Governor-General, 26 September 1910, no. 18, application by Marta and Said and related trial documents. Sutan Sjahrir also described the fear of *tjoeliks* as he witnessed it in Banda Neira, his place of exile. This mass psychosis, as he called it, made all the locals — and some Europeans — too scared to leave their houses. Wild rumours were going around. Sjahrir did everything he could to discredit them, but he ultimately decided it was a matter for 'ethnographic psychologists' (Sjahrir, *Indonesische overpeinzingen*, pp. 148–51).
7. Interview with Abdul Rachman, 19 January 1998; and Jellinek, *The Urban Cycle*, pp. 6–7.
8. *Java-bode*, 2 March 1908.
9. Gonggrijp, *Brieven van Opheffer*, pp. 77–8.
10. Schulte Nordholt and Van Till, 'Colonial Criminals in Java', p. 59.
11. Ginzburg argues that there are striking similarities between the work of the historian, the doctor, and the detective. In 'Clues: Roots of an Evidential Paradigm' he describes the late nineteenth-century 'presumptive paradigm' in the humane sciences, by which he means the acquisition of knowledge through guesswork, the ability to identify a disease, a criminal, or the character of a society on the basis of symptoms or 'clues'. Ginzburg contrasts this 'evidential' or 'conjectural' system with the method of acquiring knowledge that was dominant in the natural sciences: the Galilean paradigm, based on quantification and

repetition of phenomena. In many disciplines, such as medicine, politics, and detective work, the Galilean paradigm was of limited use, Ginzburg argues. A doctor trying to diagnose a patient has little use for statistics and must rely on his senses. Much the same thing is true of a politician trying to resolve a violent conflict or a detective hoping that a few cigarette butts in an ashtray will put him on the trail of a killer. [The page numbers cited in the footnotes refer to the Dutch translation of Ginzburg's essay, 'Sporen: Wortels van een indicie-paradigma', which is listed in the bibliography along with the English version. — trans.]

12. NA, The Hague, Ministry of Colonies, inv. no. 1274, Vb. 9 March 1914, no. 6, 'De Sarekat Islam in de residentie Batavia, speciaal in de afdeling Meester Cornelis'.
13. Ginzburg, 'Sporen', p. 242.
14. Vergouw, 'Animisme', p. 110.
15. *Bataviaasch Nieuwsblad*, 26 May 1923.
16. *Bataviaasch Handelsblad*, 10 February 1915; see also NA, The Hague, Index to registers of civil servants in the Dutch East Indies and members of the colonial navy (*Gouvernementsmarine*), item no. 2.10.07, vol. H-O, index and folio T 278.
17. NA, The Hague, Secret Archives of the Ministry of Colonies, 1911: f. 20.
18. *Bataviaasch Nieuwsblad*, 1 February 1893.
19. *Java-bode*, 26 March 1903.
20. *Java-bode*, 2 March 1908.
21. *Bataviaasch Handelsblad*, 12 and 13 April 1913.
22. Hinne's involvement in the first arrest of Gantang is reported in the *Bataviaasch Nieuwsblad*, 20 February 1903.
23. *Bataviaasch Nieuwsblad*, 17 November 1909.
24. *Bataviaasch Nieuwsblad*, 20 November 1909.
25. *Bataviaasch Handelsblad*, 10 February 1915.
26. See also Mrázak, 'The City of Light'.
27. Van Till, 'In Search of Si Pitung'.
28. Ido, 'De tentoonstelling', p. 59.
29. I made use of this 1986 reprint; the first edition does not give a publication date.
30. McClintock, *Imperial Leather*, pp. 69–71.
31. Kipling, *Kim*, p. 89.
32. Fabricius, *Tempo doeloe*, pp. 123–5.
33. James Siegel has also pointed out that Eurasian authors were interested in crime. He writes that this is because, in the late nineteenth century, people

of mixed blood were in danger of losing their privileged ties to their white fathers. These 'Indo' authors used their stories to ally themselves closely with the colonial authorities in the fight against criminals whom they portrayed as 'natives' (*inheemsen*). They claimed that these indigenous people formed a threat to the Dutch, who had not in fact been aware of any such threat. Siegel's theory does not, however, explain why Indo authors presented such stories to their Malay-speaking readers. Furthermore, the criminals they wrote about were not always indigenous to the archipelago, but might instead be Chinese, Indo, or even European. See Siegel, 'A New Criminal Type', p. 212.

Chapter 8

1. *Moesson*, 15 May 1978, p. 19.
2. See also Margreet van Till, 'In Search of Si Pitung; The History of an Indonesian Legend' (1996).
3. *Hindia Olanda*, 26 August 1892, p. 2; 28 June 1892, p. 3.
4. *Hindia Olanda*, 28 June 1892.
5. *Hindia Olanda*, 10 August 1892, p. 2; 26 August 1892, p. 2.
6. ANRI, Bogor, Algemene Secretarie, President of the Supreme Court of the Dutch East Indies to His Excellency the Governor-General, Batavia, 18 April 1893. In case file MGS, 13 May 1893 (no. 1385); Bt, 11 June 1893 (no. 8); MGS, 19 August 1893 (no. 2127); MGS, 9 September 1893 (no. 2283); MGS, 7 October 1893 (no. 2570); Bt, 7 December 1893 (no. 4).
7. *Hindia Olanda*, 26 August 1892, p. 2.
8. *Hindia Olanda*, 25 April 1893, p. 3; *Locomotief*, 25 April 1893, p. 2.
9. *Hindia Olanda*, 12 May 1893, p. 3.
10. *Hindia Olanda*, 2 May 1893, p. 2.
11. The appeal for a reprieve can be found in the ANRI, Bogor, Algemene Secretarie, MGS, December 1893, Gewestelijk Bestuur Residentie Batavia (District Executive of the Residency of Batavia) to His Excellency the Governor-General of the Dutch East Indies, 16 November 1893, own fol. 6.
12. *Hindia Olanda*, 23 September 1893, p. 2.
13. ANRI, Bogor, Algemene Secretarie, MGS, December 1893, Resident of Batavia to the Governor-General of the Dutch East Indies, 1 September 1993.
14. *Hindia Olanda*, 22 November 1892.
15. *Hindia Olanda*, 19 August 1893.
16. Dji-ie is an alternative spelling of Dji-ih.
17. *Java-bode*, 15 August 1893, p. 2.
18. Ibid.

19. *Hindia Olanda*, 1 September 1893, p. 2. The original text reads 'Itoe djoeragan koetika ketemoe Si Pitoeng betoelan tempat tepi troes. Si djoeragan menjikip pada Si Pitoeng dan dari tjipetnja Si Pitoeng troes ambil pestolnja dari pinjang, lantas tembak si djoeragan itoe menja di mati itoe tempat djoega.'
20. ANRI, Jakarta, archives of the Residency of Tangerang, inv. no. 244A. Appendix enclosed as evidence from the Resident of Batavia to the Assistant Resident of Tangerang, 20 September 1893.
21. *Locomotief*, 19 October 1893, p. 2.
22. Ibid.
23. *Hindia Olanda*, 18 October 1893, p. 2.
24. Ibid.
25. Damardini, *Cerita Si Pitung*, p. 142.
26. *Hindia Olanda*, 18 October 1893, p. 2.
27. *Locomotief*, 19 October 1893, p. 2.
28. ANRI, Bogor, Algemene Secretarie, MGS, December 1893, Gewestelijk Bestuur Residentie Batavia (District Executive of the Residency of Batavia) to His Excellency the Governor-General of the Dutch East Indies, 16 November 1893, internal fol. 6.
29. *Hindia Olanda*, 20 October 1893, p. 2.
30. Fabricius, *Tempo doeloe*, pp. 123–40.
31. Damardini, *Cerita Si Pitung*.
32. Some sources give his name as Heyne.
33. Grijns, *Jakarta Malay*, II.
34. Damardini, *Cerita Si Pitung*, p. 145.
35. Ibid., p. 144.
36. Interview with Lukman Karmani, 23 September 1994.
37. The films still exist today, but unfortunately I was unable to find anyone who still had a copy of Lukman Karmani's book (not even the author!) or of the comics featuring Si Pitung that are so frequently mentioned in Jakarta. We do find references to Si Pitung in *Cerita Rakyat Betawi*, a volume in a series of booklets with popular tales from the archipelago.
38. Rivai Hutapea, 'Jurus maut warga "Pitung"'.
39. Pramoedya Ananta Toer, *House of Glass*.
40. Ibid.
41. See for example Hilton, 'The Origins of Robin Hood' (1958); Holt, 'The Origins and Audience of the Ballads of Robin Hood' (1960); Keen, 'Robin Hood: Peasant or Gentleman?' (1961); and Aston, 'Robin Hood' (1961).
42. Sidel, 'The Usual Suspects', pp. 72–94.
43. Blok, 'The Peasant and the Brigand', p. 500.

44. The story of Si Pitung was not the only bandit's tale that gradually became more widely known and was commercialized. Another example is the story of Si Tjonat, although this outlaw did not attain the final 'phase' — that of promotion to popular hero.
45. Lie Tek Long, *Tjerita dan sair Sie Rondah atawa rampok jang gaga brani*, cover.
46. The process of the revision of a classical Malay story by the modern media is also described in Taylor, 'Nyai Dasima: Portrait of a Mistress in Literature and Film'.
47. Hobsbawm, *Bandits*, p. 14.
48. Even so, we should not deny the potential social bandits of nineteenth-century Batavia their place in history on these grounds; it would be impossible to prove that there were never any social bandits operating in that region.
49. The sources of similar nineteenth-century narratives have been described in Boomkens, *De angstmachine*, for example on pp. 41–2.

Chapter 9

1. *Bataviaasch Nieuwsblad*, 21 November 1903.
2. *Bintang Betawi*, 24 November 1903, f. 2.
3. Du Perron, *Het land van herkomst*, p. 109. The quotation continues (pp. 109–10) [in Dutch]: 'The Assistant Resident of Meester Cornelis was an elderly man named Hartelust [lit. "heart's content"], who always arrived, according to newspaper reports, exactly when the perpetrators had gone; the sheriff was called Calmer and the *controleur* Shilling; and the newspapers punned, in typically Indonesian style, that the robbers murdered and stole to their heart's content, the sheriff became calmer as time went on, and the *controleur* was not worth a shilling.'
4. *Bataviaasch Nieuwsblad*, 30 December 1902.
5. Y.L.M., *Sair Java-Bank di rampok* (1922). This *sair* contains 470 quatrains.
6. The Dutch edition gives a further account of the robbery of the Javasche Bank in appendix VII.
7. *Bintang Betawi*, 14 November 1902.
8. *Locomotief*, leading articles on 2, 3 and 4 November 1903: 'Kijkjes in het rooverland'.
9. *Bataviaasch Nieuwsblad*, 14, 19, 21 and 30 November; 1, 4, 5 and 15 December 1903.
10. *Bataviaasch Nieuwsblad*, 15 December 1903.
11. *Bataviaasch Nieuwsblad*, 30 November 1903. *Rinaldo Rinaldini*, Goeverneurs Volksboeken (1885).

12. *Bataviaasch Nieuwsblad*, 22 and 23 August 1902.
13. See also the discussion in Blok, 'The Peasant and the Brigand' (1972).
14. *Java-bode*, 21 November 1903.
15. *Bataviaasch Nieuwsblad*, 20 February 1903.
16. *Bintang Betawi*, 24 February 1904.
17. In the event, the perpetrator of the robbery of van der Capelle turned out to be one Pi-ee (see Chapter 2).
18. *Java-bode*, 6 February 1904. The term *bertillonage* refers to the system of identification devised by Alphonse Bertillon, who sought to identify law-breakers by using cards with precise descriptions (see Chapter 7).
19. *Bataviaasch Nieuwsblad*, 25 February 1904.
20. *Bintang Betawi*, 26 February 1904.
21. *Bataviaasch Nieuwsblad*, 3 March 1903.
22. *Bintang Betawi*, 14 August 1905.
23. NA, The Hague, Archives of the Ministry of Colonies, inv. no. 282, Vb. 15 December 1904, no. 64, letter from Resident Bakhuizen van den Brink of Batavia to the Director of Internal Administration, Batavia, 20 June 1904.
24. NA, The Hague, Archives of the Ministry of Colonies, inv. no. 282, Vb. 15 December 1904, no. 64, letter from Resident Bakhuizen van de Brink of Batavia to the Governor-General, Batavia, 19 December 1903.
25. *Locomotief*, 3 November 1903.
26. *Bintang Betawi*, 2 December 1903, f. 1.
27. See the diagram in Appendix I.
28. Sutherland, *The Making of a Bureaucratic Elite*, p. 25.
29. *Java-bode*, 4 December 1903.
30. ANRI, Jakarta, Archives of Tangerang, *Renvooi* 6433, Batavia, 20 September 1903, inv. no. 244A (2).
31. *Bintang Betawi*, 30 August 1901.
32. *Onderzoek naar de mindere welvaart der inlandsche bevolking op Java en Madoera*, vol. VIIIb, p. 58.
33. Kalff, 'Europees pauperisme in Indië', p. 580.
34. Du Perron, *Het land van herkomst*, p. 71. This episode is also described in Snoek, *E. du Perron*, pp. 35–6.
35. *Bintang Betawi*, 11 December 1903, f. 2.
36. *Bataviaasch Nieuwsblad*, 6 February 1906.
37. *Bataviaasch Nieuwsblad*, 7 December 1903.
38. *Java-bode*, 4 December 1903.
39. *Pemberita Betawi*, 19 December 1903, f. 2.
40. *Bataviaasch Nieuwsblad*, 2 December 1903.

41. *Bintang Betawi*, 4 December 1903, f. 2.
42. *Locomotief*, 29 December 1903.
43. *Pemberita Betawi*, 19 December 1903; *Bataviaasch Nieuwsblad*, 24 November 1903.
44. *Java-bode*, 27 November 1903.
45. *Bataviaasch Nieuwsblad*, 30 November 1903, f. 1.
46. *Locomotief*, 30 November, 1 December and 3 December 1903.
47. Van Kol, *Uit onze koloniën*, pp. 815–22.
48. From other sources it is known that these small cannons dated from Daendels' time. In those days, landowners had been obliged to fire a salute whenever the governor-general was travelling between Batavia and Buitenzorg. See for example the *Locomotief*, 2 November 1903, 'Kijkjes in het rooversland'.
49. Van Kol, *Uit onze koloniën*, p. 817.
50. Stibbe (ed.), *Encyclopaedie van Nederlandsch-Indië*, p. 349.
51. Ibid., pp. 349–50.
52. Van Motman, *Particuliere landerijen op Java*, p. 50.
53. *Handelsblad*, 12 August 1919.
54. Van Houtum, *De partikuliere landerijen (bewesten de Tjimanoek) op Java*; Van Motman, *Particuliere landerijen op Java*.
55. Van Motman, *Particuliere landerijen op Java*, p. 42.
56. Van Houtum, *De partikuliere landerijen (bewesten de Tjimanoek) op Java*, p. 10.
57. According to the landowner Van Motman, in his *Particuliere landerijen op Java*, pp. 9, 10 and 26.
58. *Soerabajaasch Handelsblad*, 2 June 1881.
59. See Schulte Nordholt, 'De jago in de schaduw'.
60. *Koloniaal verslag*, 1872, p. 58.
61. *Koloniaal verslag*, 1875, p. 75; NA, The Hague, Ministry of Colonies, Vb. 28 September 1875, no. 14.
62. *Java-bode*, 2 July 1903.
63. Handelingen van de Tweede Kamer (Proceedings of the Lower House of Parliament), 24th session, 24 November 1903, 'vaststelling van de begrooting van Nederlandsch-Indië voor 1904' (II, 469).
64. Dekker, *De politie in Nederlandsch-Indië*, p. 46.
65. For the ranks of the city police force after 1911, see Appendix I.
66. See also Locher-Scholten, 'State Violence and the Police in Colonial Indonesia', p. 100.
67. *Regeringsalmanak Nederlandsch-Indië*, 1910 vol. II, p. 168; 1915 vol. II, p. 162; 1920 vol. II, pp. 185–6.
68. Locher-Scholten, 'State Violence and the Police in Colonial Indonesia', p. 94.

69. Examples may be found in the *Nederlandsch-Indische Politiegids* (September 1917) and the *Soerabajaasch Handelsblad* (10 February 1912).
70. In 'De Jago in de schaduw', Schulte Nordholt discusses the low priority that the colonial authorities accorded to combating crime within the Indonesian community.
71. Locher-Scholten, 'State Violence and the Police in Colonial Indonesia', p. 96.
72. On this problem, see Van den Doel, *De stille macht*.
73. For example in the *Nederlandsch-Indische Politiegids*, vol. 9, September 1917.
74. NA, The Hague, Archives of the Ministry of Colonies (and KIT), *memorie van overgave* (memorandum on leaving office) by the administrative authorities for the district of Batavia on 3 March 1922, by Resident Hunger, p. 30.
75. NA, The Hague, *memorie van overgave* (memorandum on leaving office) from Batavia, by Resident Rijfsnijder, 1916.
76. *Sair Tjerita Rampok Si Ronda*, p. 31 [translated from the Dutch]. The original text is as follows:

    Tiga pelor masoek dalem iga,
    Demang preksa dengen gaga,
    Pada Oedji tida dibouat tjoeriga,
    *f*150,– di kasi persen djoega.

    Pada Oedji Demang berkata,
    Kau gaga dan denger prenta,
    Pande menembak pake sendjata,
    Djadi Oppas diangkat serenta.

77. NA, The Hague, Ministry of Colonies, inv. no. 2713, mail rapport 541–521, Vb. 9 March 1925, no. 3, 'Rapport omtrent de afdeeling en het afdeelingsverband bij de Algemeene Politie, door de hoofdopziener Scheepmaker'.
78. *Het politieschandaal te Batavia*, p. 2.
79. Locher-Scholten, 'State Violence and the Police in Colonial Indonesia', p. 95.
80. Gambetta, *The Sicilian Mafia*, p. 79, which is based on Franchetti, *Condizioni economiche e amministrative delle province napoletane* (1974 edition), pp. 90–1.
81. *Bataviaasch Nieuwsblad*, 26 January and 12 February 1939.
82. *Bataviaasch Nieuwsblad*, 24 January 1935.
83. *Locomotief*, 7 May 1937.
84. People's Council (Volksraad), zittingsjaar 1937/38, 24ste vergadering, 21 August 1937, H 609; 25ste vergadering, 3 August 1937, H 679; 2de vergadering, 3 August 1937, H 659; and appendix to the Handelingen van den Volksraad betreffende het zittingsjaar 1937/38 (Proceedings of the People's Council for

the parliamentary year 1937/38), 5 April 1937, question submitted by Prawoto, reply on 5 August 1937.

85. *Indische Gids*, no. 59, vol. 1, 1937, pp. 532–6.
86. *Bataviaasch Nieuwsblad*, 12 March 1938.
87. Misset, *In de schaduw van de gevangenis*, p. 183.
88. Gouda, 'Language of Gender and Neurosis', pp. 45–77.
89. Van Wulfften Palthe, *Over het bendewezen op Java*, p. 18.
90. Cribb, *Gangsters and Revolutionaries*, pp. 2–3.
91. Ibid., p. 24.
92. Ministry of Defence, Central Archives Depot, Archives of the 7 December Division, inv. no. 33, 'Bijzonder Inlichtingsrapport Gegevens Pandji' ('Special Intelligence Report on Pandji'), 12 May 1947.
93. Frederick, 'Shadows of an Unseen Hand', p. 161.
94. Frederick, 'Outward Appearances'.

Concluding Remarks

1. See for example the *Locomotief*, 2 November 1903, 'Kijkjes in het rooversland'.
2. Fukuyama, *Trust: The Social Virtues and the Creation of Prosperity*; Henley, 'Entrepreneurship, Individualism and Trust in Indonesia'.
3. Boomgaard and Brown (eds.), *Weathering the Storm. The Economies of Southeast Asia in the 1930s Depression.*
4. Gallant, 'Brigandage, Piracy, Capitalism, and State-Formation', p. 30.

Appendix I

1. Stibbe (ed.), *Encyclopaedie van Nederlandsch-Indië*, vol. 3, pp. 444–6.

Appendix III

1. The fixed numerical values of the ordinary weekdays and the pasar days are as follows: Monday 4, Tuesday 3, Wednesday 7, Thursday 8, Friday 6, Saturday 9, Sunday 5. Kliwon 8, Legi 5, Pahing 9, Pon 7, Wagé 4.

Abbreviations

(*including Dutch terms used in the notes*)

Nationaal Archief	Dutch National Archives, The Hague
ANRI	Arsip Nasional Republik Indonesia (National Archives of the Republic of Indonesia, in Jakarta and Bogor)
ARA	Algemeen Rijksarchief, see NA
Archief Algemene Sekretarie	Archives of the General Secretariat
Archief Batavia	Batavia Archives
BB	Binnenlands bestuur (internal administration of the Dutch East Indies)
BN	Bataviaasch Nieuwsblad (a Dutch-language newspaper)
KITLV	Koninklijk Instituut voor Taal-, Land- en Volkenkunde (Royal Netherlands Institute of Southeast Asian and Caribbean Studies, in Leiden)
Ministerie van Koloniën	Ministry of Colonies

MGS	Missive Generale Sekretarie (official letter from the General Secretariat)
NA	Nationaal Archief (National Archives in The Hague, known as the Algemeen Rijksarchief until 2002)
Nationaal Archief	*see* NA
Residentie Archief Banten	Banten Residency Archives
Vb.	Verbaal (official report)
Geheim Archief Koloniën	Secret Archives of the Ministry of Colonies
VOC	Vereenigde Oost-Indische Compagnie (Dutch East India Company)

Glossary

[*of Malay and (where noted) Javanese, Sundanese, and Dutch words used in this book*]

Indonesian (Malay) words are generally given in the new spelling. When they occur in quotes, however, the old spelling is used.

adat	custom, tradition, customary law
arsip	archive
babu	nursemaid, female domestic servant
bangsawan	traditional Malay opera
barisan preman	literally 'force of free men', citizen militia in Batavia
batik	dyed fabric
belanda	Dutch
belanda kesasar	literally 'stray Dutchman', European living in a kampong, often a *prokol*
Betawi	indigenous people of Batavia (Jakarta), descendants of people who were already living in and around the city in the 17th century

binnenlands bestuur (Dutch)	internal administration of the Dutch East Indies in the colonial period
bouw	unit of area used on Java: 1 *bouw* = 7096 m^2. Derived from *bahoeen*, which originally meant 'as much farmland as one man and his family can cultivate'.
buaya	literally 'crocodile', delinquent Eurasian youth or bandit
Budi Utomo	early indigenous political movement in the Dutch East Indies
bung	brother, father, comrade
bupati	regent, indigenous head of a regency
burchtheren (Dutch)	feudal lord, lord of a castle or fortress
camat	indigenous head of a subdistrict
controleur	colonial official responsible for a subdistrict in the Dutch East Indies
Cultuurstelsel (Dutch)	system in which the Dutch forced indigenous people to cultivate certain crops
dalang	wayang performer and expert on Javanese culture
daerah istimewa	district with special status
danjang	guardian spirit
danjang pengantenan	almost certain
demang	district chief, similar to *tehsildar* in British colonies
desa	administrative unit consisting of a village or group of villages, countryside
djalanan besar	main road
dukun	traditional healer, counsellor, religious leader
gang (Dutch)	alley, walkway, narrow street
gedong	country house, castle
gigis (Javanese)	sure of oneself, a sure thing
golok	machete

guru (goeroe)	teacher
haj	pilgrimage to Mecca
haji	Muslim who had made the pilgrimage to Mecca
hari sial	day of ill fortune
heemraad (Dutch)	public official, member of a board responsible for public works and settlement of some disputes in the Batavia region
ilmu	learning, science, skill
ilmu kebal	form of supernatural invulnerability
jago (djago)	literally 'fighting cock'; used in various senses, from charismatic leader to notorious villain
jagoan	criminal, quasi-*jago*
jaksa	indigenous public prosecutor
jalan (djalan)	road
janur kuning	leaves symbolizing evil
jimat	talisman, amulet
kalamomor (Javanese)	dubious
kalasembodjo (Javanese)	impossible
kali	river
kampak	synonym for *rampok*
kampong	urban residential district inhabited by indigenous people
kepala	chief, leader
kepala RT	hamlet chief, abbreviation of *kepala Rukun Tetanga*
ketjoe	dangerous robber; kind of armed robbery
kraton	palace
krontjong	*krontjong toegoe* (or *keroncong tugu*), a form of music influenced by Portuguese Moresco

landdrost (Dutch)	senior colonial official, chairman of the board of *heemraden*
laskar rakyat	people's militia
lenong	traditional *Betawi* folk theatre
loenggoeh	almost certain
magang	a student in the public service who was not yet drawing a salary
maling ketoet (Javanese)	literally 'muscular thief', bandit, robber
maling krowodan (Javanese)	literally 'thief of crops'; occasional thief
maling tengah (Javanese)	literally 'middle thief'; professional thief
maloe	embarrassed, embarrassment
mandoer	foreman (on a private estate)
mantri	indigenous police officer or low-ranking public official
mbak	girl, mother
menak (Sundanese)	distinguished, aristocratic
menjaga	guard, watch over
merdeka	independence, freedom
momor (Javanese)	unite
muiteling (Dutch)	rebel, mutineer
nasional	national
njai	nursemaid
Ommelanden (Dutch)	area surrounding Batavia
oppas, oppasser (Dutch)	constable
oproerling	insurgent, rabble-rouser
orang Betawi	indigenous inhabitants of Batavia, see *Betawi*

pagger	hedge, bamboo enclosure
pak (van: bapak)	father, form of address for an older man
partijganger	militia member
pasar	market
pasar Maleis	the simplified Malay spoken at the market
pemuda	young freedom fighter
pencak silat	indigenous martial art (also spelled *pentjak silat*)
pentjalang, pencalang	low-ranking indigenous official
pesantren	Muslim boarding-school
piso raout	kind of knife
preman	criminal, from the Dutch *vrijman* (free man, non-slave)
primbon	mystical Javanese book (a kind of almanac)
prokol	see *prokureur-bamboe*
prokureur-bamboe (Dutch)	wealthy bandit's adviser and representative, roughly equivalent to 'hedge-lawyer', *consigliere*
puasa	Ramadan, the Muslim month of fasting
pukulan	Batavian dialect for *pencak silat*
pusaka	regalia
raden (Javanese)	aristocratic title
radja, raja	king, ruler, sultan, master thief
radjamoekah	system used by *ketjoe*s to plan attacks
radja oetan	king of the jungle (of the wilderness)
rampok	kind of armed robbery
rancak	traditional Indonesian poem, generally for recitation
ringit	unit of currency in the Dutch East Indies
roesak	broken, injured
roesak djawi	the attacker is injured

roesak djero	the person attacked is injured
ronda	traditional law enforcement system at local level
sado	horse-drawn cab
sair	rhyming Malay poem
Sarekat Islam	first indigenous political organization in the Dutch East Indies
sarong	skirt-like garment wrapped around the waist
sawah	irrigated rice field
schout (Dutch)	sheriff, senior police officer
senapan	rifle, derived from the Dutch *snaphaan* (snaphaunce).
silat	indigenous martial art
spiun, spion (Dutch)	spy
sri (Javanese)	a very easy prize
stamboel	kind of Javanese theatrical performance
sunan	sultan of Mataram
tandak	ritual war dance
tempo doeloe	the good old days
terlaloe	too bad
tjoeké (cuke)	the portion of the harvest that the farmer must yield to the landowner as a tithe (from 1836 onward at most one-fifth, traditionally one-tenth)
tjoelik	supernatural creatures that spread sickness and ruin according to indigenous folk tales
toewan	boss, European gentleman
toewan tanah	estate owner
toko	general store
tongtong	hollowed-out wooden trunk that was struck to sound an alarm
tongtong amok	alarm sound on the tongtong in the event of a fatal attack

totok	full-blooded (often used to describe Dutch people who had just arrived in the Dutch East Indies)
towak	palm wine
towak sama ijs	palm wine with ice
tuan	sir, gentleman
veldpolitie (Dutch)	rural police
verbaal (Dutch)	official report, file
wakil	deputy
warisan	estate, inheritance
warung (waroeng)	shop, stall, small eating house
wayang	Javanese shadow puppetry
wayang golek pop	kind of wayang puppet
wedana, wedono	indigenous regional administrator

Bibliography

The sources consulted are divided into five categories:

- archival sources
- daily newspapers and periodicals from the period investigated
- interviews
- books from the period investigated or earlier
- more recent books and articles

1. Archival sources

Central Archival Depot (Centraal Archief Depot), of the Dutch Ministry of Defence (Nederlands Ministerie van Defensie), Rijswijk

Archives of the Ministry of Colonies (Ministerie van Koloniën), NA, The Hague

Archives of the General Secretariat (Archief Algemene Sekretarie), ANRI, Jakarta

Banten Residency Archives (Archief Residentie Banten), ANRI, Jakarta

Batavia Residency Archives (Archief Residentie Batavia), ANRI, Jakarta

Tangerang Residency Archives (Archief Residentie Tangerang), ANRI, Jakarta

2. Newspapers and periodicals

Algemeen Handelsblad

Archipel

Bataviaasch Nieuwsblad (1885–1942)

Bataviaasch Handelsblad

Bataviaasche Courant, Batavia (called the *Javasche Courant* from 1827 onward)

Bintang Barat, Batavia

Bintang Betawi, Batavia

Handelsblad, Rotterdam

Hindia Olanda, Batavia

De Indische Gids, Amsterdam (successor to the *Tijdschrift voor Nederlandsch-Indië*)

Indonesië

Intisari (magazine)

Jakarta, Jakarta (magazine)

Javasche Courant, Batavia (called the *Bataviaasche Courant* until 1827)

Java-bode, Nieuws-en Handels-en Advertentieblad voor Nederlandsch-Indië, Batavia (1852–1942)

Koloniale Studiën. Tijdschrift van de Vereeniging voor Studie van Koloniaal-Maatschappelijke Vraagstukken. Weltevreden (1916–41)

Locomotief, Samarangsch Handel-en Advertentieblad (1863–1942)

Moesson

Nederlandsch-Indische Politiegids. Orgaan van de Broederschap van Commissarissen van Politie in Nederl.-Indië

Nieuwe Rotterdamsche Courant (NRC), Rotterdam

Nieuws van den Dag voor Nederlandsch-Indië

Panorama, Batavia (in the Pusat Perfilman, Jakarta)

Pemberita Betawi, Batavia

Perniagaan, Batavia

Soerabajasch Handelsblad (1865–1942)

Singapore Free Press and Mercantile Advertiser (1835–1962)

Staatsblad

Telegraaf, Amsterdam

Tijdschrift voor het Binnenlandsch Bestuur

Tijdschrift voor Nederlandsch-Indië, Amsterdam (J.H. de Bussy)

Vaderland

De Zweep: een wreed weekblad: het grootste weekblad van de Oriënt. Ed. Jan Karwats (pseudonym of D.W. Beretty). Published from 1921 to 1923, then continued under the name of *d'Oriënt, een weekblad voor kunst en actualiteit.*

3. Interviews

Jali Jalud, interviewed by Purwadi Djunaedi and Pambudi Widodo, 30 December 1997.

Kusno Parto ('Om Pit'), interviewed by Purwadi Djunaedi and Pambudi Widodo, 19 January 1998.

Abdul Rachman, interviewed by Purwadi Djunaedi and Pambudi Widodo, 19 January 1998.

Sabeni, interviewed by the author, 20 January 1998.

Descendants of Police Commissioner Hinne, interviewed by the author, various locations in the Netherlands and various dates.

4. Books from the period investigated or earlier

André de la Porte, G., *Recht en rechtsbedeeling in Nederlandsch-Indië. Handleiding bij de beoefening van het Nederlandsch-Indische privaat-en strafrecht*. 2nd edition. The Hague: Belinfante, 1933.

Anwar, *Gerakan protes petani Bekasi 1913. Studi kasus awal masuknya sarekat islam di tanah partikelir*. Skripsi Jurusan Sejarah Fukultas Sastra Universitas Indonesia, 1990 [unpublished].

Babad tanah djawi. Javaansche geschiedenis. The Hague: Martinus Nijhoff, 1941.

Bodemeijer, P.H., *Waaraan de achteruitgang van de bevolking in het district Bekasie en de daarmee gepaard gaande moord en roofpartijen te wijten is*. Weltevreden: A.M. van Belkum & Co., 1905.

Boeka, *Uit Java's binnenland. Een koffieopziener*. Amsterdam: F. van Rossum, 1901.

———, *Uit Java's binnenland. Pah Troeno*. Amsterdam: F. van Rossum, 1901.

———, *Uit Java's binnenland. Beschaving*. 2 vols. Amsterdam: F. van Rossum, 1903.

———, *Pahkasinum*. Amsterdam, 1904.

Boekhoudt, W., *Rapport reorganisatie van het politiewezen op Java en Madoera (uitgezonderd de Vorstenlanden, de particuliere landerijen en de hoofdplaatsen Batavia, Semarang en Soerabaja), 1906–1907*. Batavia: Landsdrukkerij, 1908.

Coldenhoff, Ulrich [writing under the pseudonym of Ucee], *De schoonste triomf van de indo-detective*. San Francisco, The Hague: Tong-Tong International, n.d. [1920s].

Couperus, Louis, *De stille kracht* [*The Hidden Force*]. Amsterdam: Querido, 1900. Trans. Alexander Teixeira de Mattos, 1921. Revised and edited, with an introduction and notes by E.M. Beekman. Library of the Indies series. Amherst, Mass.: University of Massachusetts Press, 1985.

Darwin, Charles, *On the Origin of Species by Means of Natural Selection, or the Preservation of Favoured Races in the Struggle for Life*. London: John Murray, 1859.

Day, Clive, *The Policy and Administration of the Dutch in Java*. 1904. Reprinted in 1966.

De Haan, F., *Priangan. De Preanger-Regentschappen onder het Nederlandsch Bestuur tot 1811*. 4 vols. Batavia: G. Kolff & Co. and The Hague: Martinus Nijhoff, 1910.

De Jong, C.G.E., *De organisatie der politie in Nederlandsch-Indië*. Leiden, doctoral thesis, Leiden University, 1933.

De Jonge, J.K.J. and M.L. van Deventer, *De opkomst van het Nederlandsch gezag in Oost-Indië. Verzameling van onuitgegeven stukken uit het oud-koloniaal archief (1595–1814)*. 17 vols. The Hague: Nijhoff, 1862–95.

De Kat Angelino, A.D.A., *Staatkundig beleid en bestuurszorg in Nederlands Indië*. 2 vols. The Hague: Martinus Nijhoff, 1931.

De Klerck, E.S., *History of the Netherlands East Indies*. Rotterdam: W.L.&J. Brussee, 1938.

De la Valetta, G., 'Politiekunst', *Koloniaal Tijdschrift* 1 (1912): 465–77 and 580–93.

De Veer, W., *Particuliere landerijen en de openbare veiligheid in de residentie Batavia*. Batavia: Javasche Boekhandel & Drukkerij, 1904.

Dekker, P., with S.H. Tacoma, *De politie in Nederlandsch-Indië. Hare beknopte geschiedenis, haar taak, bevoegdheid, organisatie en optreden*. Soekaboemi: Insulinde, 1938 (2nd edition).

Drewes, G.W.J., *Drie Javaansche goeroe's. Hun leven, onderricht en messiasprediking*. Leiden: A. Vros, doctoral thesis, Leiden University, 1925.

Du Perron, E., *Het land van herkomst* [*Country of Origin*]. Amsterdam: Van Oorschot, 1935. Trans. Francis Bulhof. Library of the Indies series. Amherst: University of Massachusetts Press, 1984. For the Dutch edition of this book, use was made of the 13th, expanded edition (1989), with autobiographical notes by Du Perron.

Franchetti, Leopoldo, *Condizioni economiche e amministrative delle province napoletane*. Bari: Laterna, 1875 (reissued, 1974).

Furnivall, J.S., *Netherlands India: A Study of Plural Economy*. London, Cambridge: Cambridge University Press, 1939.

Gonggrijp, G.L., *Brieven van Opheffer. Aan de redaktie van het Bataviaasch Handelsblad*. 3rd edition. Maastricht: Leiter-Nypels, 1944.

Gonggrijp, G.F.E., *Geïllustreerde encyclopaedie van Nederlandsch-Indië*. Leiden: Leidsche Uitgeversmaatschappij, 1934.

Groneman, Isaac, *Een ketjoegeschiedenis*, in the series *Vorstenlandsche Toestanden*. Dordrecht: Revers, 1887.

Hekmeijer, F.C., *Verordeningen betreffende ontplofbare stoffen, vuurwapenen, buskruit en munitie*. In the series *Wetten en verordeningen van Ned.-Indië*, no. 21. Batavia, 1916.

Hoorweg, A., 'Politie, leger en veiligheid in Nederlandsch-Indië', *Indische Gids* 51 (1929): 357–73.

Hutton, James, *Thugs and Dacoits of India*. Delhi: Mittal Publishers, 1857. Reissued, Delhi: Gian Publications, 1981.

Ido, Victor, 'De tentoonstelling'. In *Indië in de goede oude tijd*. The Hague: Van Hoeve, 1966, reissue of 'Indië in den goeden ouden tijd: radio voordrachten voor de Nirom gehouden' (1936).

IJzerman, J.W. (ed.), *De reis om de wereld door Olivier van Noort 1598–1601.* 2 vols. Van Linschoten Vereeniging XXVII–XXVIII. The Hague, 1926.

Kalff, S., 'Europees pauperisme in Indië', *Koloniaal Tijdschrift* (1922): 573–83.

Keuchenius, W.M., *Beschrijving der Bataviasche jurisdictie en onderzoek naar de oorzaken der meerdere ongezondheid van Batavia en deszelfs rhee, alsmede waaraan de mindere bevolking, de wijnige opbrengst der producten, en de groote onveiligheid in dit anders vruchtbare gewest toe te schrijven is.* Batavia: Bruining & Wijt, 1875. Originally published in 1812.

Kipling, Joseph Rudyard, *Kim.* London: MacMillan, 1901.

Koninklijke Vereeniging Java Motor Club, *Naamlijst (residentiesgewijze en alfabetisch, van de ondernemingen, huurlanden en particuliere landerijen voorkomende op de kaart van Java en Madoera.* Weltevreden: Top. Dienst, 1926.

Lamster, J.C., 'De veiligheid van personen en goederen op Java en de noodzakelijkheid eener systematische politiereorganisatie'. In *De Indische Gids* (also the new series of the *Tijdschrift voor Nederlansch-Indië*), vol. 33, II, Amsterdam: J.H. de Bussy, 1911, pp. 1462–500.

Laporan-laporan tentang gerakan protes di Jawa pada abad-XX. Arsip Nasional Republik Indonesia, Penerbitan sumber-sumber sejarah. Jakarta, 1981.

Lie Tek Long, *Tjerita dan sair Sie Rondah.* Batavia, 1921. Catalogue, Claudine Salmon, p. 236.

———, *Gouw Soei Ho soedah binasaken ... Sie Rondah, perampok jang gagah Brani.* Batavia, 1913. Catalogue, Claudine Salmon, p. 377.

Maijer, L.Th., *De pigment-vlekken op het menschelijk lichaam en hare waarde en beteekenis naar het algemeen onder de Javanen heerschende bijgeloof. Een ethnografische bijdrage.* Weltevreden: Visser & Co., 1907.

Meijer, D.H., 'Dactyloscopie voor Nederlandsch-Indië', *Koloniale Studiën* 10, no. 2 (1926): 930–1.

———,'Twee Javaanse kapiteins van Köpenick', *Koloniaal Tijdschrift* (1930).

———, 'Politie en politiek', *Koloniale Studiën* 15 (1931): 578–610.

———, 'Ketongan en veiligheid', *Nederlandsch-Indische Politiegids*, no. 4 (April 1932): 104–97.

Neijtzell de Wilde, A., *Een en ander omtrent den welvaartstoestand der inlandsche bevolking in de Gouvernementslanden van Java en Madoera (de particuliere landerijen uitgezonderd).* Weltevreden: Visser & Co., 1913.

Oey Bo Eng, 'Sair Si Tjonat ...'. In *Sair Djamoer Aneh.* Batavia, 1931. Catalogue, Claudine Salmon, p. 369.

———, *Sair Djamoer Aneh.* Batavia, 1931. Catalogue, Claudine Salmon, p. 369.

Onderzoek naar de mindere welvaart der inlandsche bevolking op Java en Madoera. 12 vols. Batavia (various publishers), 19XX–14.

Ottow, S.J., *De oorsprong der conservatieve richting. Het kolonisatierapport Van der Cappellen, uitgegeven en toegelicht door S.J. Ottow.* Utrecht: Oosthoek, doctoral thesis, 1937.

Het Politieschandaal te Batavia, The Hague: Alex B. Benfer, n.d.

Het pauperisme onder de Europeanen in Nederlandsch-Indië. 5 vols. Batavia, 1901.

Pangemanann, F.D.J., *Tjerita Si Tjonat. Satoe kapala penjamoet di djaman dahoeloe tempo tahon 1840.* Batavia: Tjoe Teoi Yang, 1900.

Pannekoek, G.H., 'De viering van het 250-jarig bestaan van Batavia in 1869', *Tijdschrift voor Nederlandsch Indië* 18, 2 (1889): 161–205.

Paré, 'Rampokkers'. In *Nederlandsch-Indische Politiegids*, December 1917.

Particuliere landbouwnijverheid. Lijst van ondernemingen. Departement van Binnenlandsch Bestuur. Batavia, 1915–22.

Prawoto, Raden. 'Dievenbijgeloof op Midden-Java', *Tijdschrift voor Indische Taal-, Land- en Volkenkunde* 58 (1919): 169–212.

Regeringsalmanak Nederlandsch-Indië. Batavia, many vols.

Riesz, C.H.F., *De particuliere landerijen van Westelijk-Java.* 2 vols. Batavia: G. Kolff en Ernst, 1883–7.

Reitsma, S.A., *S.E.W. Roorda van Eysinga, de dichter van Sentot's vloekzang*. Offprint from the *Haagsch Maandblad*, March–April 1941, vol. 35, nos. 3 & 4. Leiden: A.W. Sijthoff, n.d.

Rinaldo Rinaldini, Gouverneurs Volksboeken, vols. 31–66. Leiden, 1885.

[Anonymous] *Roepa-roepa sair rame, Si Pitoeng, orang maen kartoe, senang hati.* Batavia, 193X. Catalogue, Claudine Salmon, p. 382.

Roorda van Eysinga, S.E.W., *Mijne verbanning en mijn vloekzang. Een andere waarheid dan de officiële.* Amsterdam: J.C. Schlömann, 1866.

Sentol, M. bin Moehamad, *Rantjak Si Pitoeng*. Batavia, 193X. Catalogue, Claudine Salmon, p. 459.

Tillema, H.F., *'Kromoblada': Over 't vraagstuk van "het wonen" in Kromo's groote land.* 2 vols. The Hague: De Atlas, 1915–6.

Ucee [pseudonym of Ulrich Coldenhoff], *De schoonste triomf van de indo-detective.* San Francisco, The Hague: Tong-Tong International, n.d. [1920s]. Use was made of the 2nd edition, dated 1986.

Van de Heijden, J., *Batavia bij nacht. Realistische roman uit het nachtleven van Indië.* The Hague: Confidentia, 1940.

Van de Wall, V.I., *Oude Hollandsche buitenplaatsen van Batavia.* Deventer: Van Hoeve, 1943.

Van Delden, Emile, *De particuliere landerijen op Java*. Leiden: S.C. van Doesburgh, 1911, doctoral thesis, Leiden University.

Van den Bovenkamp, A., 'Het dactyloscopeeren als algemeene Regeeringsmaatregel ter tijdelijke vervanging van een Burgerlijken stand voor de Inlandse bevolking', *Koloniale Studiën* 3, no. 2 (1919): 156–64.

Van Helsdingen, W.H. (ed.), *Daar wèrd wat groots verricht … Nederlandsch Indië in de XXste eeuw*. Amsterdam: Elsevier, 1941.

Van Houtum, A., *De particuliere landerijen (bewesten de Tjimanoek) op Java*. Amsterdam: M.H. de Bussy, 1905.

Van Kol, H., *Uit onze koloniën. Uitvoerig reisverhaal*. Leiden: A.W. Sijthoff, 1903.

———, *Nederlandsch-Indië in de Staten-Generaal van 1897 tot 1909. Een bijdrage tot de geschiedenis der koloniale politiek in Nederland*. The Hague: Martinus Nijhoff, 1911.

Van Motman, C.J., *Particuliere landerijen op Java*. The Hague: De Groot & Dijkhoffz, 1906 [reprint of documents published between 1904 and 1906].

Vergouw, W.G., 'Animisme in de Javaansche dievenwereld', *Koloniale Studiën* 13, no. 1 (1929): 82–110.

Verslag over de Hervormingen van het Gevangeniswezen in Nederlandsch-Indië, over 1921–1925. Batavia: G. Kolff & Co., 1926.

Veth, Bas, *Het leven in Nederlandsch-Indië*. Amsterdam: P.N. van Kampen, 1900.

Von Faber, G.H., *A Short History of Journalism in the Dutch East Indies*. 1931.

Voorhoeve, R., *Inlandsche jagers*. The Hague: De Hofstad, 1940.

De vuurwapenordonnanties 1925. De vuurwapenbelasting en de daarmede verband houdende voorschriften van administratieven aard. Bewerkt door B.G. ter Brake & F.J.W.H. Sandbergen. Weltevreden: Bureau tot Uitgave van Werken op Politicgebied, 1925.

Wiggers, F., *Boekoe peringatan. Di tjeritain dari halnja saorang prampewan Islam Tjeng Kao bernama Fatima*. Batavia, 1916 [in the collection of the Perpustakaan Nasional RI in Jakarta].

Wormser, C.W., 'De pers in Indië', in *Daar wèrd wat groots verricht … Nederlandsch Indië in de XXste eeuw*, ed. W.H. van Helsdingen. Amsterdam: Elsevier, 1941, pp. 438–45.

Wormser, C.W., *Drie en dertig jaren op Java*. Vol. 3: *In het dagbladwezen*. Amsterdam: W. ten Have, 1935.

Y.L.M., *Sair Java-Bank di rampok*. 1922. Catalogue, Claudine Salmon, p. 369.

5. Recent books and articles

Abdullah, Hamid, 'Potret tingkah laku pemuda dalam revolusi'. Paper delivered at the seminar *Sejarah Peranan Generasi Muda dalam Perjuangan Bangsa 1942–1945*. Yogyakarta, 20–21 December 1989.

Abdullah, Taufik, H. Misbach Yusa Biran, and S.M. Ardan, *Film Indonesia Bagian I, 1900–1950*. Jakarta: Perum Percetakan Negara Republik Indonesia, 1993.

Abeyasekere, Susan, *Jakarta: A History*. Singapore, Oxford and New York: Oxford University Press, 1987.

Adam, Ahmat B., *The Vernacular Press and the Emergence of Modern Indonesian Consciousness (1855–1913)*. Ithaca and New York: Cornell University Press, 1995.

Adas, Michael L., 'From Avoidance to Confrontation. Peasant Protest in Pre-Colonial South East Asia', in *Comparative Studies in Society and History*, vol. 23. Cambridge: Cambridge University Press, 1981, pp. 217–47.

———, 'Bandits, Monks, and Pretender Kings: Patterns of Peasant Resistance and Protest in Colonial Burma, 1826–1941', in *Power and Protest in the Countryside*, ed. R.P. Weller and S.E. Guggenheim. Durham, N.C.: Durham University Press, 1982.

Ahmad, I., *Thugs, Dacoits, and the Modern World-System in Nineteenth Century India*. Doctoral dissertation, State University of New York at Binghamton.

Alatas, Syed Hussein, *The Myth of the Lazy Native: A Study of the Image of the Malays, Filipinos and Javanese from the 16th to the 20th Century and its Function in the Ideology of Colonial Capitalism*. London: Frank Cass, 1977.

Alexander, Howard, Quintin Chambers, and Donn F. Draeger, *Pentjak-Silat, de Indonesische vechtkunst*. Amsterdam: Bert Bakker, 1980.

Alexander, Paul, Peter Boomgaard, and Ben White (eds.), *In the Shadow of Agriculture: Non-Farm Activities in the Javanese Economy, Past and Present*. Amsterdam: Royal Tropical Institute, 1991.

Ali, Rahmat, *Cerita rakyat betawi I*. Jakarta: PT Gramedia Widiasarana Indonesia, 1993.

Anderson, Benedict, *The Pemuda Revolution: Indonesian politics 1945–1946*. Doctoral dissertation, Cornell University, 1967.

———, *Java in a Time of Revolution: Occupation and Resistance, 1944–1946*. Ithaca and London: Cornell University Press, 1972.

———, 'The Idea of Power in Javanese Culture', in *Culture and Politics in Indonesia*, ed. Claire Holt, Benedict R.O'G. Anderson and James Siegel. Ithaca, NY: Cornell University Press, 1972, pp. 1–69.

———, *Imagined Communities: Reflections on the Origin and Spread of Nationalism*: London: Verso, 1983.

———, *Language and Power: Exploring Political Cultures in Indonesia*. Ithaca and London: Cornell University Press, 1990.

Anderson, Benedict (ed.), *Violence and the State in Suharto's Indonesia*. Studies on Southeast Asia 30. Ithaca, NY: Cornell University, 2001.

Anderson, David M. and David Killangray (eds.), *Policing the Empire: Government, Authority and Control, 1830–1940*. Manchester and New York: Manchester University Press, 1991.

——— (eds.), *Policing and Decolonisation: Politics, Nationalism and the Police, 1917–1965*. Manchester and New York: Manchester University Press, 1992.

Anderson, J.L., 'Piracy and World History: An Economic Perspective on Maritime Predation', *Journal of World History* 6: 175–99.

Ankersmit, F.R., *Denken over geschiedenis. Een overzicht van moderne geschiedfilosofische opvattingen*. Groningen, 1984.

Arnold, David, *Police Power and Colonial Rule; Madras 1859–1947*. Delhi: Oxford University Press, 1986.

———, 'Dacoity and Rural Crime in Madras, 1860–1940', *Journal of Peasant Studies* 6 (1979): 140–67.

———, 'The Colonial Prison: Power, Knowledge and Penology in Nineteenth-Century India', in *Subaltern Studies 8: Essays in Honour of Ranajit Guha*, ed. David Arnold and David Hardiman. Delhi: Oxford University Press, 1994, pp. 148–87.

Arnold, David and David Hardiman (eds.), *Subaltern Studies 8: Essays in Honour of Ranajit Guha*. Delhi: Oxford University Press, 1994.

Arthur, T.C., *Reminiscences of an Indian Police Official*. London: Sampson Low, Marston & Co., 1894.

Aston, T.H., 'Robin Hood', *Past and Present* 20 (November 1961): 7–9.

Atkinson, Jane Monnig, and Shelly Errington (eds.), *Power and Difference: Gender in Island Southeast Asia*. Stanford, Calif.: Stanford University Press, 1990.

Babad tanah djawi. Javaansche geschiedenis. The Hague: Martinus Nijhoff, 1941.

Banfield, Edward, *The Moral Basis of a Backward Society*. Glencoe: Free Press, 1958.

Bankoff, Greg, 'Bandits, Banditry and Landscapes of Crime in Nineteenth-Century Philippines', *Journal of Southeast Asian Studies* 29, 2 (September 1998): 319–39.

Barker, Joshua, 'Surveillance and Territoriality in Bandung', in *Figures of Criminality in Indonesia, the Philippines, and Colonial Vietnam*, ed. Vicente L. Rafael. Ithaca and New York: Cornell University Press, 1999, pp. 95–127.

Billingsley, Phil, *Bandits in Republican China*. Stanford, Calif.: Stanford University Press, 1988.

Bloembergen, Marieke, 'Een koffieopziener in de desa. P.C.C. Hansen en zijn beeld van Java's binnenland', Master's thesis, Amsterdam University, 1993.

———, 'Koloniale staat, politiestaat? Politieke politie en het rode fantoom in Nederlands-Indië, 1918–1927'. In *Leidschrift*, 2006.

Blok, Anton, *The Mafia of a Sicilian Village (1860–1960): An Anthropological Study of Political Middlemen*. Amsterdam, doctoral thesis, 1972.

———, 'The Peasant and the Brigand: Social Banditism Reconsidered', *Comparative Studies in Society and History* 4 (1972): 494–503. Dit artikel wordt gevolgd door een respons van Hobsbawm, pp. 503–5.

———, 'Wie waren de Bokkerijders?' *Tijdschrift voor Sociale Geschiedenis* 14 (1979): 168–200.

———, 'Eer en de fysieke persoon', *Tijdschrift voor Sociale Geschiedenis* 18 (June 1980): 211–30.

———, 'Zinloos en zinvol geweld', in *Alledaags en ongewoon geweld*, ed. H. Franke, N.W. Wilterdink, and Christien Brinkgreve. Groningen, 1991.

———, *De Bokkerijders. Roversbenden en geheime genootschappen in de Landen van Overmaas (1730–1774)*. Amsterdam, 1993.

Blussé, Leonard, 'An Insane Administration and an Unsanitary Town: The Dutch East India Company and Batavia (1619–1799)', in *Colonial Cities*, ed. Robert J. Ross and G.J. Telkamp. Dordrecht, Boston and Lancaster: Martinus Nijhoff, 1985, pp. 65–85.

———, *Strange Company: Chinese Settlers, Mestizo Women and the Dutch in VOC Batavia*. Dordrecht-Holland: Foris Publications, 1986.

———, *Bitters bruid. Een koloniaal huwelijksdrama in de Gouden Eeuw*. Amersfoort: Balans, 1997.

Boissevain, Jeremy, *Friends of Friends: Networks, Manipulators and Coalitions*. Oxford: Basil Blackwell, 1974.

Boomgaard, Peter, 'Buitenzorg in 1805: The Role of Money and Credit in a Colonial Frontier Society', *Modern Asian Studies* 20 (1986): 33–58.

———, *Children of the Colonial State: Population Growth and Economic Development in Java, 1795–1880*. Amsterdam: Free University Press, 1989.

———, *Frontiers of Fear: Tigers and People in the Malay World, 1600–1950*. New Haven, London: Yale University Press, 2001.

———, 'From Subsistence Crises to Business Cycle Depressions', *Itinerario* 36, nos. 3–4 (2002): 35–50.

Boomgaard, Peter and Ian Brown (eds.), *Weathering the Storm: The Economies of Southeast Asia in the 1930s Depression*. Leiden: KITLV Press and Singapore: Institute of Southeast Asian Studies, 2000.

Boomkes, René, *De angstmachine. Over geweld in films, literatuur en popmuziek*. Amsterdam: De Balie, 1996.

Booth, Anne, *The Indonesian Economy in the Nineteenth and Twentieth century: A History of Missed Opportunities*. London: MacMillan Press, 1998.

Bosma, Ulbe, *Karel Zaalberg, journalist en strijder voor de Indo*. Leiden: KITLV Uitgeverij, 1997.

Bosma, Ulbe and Remco Raben, *De oude Indische wereld 1500–1920*. Amsterdam: Prometheus, Bert Bakker, Van Goor, 2003.

Bosma, Ulbe, Angelie Sens, and Gerard Termorshuizen, *Journalistiek in de Tropen: De Indische en Indonesisch Nederlandse pers 1850–1958*. Amsterdam: Aksant; Persmuseum, 2005.

Breman, Jan (ed.), *Imperial Monkey Business: Racial Supremacy in Social Darwinist Theory and Colonial Practice.* CASA Monographs. Amsterdam: Free University Press, 1990.

Brown, Nathan, 'Brigands and State Building: The Invention of Banditry in Modern Egypt', *Comparative Studies in Society and History* 32 (April 1999): 258–81.

Bruinink-Darlang, Anne Marie Christien, *Het penitentiair stelsel in Nederlands-Indië van 1905 tot 1940.* Utrecht, doctoral thesis, 1986.

Brunk, S., '"The Sad Situation of Civilians and Soldiers": The Banditry of Zapatismo in the Mexican Revolution', *American Historical Review* 101 (1996): 334–54.

Burke, Peter, *Popular Culture in Early Modern Europe.* London: Temple Smith, 1978.

———, *Varieties of Cultural History.* Cambridge: Polity Press, 1998.

Campbell, Bruce B. and Arthur D. Brenner (eds.), *Death Squads in Global Perspective: Murder with Deniability.* New York: St. Martin's Press, 2000.

Castles, Lance, *Religion, Politics and Economic Behaviour in Java: The Kudus Cigarette Industry.* Yale University Southeast Asia Studies Cultural Report Series, no. 15.

Caverle, J., *Pencak silat, de Indonesische vechtsport.* Rijswijk: Uitgeverij Elmar, 1996.

Chambers, Quintin and Donn F. Draeger, *Javanese Silat: The Fighting Art of Perisai Diri.* Tokyo, New York and San Francisco: Kodansha International, 1978.

Chandler, Billy Jaynes, *The Bandit King: Lampião of Brazil.* College Station and London: Texas A&M University Press, 1978.

Cheah Boon Kheng, *The Peasant Robbers of Kedah 1900–1929: Historical and Folk Perceptions.* East Asian Historical Monographs. Singapore, Oxford and New York: Oxford University Press, 1988.

Clancy-Smith, Julia and Frances Gouda, *Domesticating the Empire: Race, Gender, and Family Life in French and Dutch Colonialism.* Charlottesville and London: University of Virginia Press, 1998.

Cobb, R.C., *The Police and the People: French Popular Protest 1789–1820.* Oxford: Clarendon Press, 1970.

———,'La Bande d'Orgères', in *Reactions to the French Revolution*, ed. R.C. Cobb. London and New York: Oxford University Press, 1972, pp. 181–215.

Cobb, R.C. (ed.), *Reactions to the French Revolution.* London and New York: Oxford University Press, 1972.

Colombijn, Freek and J. Thomas Lindblad (eds.), *Roots of Violence in Indonesia: Contemporary Violence in Historical Perspective.* Proceedings of the KITLV 194. Leiden: KITLV Press, 2002.

Cohen, Matthew Isaac, *Komedie Stamboel: Popular Theater in Colonial Indonesia 1891–1903*. Leiden: KITLV Press, 2006.

Cohen, S., *Folk Devils and Moral Panics: The Creation of the Mods and Rockers*. Sociology and the Modern World. London: MacGiboon & Kee, 1972.

Cohen, S. and J. Young (eds.), *The Manufacture of News: Deviance, Social Problems and the Mass Media*. London: Constable, 1973.

Colombijn, Freek and J. Thomas Lindblad (eds.), *Roots of Violence in Indonesia: Contemporary Violence in Historical Perspective*. Proceedings of the KITLV 194. Leiden: KITLV Press, 2002.

Colombijn, Freek, 'Maling, Maling! The Lynching of Petty Criminals', in *Roots of Violence in Indonesia: Contemporary Violence in Historical Perspective*, ed. Freek Colombijn and J. Thomas Lindblad, Proceedings of the KITLV 194. Leiden: KITLV Press, 2002, pp. 299–329.

Consten, Paul, *De functie van de straf van rottingslagen bij de politierechtspraak op Java tijdens het cultuurstelsel*. Unpublished paper. Amsterdam n.d.

Cribb, Robert, *Gangsters and Revolutionaries: The Jakarta People's Militia and the Indonesian Revolution 1945–1949*. Kensington, Australia, 1991.

Cribb, Robert (ed.), *The Late Colonial State in Indonesia: Political and Economic Foundations of the Netherlands Indies 1880–1942*. Proceedings of the KITLV 163. Leiden: KITLV Press, 1994.

Damardini, Palupi, *Cerita Si Pitung sebagai sastra lisan: Analisis terhadap struktur cerita*. Depok, 1993 [final paper, Fakultas Sastra Universitas Indonesia, Depok].

Darnton, Robert, *The Great Cat Massacre and Other Episodes in French Cultural History*. New York, Toronto: Random House, Inc., 1984.

Davis, Natalie Zemon, *Society and Culture in Early Modern France: Eight Essays*. Stanford, Calif.: Stanford University Press, 1975.

De Graaff, Bob, *'Kalm temidden van woedende golven': Het Ministerie van Koloniën en zijn taakomgeving, 1912–1940*. The Hague: SDU, 1997.

De Graaf, H.J., *Geschiedenis van Indonesië*. The Hague, Bandoeng: W. van Hoeve, 1949.

De Vries, G. and B.J. Martens, *Nederlandse vuurwapens. KNIL en militaire luchtvaart, 1897–1942*. Amsterdam, 1995.

De Jong, J.J.P., *De waaier van het fortuin. Van handelscompagnie tot koloniaal imperium. De Nederlanders in Azië en de Indonesische archipel 1595–1950*. The Hague: SDU, 1998.

De Misset, I.H., *In de schaduw van de gevangenis*. Baarn: De Boekerij, 1952.

Dhakidae, Daniel, 'Criminals and the State in Indonesia'. n.p., 1987 [talk given to the Southeast Asia Program, Cornell University, 16 April 1987].

di Leonardo, Micaela (ed.), *Gender at the Crossroads of Knowledge*. Berkeley: University of California Press, 1991.

Dick, Howard, Vincent Houben, Thomas Lindblad, and Thee Kian Wie, *The Emergence of a National Economy: An Economic History of Indonesia, 1800–2000*. Leiden: KITLV Press, 2002.

Djajadiningrat-Nieuwenhuis, Madelon, 'Ibuism and Priyayization: Path to Power', in *Indonesian Women in Focus: Past and Present Notion*, ed. Elsbeth Locher-Scholten and Anke Niehof. Proceedings of the KITLV 127. Dordrecht, Holland and Providence, USA: Foris Publications, 1987, pp. 43–51.

Dobbin, Christine, 'Accounting for the Failure of the Muslim Javanese Business Class: Examples from Ponorogo and Tulungagung (c. 1880–1940)', *Archipel* 48: 87–101.

Draeger, Donn F., *Weapons and Fighting Arts of the Indonesian Archipelago*. Rutland: Vermont, Tokyo: Charles E. Tuttle Company, 1972.

Egmond, Florike, *Banditisme in de Franse Tijd. Profiel van de Grote Nederlandse Bende 1790–1799*. Soest: De Bataafsche Leeuw, 1986.

———, *Underworlds: Organized Crime in The Netherlands 1650–1800*. Cambridge: Polity Press, 1993.

Einstadter, Werner J., 'The Social Organization of Armed Robbery', in *Professional Criminals*, ed. Dick Hobbs. Aldershot: Dartmouth, 1995, pp. 64–83.

Elias, Norbert, *Ueber den Prozess der Zivilisation. Soziogenetische und psychogenetische Untersuchungen*. Basel, 1939. Edition used: *Het civilisatieproces. Sociogenetische en psychogenetische onderzoekingen*. Utrecht: Antwerp, 1982.

Engelen, Theo, 'De Bokkerijders. Banditisme tijdens het Ancien Régime', *Tijdschrift voor Sociale Geschiedenis* 8 (1977): 169–96.

———, 'De Bokkerijders. Banditisme tijdens het Ancien Régime II. Een repliek', *Tijdschrift voor Sociale Geschiedenis* 14 (1979a): 160–7.

———, 'De Bokkerijders. Banditisme tijdens het Ancien Régime III. Een tripliek', *Tijdschrift voor Sociale Geschiedenis* 16 (1979b): 313–20.

Errington, Shelly, 'Recasting Sex, Gender, and Power: A Theoretical and Regional Overview', in *Power and Difference: Gender in Island Southeast Asia*, ed. Shelly Errington and Jane Monnig Atkinson. Palo Alto: Stanford University Press, 1990, pp. 1–58.

Erwiza, *Miners, Managers and the State: A Socio-Political History of the Ombilin Coal-Mines, West Sumatra, 1892–1996*. Doctoral thesis, Amsterdam University, 1999.

Fabricius, Jan, *Tempo doeloe. Uit de goeie ouwe tijd*. The Hague: H.P. Leopold, 1949.

Fasseur, Cees, *De indologen. Ambtenaren voor de Oost, 1825–1950*. Amsterdam, 1993.

Foucault, Michel, *Surveiller et punir. Naissance de la prison.* Paris: Gallimard, 1975.

Frederick, William H., *Visions and Heat: The Making of the Indonesian Revolution.* Athens: Ohio University Press, 1989.

———, 'The Appearance of Revolution: Cloth, Uniform, and the Pemuda Style in East Java, 1945–1949', in *Outward Appearances: Dressing State and Society in Indonesia,* ed. Henk Schulte Nordholt. Leiden: KITLV Press, 1997, pp. 181–99.

———,'Shadows of an Unseen Hand. Some Patterns of Violence in the Indonesian Revolution, 1945–1949', in *Roots of Violence in Indonesia: Contemporary Violence in Historical Perspective*, ed. Freek Colombijn and J. Thomas Lindblad. Proceedings of the KITLV 194. Leiden: KITLV Press, 2002, pp. 143–72.

Fukuyama, Francis, *Trust: The Social Virtues and the Creation of Prosperity.* New York: Simon & Schuster, 1995.

Furnivall, J.S., *Colonial Policy and Practice: A Comparative Study of Burma and Netherlands India.* Cambridge: Cambridge University Press, 1948.

Gallant, Thomas W., 'Brigandage, Piracy, Capitalism, and State-Formation: Transnational Crime From a Historical World-Systems Perspective', in *States and Illegal Practices*, ed. Josiah McC. Heyman. Oxford, New York: Berg, 1999, pp. 25–62.

Gambetta, Diego, *The Sicilian Mafia: The Business of Private Protection*. Cambridge, Mass. and London: Harvard University Press, 1993.

Gambetta, Diego (ed.), *Trust: Making and Breaking Cooperative Relations.* Cambridge: Basil Blackwell, 1990.

Geertz, Hildred (ed.), *State and Society in Bali.* Leiden: KITLV Press, 1991.

Geertz, Clifford, *The Social History of an Indonesian Town.* Cambridge, Mass.: M.I.T. Press, 1965.

———, *The Religion of Java.* Chicago and London: University of Chicago Press, Phoenix Edition, 1976.

Gianno, Rosemary, '"Women Are Not Brave Enough". Semalai Male Midwives in the Context of Southeast Asian Cultures', *Bijdragen tot de Taal- , Land-en Volkenkunde* 160, no. 1 (2004): 31–71.

Ginzburg, Carlo, 'Morelli, Freud and Sherlock Holmes: Clues and Scientific Method', *History Workshop Journal* 9 (1980): 5–36, reprinted as 'Clues: Roots of an Evidential Paradigm', in Carol Ginzburg, *Myths, Emblems, Clues*. London, 1990, pp. 96–127.

Gobbé, E. and C. Adriaans (eds.), *Ambtelijke adviezen van Snouck Hurgronje*, 2 vols. The Hague: M. Nijhoff, 1959.

Gouda, Frances, 'Language of Gender and Neurosis in the Indonesian Struggle for Independence 1945–1948', *Indonesia*, no. 64 (October 1997): 45–77.

Gould, *Ontogeny and Phylogeny*. Cambridge, Mass.: Harvard University Press, 1977.

Grijns, C.D., *Jakarta Malay: A Multidimensional Approach to Spatial Variation, Part II*. Proceedings of the KITLV 149. Leiden: KITLV Press, 1991.

Grijns, Kees and Peter J.M. Nas (eds.), *Jakarta-Batavia: Socio-Cultural Essays*. Leiden: KITLV Press, 2000.

Guha, Ranajit (ed.), *A Subaltern Studies Reader 1986–1995*. Minneapolis: University of Minnesota Press, 1997.

Gunawan, F.X. Rudy and Nezar Patria, *Premanisme Politik*. Jakarta: ASAI (Institut Studi Arus Informasi), 2000.

Hall, D.G.E., *A History of South-East Asia*. London: MacMillan, 1991 (4th edition).

Hatley, Ron *et al.*, *Other Javas Away From the Kraton*. Clayton, Vic.: Centre of Southeast Asian Studies, 1984.

Henley, David, 'Entrepreneurship, Individualism and Trust in Indonesia'. Unpublished paper for the Seminar on Indonesian Social History, Jakarta/Depok, 8–11 December 1997.

Heuken, Adolf S.J., *Historical Sights of Jakarta*. Singapore: Times Books International, 1982 (3rd edition used).

Heyman, Josiah McC. (ed.), *States and Illegal Practices*. Oxford, New York: Berg, 1999.

Hilton, R.H., 'The Origins of Robin Hood', *Past and Present* 14 (November 1958): 30–43.

Hobbs, Dick (ed.), *Professional Criminals*. The International Library of Criminology, Criminal Justice and Penology. Aldershot: Dartmouth, 1995.

Hobsbawm, Eric J., *Primitive Rebels: Studies in Archaic Forms of Social Movement in the 19th and 20th Centuries*. Manchester: Manchester University Press, 1959.

———, *Bandits*. London: Weidenfeld & Nicolson, 1969.

Holt, J.C., 'The Origins and Audience of the Ballads of Robin Hood', *Past and Present* 18 (November 1960): 89–110.

———, 'Robin Hood: Some Comments', *Past and Present* 19 (April 1961): 16–9.

Holt, Claire, Benedict R. O'G. Anderson, and James Siegel, *Culture and Politics in Indonesia*. Ithaca, NY and London: Cornell University Press, 1972.

Hoogerwerf, Evert-Jan, *Persgeschiedenis van Indonesië tot 1942. Geannoteerde bibliografie*. Leiden: KITLV Uitgeverij, 1990.

Hutapea, Rivai, 'Jurus maut warga "Pitung"'. In *Sabili*, no. 21, tahun VIII, 11 April 2001. [In the collection of the KITLV library in Leiden.]

Hyam, Ronald, *Empire and Sexuality: The British Experience*. Manchester and New York: Manchester University Press, 1990.

Jellinek, Lea, 'The Urban Cycle — Jakarta: Memories of Kebun Kacang 1930s–1980s'. In Royal Institute of Linguistics and Anthropology, *International Workshop on Indonesian Studies*, no. 4: *Western Java in Development Perspective*. Leiden, 11–15 September 1989.

Jong, J.J.P. de, *De waaier van het fortuin. Van handelscompagnie tot koloniaal imperium. De Nederlanders in Azië en de Indonesische archipel 1595–1950*. Den Haag: SDU, 1998.

Kahin, Audrey R. (ed.), *Regional Dynamics of the Indonesian Revolution: Unity from Diversity*. Honolulu: University of Hawaii Press, 1985.

Karim, Mulyawan, 'Dokumen Batavia 1893', *Jakarta, Jakarta* 19, no. 6: 62–9.

Kartodirdjo, Sartono, *The Peasants' Revolt of Banten in 1888; Its Conditions, Course and Sequel: A Case Study of Social Movements in Indonesia*. The Hague: Martinus Nijhoff, 1966.

———, *Protest Movements in Rural Java: A Study of Agrarian Unrest in the Nineteenth and Early Twentieth Centuries*. Singapore: Oxford University Press, 1973.

Katz, F., *Riot, Rebellion, and Revolution: Rural Social Conflict in Mexico*. Princeton, NJ: Princeton University Press, 1988.

Keeler, Ward, 'Speaking of Gender in Java', in *Power and Difference: Gender in Island Southeast Asia*, ed. Jane Monnig Atkinson and Shelly Errington. Stanford, Calif.: Stanford University Press, 1990, pp. 127–52.

Keen, Maurice, 'Robin Hood – Peasant or Gentleman?' *Past and Present* 19 (April 1961): 7–15.

Kempers, R.T.W., *Antieke vuurwapens*. Haarlem, 1977.

Kleden-Probonegoro, Ninuk, 'Wacana sejarah dalam ungkapan teater betawi', *Mayarakat dan Budaya, Jurnal Masalah Kemasyarakatan dan Kebudayaan* 2, no. 2 (1999): 145–73.

———, 'Teater tradisional sebagai dokumen komunitas', *Mayarakat dan Budaya, Jurnal Masalah Kemasyarakatan dan Kebudayaan* 3, no. 1 (2000): 63–90.

Koesasi, B., *Lenong and Si Pitung*. Working Paper 73, Centre of Southeast Asian Studies. Clayton: Monash University, 1992.

Koliopoulos, J.S., *Brigands with a Cause: Brigandage and Irredentism in Modern Greece, 1821–1912*. Oxford: Clarendon Press, 1987.

———, 'Brigandage and Irredentism in Nineteenth-Century Greece', *European History Quarterly* 19: 193–228.

Kommers, Jean Hubertus Maria, *Besturen in een onbekende wereld. Het Europese binnenlands bestuur in Nederlands Indië 1800–1830*. Meppel: Krips Repro, doctoral thesis, Katholieke Universiteit Nijmegen, 1979.

Korver, A.P.E., *Sarekat islam 1912–1916. Opkomst, bloei en structuur van Indonesië's eerste massabeweging*. Amsterdamse Historische Reeks 3. Amsterdam: Historisch Seminarium, Amsterdam University, 1982.

Kousbroek, Rudy, *Het Oostindisch kampsyndroom*. Amsterdam, 1992.

Kuman, Ann, *Suropati: Man and Legend*. Leiden: Brill, 1975.

Laporan-laporan tentang gerakan protes di Jawa pada abad-XX. Arsip Nasional Republik Indonesia, Penerbitan sumber-sumber sejarah. Jakarta, 1981.

Lenselink, J., *Vuurwapens van 1840 tot heden*. Bussum: Van Dishoeck, 1966.

Lewin, Linda, 'The Oligarchical Limitations of Social Banditry in Brazil: The Case of the "Good" Thief Antonio Silvino', *Past and Present* 82 (1979): 116–46.

Lewis, Gwynne and Colin Lucas (eds.), *Beyond the Terror: Essays in French Regional and Social History, 1794–1815*. Cambridge: Cambridge University Press, 1983.

Linebaugh, Peter, *The London Hanged: Crime and Civil Society in the Eighteenth Century*. London: Penguin, 1991.

Locher-Scholten, Elsbeth, *Women and the Colonial State: Essays on Modernity in the Netherlands Indies 1900–1942*. Amsterdam: Amsterdam University Press, 2000.

———, 'State Violence and the Police in Colonial Indonesia Circa 1920. Exploration of a Theme', in *Roots of Violence in Indonesia: Contemporary Violence in Historical Perspective*, ed. Freek Colombijn and J. Thomas Lindblad, Proceedings of the KITLV 194. Leiden: KITLV Press, 2002, pp. 81–104.

Locher-Scholten, Elsbeth and Anke Niehof (eds.), *Indonesian Women in Focus: Past and Present Notions*. Proceedings of the KITLV 127. Dordrecht, Holland/ Providence, USA: Foris Publications, 1987.

Loven, Klarijn, *Si Doel and Beyond: Discourse on Indonesian Television in the 1990s*. Doctoral thesis, Leiden University, 2003.

Lucas, Anton, 'Kyai, Jago, Guru: Three Life Histories From Tegal', in Ron Hatley *et al.*, *Other Javas Away From the Kraton*. Australia: Monash University Press, 1983, pp. 41–8.

Lucas, Nicole, 'Trouwverbod, inlandse huishoudsters en Europese vrouwen. Het concubinaat in de planterswereld aan Sumatra's Oostkust', in *Vrouwen in de Nederlandse koloniën*, ed. Jeske Reijs *et al.* Nijmegen: SUN, 1986, pp. 78–97.

Luiten van Zanden, Jan, 'The Growing Maturity of Indonesian Economic History', *Itinerario* 26, nos. 3–4 (2002): 9–34.

Maddicott, J.R., 'The Birth and Setting of the Ballads of Robin Hood', *English Historical Review* 93, no. 367 (April 1978): 276–99.

Maxwell, Gavin, *God Protect Me From My Friends*. London, New York and Toronto: Longmans, Green & Co., 1956.

Maters, Mirjam, *Van zachte wenk tot harde hand. Persvrijheid en persbreidel in Nederlands-Indië 1906–1942*. Hilversum: Verloren, 1998.

McClintock, Anne, *Imperial Leather: Race, Gender and Sexuality in the Colonial Contest*. New York and London: Routledge, 1995.

McCown, Theodore D. and Kenneth A.R. Kennedy, *Climbing Man's Family Tree: A Collection of Writings on Human Phylogeny, 1699–1971*. Engelwood Cliffs, NJ: Prentice, 1972.

McGrath, R.D., *Gunfighters, Highwaymen, and Vigilantes: Violence on the Frontier*. Berkeley: University of California Press, 1984.

McVey, Ruth T., 'Introduction: Local Voices, Central Power', in *Southeast Asian Transitions: Approaches Through Social History*, ed. McVey, Ruth T. New Haven and London: Yale University Press, 1978.

McVey, Ruth T. (ed.), *Southeast Asian Transitions: Approaches Through Social History*. New Haven and London: Yale University Press, 1978.

Meijer, D.H., 'Over het bendewezen op Java', *Indonesië* 3 (1949–50): 178–89.

Melalatoa, Junus and Rivai Abu, *Sistem kesatuan hidup setempat daerah DKI Jakarta*. Proyek inventarisasi dan dokumentasi kebudayaan daerah 1980/1981. Jakarta: Departemen Pendidikan dan Kebudayaan, 1981.

Merrillees, Scott, *Batavia in Nineteenth Century Photographs*. Richmond: Curzon Press, 2001.

Mrázek, Rudolph, *The United States and the Indonesian Military, 1945–1965*, vol. 1. Prague: Oriental Institute, Publishing House of the Czechoslovak Academy of Sciences, 1978.

———, 'From Darkness to Light', 1997 [unpublished].

Nagtegaal, Luc and Peter J.M. Nas, 'Jakarta Greenery: An Essay on Urban Natural Environment', in *Jakarta–Batavia: Socio-Cultural Essays*, ed. Kees Grijns and Peter J.M. Nas (eds.). Leiden: KITLV Press, 2000, pp. 263–90.

Nagtegaal, Luc, *Riding the Dutch Tiger: The Dutch East Indies Company and the Northeast Coast of Java, 1680–1743*. Leiden: KITLV Press, doctoral thesis, 1996.

Nas, Peter J.M., 'Jakarta, stad vol symbolen'. Paper for the KOTA X conference *Ritueel en politiek in Azië*, 14–15 June 1990, Amsterdam (at the KITLV Library, Leiden).

Nas, Peter J.M. (ed.), *Urban Symbolism*. Leiden: Brill, 1993.

Niemeijer, H.E., *Calvinisme en koloniale stadscultuur, Batavia 1619–1715*. Doctoral thesis, Free University of Amsterdam, Amsterdam, 1996.

———, 'The Free Christian Asian Community and Poverty in Pre-Modern Batavia', in *Jakarta–Batavia: Socio-Cultural Essays*, ed. Kees Grijns and Peter J.M. Nas. Leiden: KITLV Press, 2000, pp. 75–92.

———, *Batavia, een koloniale samenleving in de 17de eeuw*. Amsterdam: Balans, 2005.

Nieuwenhuys, J. Rogier, 'De Tjiomas-zaak. Een Indische "cause célèbre" uit 1886'. Master's thesis, cultural anthropology, 1973.

Nieuwenhuys, Rob, 'Tempo doeloe (1870–1920)', in Rob Nieuwenhuys, *Tussen twee vaderlanden*. 1979. Amsterdam: G.A. van Oorschot, 1988 (3rd, revised edition; 1st edition 1959), pp. 5–84.

O'Malley, W.J.O., 'Criminals, Society, and Politics in Java', 1984 [unpublished].

O'Malley, P., 'Class conflict, Land and Social Banditry: Bushranging in Nineteenth Century Australia', *Social Problems*, no. 26 (1979): 271–83.

———, 'Social Bandits, Modern Capitalism and the Traditional Peasantry', *Journal of Peasant Studies*, no. 6 (1979): 410–22.

———, 'The Class Production of Crime: Banditry and Class Strategies in England and Australia', *Research in Sociology and Law*, no. 3 (1980): 181–99.

Onghokham, 'The Inscrutable and the Paranoid: An Investigation into the Sources of the Brotodiningrat Affair', in *Southeast Asian Transitions: Approaches through Social History*, ed. Ruth T. McVey. New Haven and London: Yale University Press, 1978, pp. 112–57.

———, 'The *Jago* in Colonial Java, Ambivalent Champion of the People', in *History and Peasant Consciousness in South East Asia*, ed. Andrew Turton and Shigeharu Tanabe. Senri Ethnological Studies, no. 13. Osaka: National Museum of Ethnology, 1984, pp. 327–44.

'De onveiligheid op de particuliere landen in West-Java', *De Indische Gids* 59 (1937): 532–7.

O'ong Maryono, *Pencak silat. Merentang waktu.* Yogyakarta: Pustaka Pelajar, 1998.

———, 'Jago, Friend or Foe' [unpublished].

Pandey, Gyanendra, 'In Defense of the Fragment: Writing about Hindu-Muslim Riots in India Today', in *A Subaltern Studies Reader 1986–1995*, ed. Ranajit Guha. Minneapolis: University of Minnesota Press, 1997, pp. 1–33.

Panorama, Batavia. Jakarta: Pusat Perfilman.

Pattynama, Pamela, 'Secrets and Danger: Interracial Sexuality in Louis Couperus's *The Hidden Force* and Dutch Colonial Culture Around 1900', in *Domesticating the Empire: Race, Gender, and Family Life in French and Dutch Colonialism*, ed. Julia Clancy-Smith and Frances Gouda. Charlottesville and London: University of Virginia Press, 1998, pp. 84–107.

Het Pauperisme onder de Europeanen in Nederlandsch–Indië. Voor den dienst. 3 vols. Batavia: Landsdrukkerij, 1901–2.

Pemberton, John, *On the Subject of 'Java'*. Ithaca and London: Cornell University Press, 1994.

Pérez, Louis A., Jr., *Lords of the Mountain: Social Banditry and Peasant Protest in Cuba, 1878–1918.* Pitt Latin American Series. Pittsburgh, PA: University of Pittsburgh Press, 1989.

Pettigrew, Joyce, *Robber Noblemen: A Study of the Political System of the Sikh Jats.* London and Boston: Routledge & Kegan Paul, 1975.

Pick, Daniel, *Faces of Degeneration: A European Disorder, c. 1848–c. 1918.* Cambridge: Cambridge University Press, 1989.

Pollmann, Tessel, 'Bruidstraantjes. De koloniale roman, de njai en de apartheid', in *Vrouwen in de Nederlandse koloniën*, ed. Jeske Reijs *et al.* Nijmegen: SUN, 1986, pp. 98–125.

Pramoedya Ananta Toer, *Tjerita dari Djakarta. Sekumpulan karikatur deadaan dan manusianja.* Jakarta: Penerbit Grafica, 1957.

———, *Rumah kacah. Sebuah roman sejarah, buku keIV.* Jakarta: Hastra Mitra, 1988. Translated into Dutch under the title of *Het glazen huis.* Houten: Wereldvenster/Unieboek, 1988. NOVIB, Derde Spreker series. Vol. 4 of a four-volume series, *Aarde der mensen.*

———, *De pionier. Biografie van Tirto Adhisoerjo.* Amsterdam: Manus Amici BV–NOVIB, 1988. Translated into Dutch by Marjanne Termorshuizen.

Purdey, Jemma, 'Describing Kekerasan. Some Observations on Writing about Violence in Indonesia after the New Order', *Bijdragen tot de Taal- , Land-en Volkenkunde* 160, no. 2/3 (2004): 189–225.

Raben, Remco, *Batavia and Colombo: The ethnic and spatial order of two colonial cities, 1600–1800.* Doctoral thesis, Leiden University, Leiden, 1996.

———, 'Round about Batavia: Ethnicity and Authority in the Ommelanden, 1650–1800', in *Jakarta–Batavia: Socio-Cultural Essays,* ed. Kees Grijns and Peter J.M. Nas. Leiden: KITLV Press, 2000, pp. 93–114.

Rafael, Vicente L. (ed.), *Figures of Criminality in Indonesia, the Philippines, and Colonial Vietnam.* Ithaca and New York: Cornell University Press, 1999.

Redfield, Robert, *Peasant Society and Culture: An Anthropological Approach to Civilization.* Chicago: University of Chicago Press, 1956.

Reid, Anthony, 'Europe and Southeast Asia: The Military Balance'. James Cook University of North Queensland, Occasional Paper no. 16. Townsville, Queensland, 1982.

Reijs, Jeske, Els Kloek, Ulla Jansz *et al.*, *Vrouwen in de Nederlandse koloniën. Zevende jaarboek voor vrouwengeschiedenis.* Nijmegen: SUN, 1986.

Ricklefs, M.C., *A History of Modern Indonesia, c. 1300 to the Present.* Houndmills, London: Macmillan, 1981.

Rock, Paul (ed.), *History of Criminology.* Dartmouth: Dartmouth Publishing Company, 1994.

Roebuck, Julian and Ronald Johnson, 'The Jack-of-All-Trades Offerder', in *Professional Criminals,* ed. Dick Hobbs. Aldershot: Dartmouth, 1995, pp. 305–14.

Rogers, John D., *Crime, Justice and Society in Colonial Sri Lanka.* London Studies on South Asia, no. 5. London: Curzon Press, The Riverdale Company, 1987.

Ross, Robert J. and G.J. Telkamp (eds.), *Colonial Cities.* Dordrecht, Boston and Lancaster: Martinus Nijhoff, 1985.

Rush, James Robert, *Opium Farms in Nineteenth Century Java: Institutional Continuity and Change in a Colonial Society 1860–1910*. Doctoral dissertation, Yale University, 1977.

———, *Opium to Java: Revenue Farming and Chinese Enterprise in Colonial Indonesia, 1860–1910*. Ithaca and London: Cornell University Press, 1990.

Sabeni, *Ihtisar keluarga pendekar Sabeni*. Jakarta, 1998 [unpublished].

Said, Edward W., *Orientalism: Western Conceptions of the Orient*. New York: Pantheon Books, 1978.

———, *Culture and Imperialism*. New York: Knopf, 1993.

Said, Salim, *Profil dunia film Indonesia*. Jakarta: PT Pustakakarya Grafikatama, 1991.

Salmon, Claudine, *Catalogus*.

Sarekat Islam lokal. Penerbitan sumber–sumber sejarah, no. 7. Arsip Nasional Republik Indonesia. Jakarta: ARNAS, 1975.

Schulte Nordholt, Henk, with Margreet van Till, 'Colonial criminals in Java, 1870–1910', in *Figures of Criminality in Indonesia, the Philippines, and Colonial Vietnam*, ed. Vicente L. Rafael. Ithaca and New York: Cornell University Press, 1999, pp. 47–69.

Schulte Nordholt, Henk, 'De jago in de schaduw; Misdaad en "orde" in de koloniale staat op Java', *De Gids* 146–8/9 (1983): 664–75.

———, *The Spell of Power: A History of Balinese Politics, 1650–1940*. Doctoral thesis, Leiden University, Leiden, 1996.

———, 'Een staat van geweld'. Inaugurele rede Erasmus Universiteit Rotterdam, 2000.

———, 'A Genealogy of Violence', in *Roots of Violence in Indonesia: Contemporary Violence in Historical Perspective*, ed. Freek Colombijn and J. Thomas Lindblad. Proceedings of the KITLV 194. Leiden: KITLV Press, 2002, pp. 33–61.

Schulte Nordholt, Henk (ed.), *Outward Appearances: Dressing State and Society in Indonesia*. Leiden: KITLV Press, 1997.

Scott, James C., *Weapons of the Weak: Everyday Forms of Peasant Resistance*: New Haven and London: Yale University Press, 1985.

Sears, Laurie J. (ed.), *Fantasizing the Feminine in Indonesia*. Durham and London: Duke University Press, 1996.

Sejarah Kampung Marunda. Jakarta: Pemerintah Daerah Khusus Ibukota Jakarta, Dinas Museum dan Sejarah, 1985.

Shannon, T.R., *An Introduction to the World-System Perspective*. Boulder, CO: Westview Press, 1996.

Sidel, John T., 'The Usual Suspects: Nardong Putik, Don Pepe Oyson, and Robin Hood', in *Figures of Criminality in Indonesia, the Philippines, and Colonial*

Vietnam, ed. Vicente L. Rafael. Ithaca and New York: Cornell University Press, 1999, pp. 70–94.

Siegel, James T., 'A New Criminal Type in Jakarta: The Nationalization of "Death"', in *Figures of Criminality in Indonesia, the Philippines, and Colonial Vietnam*, ed. Vicente L. Rafael. Ithaca and New York: Cornell University Press, 1999, pp. 210–30.

Sindall, Robert, *Street Violence in the Nineteenth Century: Media Panic or Real Danger?* Leicester, London and New York: Leicester University Press, 1990.

Singh, R.G., *Terror to Reform: A Study of Dacoits of Central India*. New Delhi: Intellectual Publishing House, 1980.

Sjahrir, Sutan, *Indonesische overpeinzingen*. Amsterdam: Bezige Bij, 1966.

Slatta, Richard W. (ed.), *Bandidos: The Varieties of Latin American Banditry*. Westport, Conn.: Greenwood, 1987.

Smail, John R.W., *Bandung in the Early Revolution, 1945–1946: A Study in the Social History of the Indonesian Revolution*. Ithaca and New York: Cornell University, 1964.

Snoek, Kees, *E. du Perron. Het leven van een smalle mens*. Amsterdam: Nijgh & Van Ditmar, 2005.

Snowden, F.M., *Violence and Great Estates in the South of Italy: Apulia 1900–1922*. Cambridge: Cambridge University Press, 1986.

Soe Hok Gie, *Orang-orang di persimpangan kiri jalan. Kisah pemberontakan maiun September 1948*. Yogyakarta: Yayasan Bentang Budaya, 1997.

Soedjatmoko, Mohammad Ali, G.K. Resink, and George M. Kahin (eds.), *An Introduction to Indonesian Historiography*. Ithaca, NY: Cornell University Press, 1965.

Steinberg, David Joel (ed.), *In Search of Southeast Asia: A Modern History*. Rev. ed, Honolulu: University of Hawaii Press, 1987.

Stepan, Nancy, 'Race and Gender: The Role of Analogy in Science', *Isis* 77 (June 1986): 261–77.

Stibbe, D.G. (ed.), *Encyclopaedie van Nederlandsch-Indië*. The Hague: Martinus Nijhoff and Leiden: NV v/h E.J. Brill, 1919. 2nd edition, 4 vols.

Stoler, Ann Laura, 'Carnal Knowledge and Imperial Power. Matrimony, Race, and Morality in Colonial Asia', in *Gender at the Crossroads of Knowledge*, ed. Micaela di Leonardo. Berkeley: University of California Press, 1991.

———, *Race and the Education of Desire: Foucault's History of Sexuality and the Colonial Order of Things*. Durham, London: Duke University Press, 1995.

Suhartono, *Bandit-bandit pedesaan di Jawa. Studi historis 1850–1942*. Yogyakarta: Aditya Media, 1995.

Suleiman, Satyawati, 'The Last Days of Batavia', *Indonesia* 28 (October 1979): 55–64.

Suryadinata, Leo, 'A Short History of the Indonesian Chinese Press', in Leo Suryadinata, *The Chinese Minority in Indonesia: Seven papers*. Singapore: Chopmen Enterprises, 1978, pp. 129–41.

———, *The Chinese Minority in Indonesia: Seven papers*. Singapore: Chopmen Enterprises, 1978.

Sutherland, H., *The Making of a Bureaucratic Elite: The Colonial Transformation of the Javanese Priyayi*. Singapore, Kuala Lumpur, Hong Kong: Heinemann, 1979.

Tagliacozzo, Eric, *Secret Trades of the Straits: Smuggling and State-Formation Along a Southeast Asian Frontier 1870–1910*. Doctoral dissertation, Yale University, 1999.

Taylor, Jean Gelman, *The Social World of Batavia: European and Eurasian in Dutch Asia*. Madison, Wisc.: University of Wisconsin Press, 1983.

———, 'Nyai Dasima. Portrait of a Mistress in Literature and Film', in *Fantasizing the Feminine in Indonesia*, ed. Laurie J. Sears. Durham and London: Duke University Press, 1996, pp. 225–48.

Teitler, G. *The Dutch Colonial Army in Transition: The Militia Debate, 1900–1921*. Townsville, Qld.: James Cook University of North Queensland, 1981.

Termorshuizen, Gerard, P.A. *Daum, Journalist en romancier van tempo doeloe*. Amsterdam: Nijgh & Van Ditmar, 1988.

Termorshuizen, Gerard, *Journalisten en heethoofden. Een geschiedenis van de Indisch Nederlandse dagbladpers 1744–1905*. Leiden: KITLV and Amsterdam: Nijgh en Van Ditmar, 2001.

Tideman, J., 'De bevolking van de regentschappen Batavia, Meester Cornelis en Buitenzorg', *Koloniaal Tijdschrift* 22: 140–68.

Tilly, Charles, *Coercion, Capital, and European States, AD 990–1990*. Cambridge, Mass., Oxford: Blackwell Publishers, 1990.

Titus, M.J., *Urbanisatie, integratie en demografische respons in Jakarta: Een empirisch onderzoek naar de stedelijke moderniseringsrol in de periode 1961–1976*. Nederlandse Geografische Studies 3. Amsterdam, Utrecht: Geografische Instituut, Rijksuniversiteit Utrecht, 1985.

Turley, Hans, *Rum, Sodomy and the Lash: Piracy, Sexuality, and Masculine Identity*. New York and London: New York University Press, 1999.

Turton, Andrew and Shigeharu Tanabe (eds.), *History and Peasant Consciousness in South East Asia*. Senri Ethnological Studies, no. 13. Osaka: National Museum of Ethnology, 1984.

Van Ballegoijen de Jong, Michiel, *Spoorwegstations op Java*. Amsterdam: De Bataafsche Leeuw, 1993.

Van de Loo, Vilan and Esther Wils, *Indië ongekuist*. Amsterdam: KIT, 2004.

Van den Doel, Wim, *De stille macht. Het Europese binnenlands bestuur op Java en Madoera 1808–1942*. Amsterdam: Bakker, 1994.

Van der Eng, Pierre, 'Halting Progress. Indonesia's Economic Development Since 1880', *Itinerario* 26, nos. 3–4 (2002): 15–34.

Van Diessen, J.R., *Jakarta/Batavia. Het centrum van het Nederlandse koloniale rijk in Azië en zijn cultuurhistorische nalatenschap*. De Bilt: Cantecleer, 1989.

Van Dijk, Kees, 'The Good, the Bad and the Ugly. Explaining the Unexplainable: *amuk massa* in Indonesia', in *Roots of Violence in Indonesia: Contemporary Violence in Historical Perspective.*, ed. Freek Colombijn and J. Thomas Lindblad. Proceedings of the KITLV 194. Leiden: KITLV Press, 2002, pp. 277–98.

———, 'Magic and Violence' [unpublished].

Van Doorn, Jacques, *The Engineers and the Colonial System: Technocratic Tendencies in the Dutch East Indies*. Comparative Asian Studies Programme (CASP). Rotterdam: Erasmus University, 1982.

Van Doorn, J.J.A., *De laatste eeuw van Indië. Ontwikkeling en ondergang van een koloniaal project*. Amsterdam: Bert Bakker, 1994.

Van Doorn, J.J.A., 'A Divided Society. Segmentation and Mediation in Late Colonial Society', *Papers of the Dutch Indonesian Historical Conference* (1974).

Van Leeuwen, Lizzy, *Airconditioned lifestyles. De nieuwe rijken in Jakarta*. Amsterdam, 1997.

Van Niel, Robert, *The Emergence of the Modern Indonesian Elite*. The Hague, Bandung: W. van Hoeve, 1960.

Van Stenus, L.E., 'Tjerita Si Tjonat: Sastra assimilatif in bahasa pra-Indonesia'. Master's thesis, Indonesian Letters, Leiden University, Leiden, 1986.

Van Till, Margreet, 'In Search of Si Pitung; The History of an Indonesian Legend', *Bijdragen tot de Taal-, Land-en Volkenkunde in Bijdragen tot de Taal-, Land- en Volkenkunde (Journal of the Royal Institute of Linguistics and Anthropology)* 152, no. 3 (1996): 461–82.

Van Till, Margreet and Roel van der Veen, 'Kennis en controle: De politie en inheemse bevolking in Nederlandsch-Indië rond 1900', in *Cultuurcontacten. Ontmoetingen tussen culturen in historisch perspectief*, ed. Arend Huussen, Janny de Jong and Gé Prince. Historische Studies IV. Groningen: Rijksuniversiteit Groningen, 2001.

Van Wulfften Palthe, P.M., *Over het bendewezen op Java*. Verslagen van het Psychiatrisch-Juridisch Gezelschap 29. Amsterdam: F. van Rossum, 1948 [text of lecture, 6 November 1948].

———, *Psychological Aspects of the Indonesian Problem*. Leiden: E.J. Brill, 1949.

Vanderwood, Paul J., *Disorder and Progress: Bandits, Police, and Mexican Development*. Lincoln and London: University of Nebraska Press, 1981.

Vanvught, Ewald, *Een propagandist van het zuiverste water. H.F. Tillema (1870–1952), en de fotografie van tempo doeloe*. Amsterdam: Jan Mets, 1993.

Verkaaik, Oskar, *Inside the Citadel, Violence and Religious Nationalism in Hyderabad, Pakistan*. PhD dissertation, University Amsterdam, 1999.

Vlekke, Bernard H.M., *Geschiedenis van den Indischen archipel. Van het begin der beschaving tot het doorbreken der nationalen revolutie*. Roermond-Maaseik: J.J. Romen, 1947.

Wallerstein, I., *The Modern World-System: Capitalist Agriculture and the Origins of the European World-Economy in the Sixteenth Century*. New York: Academic Press, 1974.

Warren, James Francis, *Rickshaw Coolie: A People's History of Singapore (1880–1940)*. Singapore, Oxford and New York: Oxford University Press, 1986.

Weber, Eugen, *Peasants into Frenchmen: The Modernization of Rural France 1870–1914*. Stanford, Calif.: Stanford University Press, 1976.

Wertheim, W.F., *Indonesian Society in Transition: A Study of Social Change*. The Hague and Bandung: W. van Hoeve, 1956.

———, 'Het sociologisch karakter van de indo-maatschappij'. Amsterdam: Uitg. Vrij Nederland, 1947.

Wessel, Ingrid, and Georgia Wimhöfer (eds.), *Violence in Indonesia*. Hamburg: Abera, 2001.

Wolf, Eric R. and Sidney Mintz, 'Haciendas and Plantations in Middle America and the Antilles', *Social and Economic Studies* 6, no. 3 (1957): 380–412.

Yang, Anand C., *Crime and Criminality in British India*. Tucson: University of Arizona Press, 1985.

Zaitch, Damián, *Trafficking Cocaine: Colombian Drug Entrepreneurs in the Netherlands*. Studies of Organized Crime. The Hague, London and New York: Kluwer Law International, 2002.

Zinoman, Peter, 'The History of the Modern Prison and the Case of Indochina', in *Figures of Criminality in Indonesia, the Philippines, and Colonial Vietnam*, ed. Vicente L. Rafael. Ithaca and New York: Cornell University Press, 1999, pp. 152–74.

———, *The Colonial Bastille: A History of Imprisonment in Vietnam, 1862–1940*. Berkeley, Los Angeles and London: University of California Press, 2001.

Index

Index of personal names

The spelling used in the book (which may be the old or the modern spelling) is given first, followed by any other relevant ways of spelling the name. Bandits were often popularly referred to with the prefix 'Si', which is omitted in this index. Muslims who had made the pilgrimage to Mecca often had 'Hadji' attached to their names, and are listed here.

Abdoelah, 163
Abdul Rachman, 137
Adam, 107
Adas, Michael, 12, 77
Adil, 130
Adiwaris, 116, 117–9
Aimard, Gustave, 103
Ali Biman, 26
Amand, C.A.A., 12, 65
Ambot, 56
Anderson, Benedict, 76, 94
Arsad, 55
Ateh, 54

Bakhuizen van den Brink, Ch.R., 8
Bankoff, Greg, 69
Baudet, H., 120
Bertillon, Alphonse, 128
Blok, Anton, 6, 14, 54, 57, 67, 90, 101, 147
Bodewitz, 81
Boeka (pen name of Peter Hansen), 11, 12
Bohong, 112
Boin, 181
Boomgaard, Peter, 48, 82, 190, 196
Boon, C.J., 174
Bosscher, C.N., 168
Briti, 56
Brown, Nathan, 7, 54
Brown (a police officer), 81
Bruinink-Dalang, A.N.M., 59
Burke, Peter, 148
Buwalda, 67

Cobbs, Richard, 90
Coen, Jan Pieterszoon, 19, 22, 24, 31, 165
Cohen, S., 47–8
Coldenhoff, Ulrich (Ucee), 133–4
Colombijn, Freek, 56
Conrad, Joseph, 109
Cortenhoeff, 19
Couperus, Louis, 1, 22, 70, 114
Couperus, J.R., 70, 162
Cribb, Robert, 77, 78, 88, 95–6, 181–2, 183, 187

Daendels, Herman Willem, 24
Damardini, Palupi, 142
Darip (Hadji Darip), 183–4
Daum, P.A., 36
De Kuijper, E.R.J.C., 20, 21, 85
De la Valetta, G., 122
De Veer, W., 109–10
Dekker, Eduard Douwes (Multatuli), 12
Djabar, 61
Djakaria (Mas Djakaria), 28–9
Djamangin, 88
Djaisin, 54
Djelane, 67
Djeram Latip, 139
Dji-ih (also Dji, Dji-ie, Dji-ieh), 58, 71, 98, 137–9, 143
Djoemaan, 67
Dobbin, Christine, 63
Doyle, Arthur Conan, 109, 126
Du Perron, E., 1, 22, 25, 26, 155–6, 162
Du Perron (father of E. du Perron), 26, 27, 80, 162

Egmond, Florike, 14, 54, 90
Entong Gendut, 81, 123–4
Errington, Shelly, 94

Fabricius, Jan, 135, 136, 141, 142
Fabricius, Johan, 141
Fairbanks, Douglas, 102
Fasseur, Cees, 121
Fatima, 131, 132, 133, 173
Fock, D., 168–9
Fouché, Joseph, 122, 123
Frederick, William, 184, 185
Freys, Georgine, 67
Fukuyama, Francis, 63

Gallant, Thomas W., 4–7, 32, 50, 51, 190–1
Gantang, 8, 59, 60, 89, 98, 102–3, 112–3, 119, 126, 128, 131, 142, 156–60, 163, 164, 178, 189
Gambetta, Diego, 14, 65
Geertz, Clifford, 63
Gentis, Cornelis, 156
Gentis, Herman, 156
Gering, 137
Giesberg, 115–6
Ginzburg, Carlo, 126, 128
Gloux, Olivier, 103
Condit, 112
Gonggrijp, G.L. (Ophcffer), 47, 72, 83, 125
Gouda, Frances, 102, 182
Groneman, I., 91

Hadji Anwar, 56
Hadji Hamid, 198
Hadji Liang, 201
Hadji Naidi, 197
Hadji Naipin, 143
Hadji Sapioen, 58
Hadji Sapiudin, 137, 138, 143
Hansen, Peter (wrote under the pseudonym of Boeka), 11–2
Hinne, Adolf Wilhelm Verbond (also Heyne), 53–4, 100, 129–36, 139–43, 150, 177

Hobsbawm, Eric, 2, 5, 6, 54, 71, 99, 112–3, 114, 116, 147–50, 182
Holmes, Sherlock, 126, 131, 132
Hood, Robin, 144, 147
Hoorweg, A., 127, 135, 170, 172, 174, 175, 176
Hunger, J.D., 173, 174
Hutton, James, 99
Hyam, Ronald, 114

Ido, Victor, 133
Ijzerman, 166

Jebul, 143
Johan, W.H.L., 131, 173
Judex, 116

Kario, 73
Karmani, Lukman, 144
Kartodirdjo, Sartono, 28–30, 182
Kaslan, 27
Kesen, 38, 90, 112, 116–9
Kiami, 181
Kieffer, J., 118
Kim, 134–5
Kipling, Rudyard, 134
Ko Haij Soei, 130
Koliopolous, J.S., 6
Komin, 180–1
Kortenhoeff, 23
Kousbroek, Rudy, 102
Kromo, 83–4, 125

Lampião, 114
Lawick van Pabst, C.N.H., 85
Leo, 134
Lias, 55, 56, 60, 93, 178, 182
Liham, 67
Lombroso, Cesare, 108, 109

Macdonald, Dwight, 148
Majoor Jantje, 34–5, 114
Mangoon, 80, 85
Masi, 52
Maxwell, Gavin, 15, 147
McClintock, Anne, 134, 135
Medomo, 129–30
Meijer, D.H., 64, 65, 76, 78, 87
Merais, 137
Mie, 139
Minke (Raden mas Minke), 145–6
Mintz, Sidney, 34
Mirah, 98
Misset, I.H., 100, 102, 136, 182
Moedjeran, 137
Moedjimi, 139, 161, 162
Moesanip, 67
Mrázek, Rudolph, 76
Multatuli (pen name of Eduard Douwes Dekker), 12

Napoleon, 122
Nata, 20, 23
Natadisastra, 156
Nawi, 56, 210
Nomo, 118
Nonya de C., 137

Oedji, 173
Oeij Tjioe Sion, 52
Oesoep, 55, 56, 60, 61, 74, 111, 178
Onghokham, 76, 78, 118
Opheffer (G.L. Gonggrijp), 47, 72, 83, 125

Pa Tirto, 83
Pa-I (Paih), 57–8, 180, 184
Pandji, 180, 183
Pangemann, 145, 146
Pannekoek, G.H., 22
Pawirono, 73
Perelaer, 21
Pinah (Mbak Pinah, mother of Si Pitung), 143

Pitung (also Pitoeng, Bitoeng, Pitang), 49, 55, 85–6, 93, 94, 95, 98, 112–3, 119, 126, 128, 130, 131, 132, 136–51, 155, 157–8, 161, 164
Piung (Bung Piung, father of Si Pitung), 143
Pramoedya Ananta Toer, 145, 146, 180
Prawoto (Raden Prawoto), 135, 180
Priester, L.R., 169
Putik, 147

R, 55, 74
Rais (Hadji R. Rais), 53, 54, 143
Reisner, 81
Rinaldini, Rinaldo, 149, 158
Robinson, Tjalie, 133
Ronda, 148, 173
Roorda van Eysinga, S.E.W., 22
Rijfsnijder, H., 110, 173

Saaba Entjak, 67
Sabam, 52, 181
Sabindjak, 56
Saipa, 112
Sakam, 126, 128, 132, 158
Salvatore, Giuliano, 15, 114, 147
Sapri, 67
Satian, 184
Schinderhannes, 158
Schulte Nordholt, Henk, 12–5, 76–8, 118
Scipio, 129
Sidel, John T., 147
Sindall, Robert, 47
Slatta, Richard W., 54
Smail, John R.W., 76
Snouck Hurgronje, C., 96
Soeriokoesoemo, S., 97
Soeroto, Noto, 97
Specks, Sara, 19
Steuerwald, 53, 54, 74
Stoler, Ann, 115
Surapati, 27–8

Tillema, A.F., 121
Tirtoadisoerjo, 38
Tjonat, 112, 148
Toit, 56

Ucee (Ulrich Coldenhoff), 133, 134, 135
Untung, 28

Van den Hoek, L.G.C.A., 180
Van der Capelle, 58, 159
Van der Eng, Pierre, 49
Van Dijk, Kees, 56, 75, 77, 78
Van Kol, H., 164, 165, 168
Van Motman, C.J., 166
Van Wulfften Palthe, P.M., 76, 78, 182–3, 187
Velia, Rudi, 98
Vergouw, W.G., 97, 128, 194
Verkaaik, Oscar, 103
Voigt, Wilhelm (the captain of the *Köpenick*), 103, 149

Wallerstein, Immanuel, 5, 32, 190
Weber, Eugen, 109
Wiggers, F., 132, 135
Wolf, Eric, 34

Zaalberg, Karel, 30, 157
Zinoman, Peter, 59

Index of place names

All Indonesian place names are given in the modern spelling. Where relevant, the old spelling follows. Country estates shown on the map that follows Chapter 1 are listed with their number on that map.

Aceh, 81, 129, 160
Amsterdam, 171
Anyer / Anyer-Kidul, 52, 66, 73

Babakan Bekasi, 91
Babalam, 74
Banten (Bantam), 24, 28, 29, 30, 109
Batoetoelis, 124
Bekasi, 4, 20–1, 29, 41, 53, 69, 74, 91, 110, 143, 150, 160–3, 183, 189, 200, 206–9
Bogor (Buitenzorg), 4, 23, 24, 29, 32, 35, 39, 68–71, 84, 91, 96, 123, 138, 145–6, 156–7, 164, 165, 180, 181, 201, 203, 208
Bolang (map of Buitenzorg, VIII), 42, 166
Borneo, 129
Buitenzorg (Bogor), 4, 23, 24, 29, 32, 35, 39, 68–71, 84, 91, 96, 123, 138, 145–6, 156–7, 164, 165, 180, 181, 201, 203, 208
Burma (Myanmar), 81

Calabria, 149
Central Java, 14, 32, 91, 101, 129, 159
Ceylon (Sri Lanka), 28, 72
China, 81, 150
Ciasem, 165
Cibarusa (Tjibaroesa, map of Buitenzorg, XXV), 42, 58, 145, 178, 179, 180
Cibinong (Tjibinong), 145
Cibodas (Tjibodas, map of Buitenzorg, XI), 42, 165, 166
Cikini (Tjikini), 87, 164
Cileungsi (Tjileungsi), 57, 145, 181
Cililitan (Tjililitan, map of Batavia, XLV), 41, 113, 201, 202, 206
Cilincing, 142
Cimanggis (Tjimanggis, map of Buitenzorg, XXII), 42, 167, 204
Cimanuk, 33
Ciomas (Tjiomas, map of Buitenzorg, 3), 29, 42, 84, 192, 200
Cipandai (Tjipandai), 202
Cipinang (Tjipinang), 60, 201, 207
Cisalak, 181
Citrap (Tjitrap), 34, 114

East Java, 25, 33, 184
East Tanjung (Tandjoeng-oost, map of Batavia, XLIII), 41, 202
Egypt, 7
Europe, 5, 19, 36, 59, 82, 114, 115, 121, 127–8, 148

France, 90
Freudian psychoanalysis, 126
Friesland, 121

Gabus / Gabus Dukuh, 53, 55
Gang Baru, 53
Gedong Panjang, 53
Glodok, 59–61
Greece, 6

The Hague (Den Haag, 's-Gravenhage), 165, 168
Halmahera, 130

India (British India), 6, 64, 99, 111, 114, 128, 134
Indramayu, 24
Italy, 6

Jakarta, 25, 75, 98, 136, 143, 161, 167, 183, 192
Janglapa (Djanglapa, map of Buitenzorg, V), 27, 42
Japan, 8, 81
Jasinga, 165
Java, 2, 4, 10–4, 22, 24–8, 30–5, 39, 47–50, 52, 60, 72, 75, 76, 81, 82, 91, 94, 95, 96, 98, 99, 101, 130, 145, 158, 161, 166, 180, 182, 183, 185, 188, 190
Jeddah, 37
Jembatan, 53

Kali Pasir, 53, 61, 210
Kampong Bambu, 140
Kampong Melayu (Kampong Melajoe), 1, 199, 202, 203
Kampong Sukabumi (Kampong Soekaboemi), 137
Kandanghauer, 165
Karawang, 49
Kartasura, 28
Kebayoran (Kebajoran), 25, 69, 131, 137, 139, 180, 197, 198, 199, 203, 204, 205, 206, 209, 210
Kebon Jeruk (Kebon Djeroek), 197, 198, 204
Kebun Kacang, 23, 124
Kendal, 159
Klender, 183
Klenteng, 51, 52
Koningsplein (Lapangan Medan Merdeka), 23, 25, 115
Köpenick, 103
Kramat, 40, 67, 201
Kramat Jati, 69
Krawang, 35, 41, 135, 201
Krekot, 112, 143
Kuningan, 25, 164

Lapangan Medan Merdeka (Koningsplein), 23, 25, 115
Latin America, 6, 25, 54
Lebak Bulus, 25
Leuwiliang, 166
Limburg, 90
London, 171

Mangga Besar, 130
Marunda, 86, 98, 137, 138, 142, 143
Mataram, 24, 28, 31
Matraman, 61
Mauk, 40, 116, 201
Meester Cornelis, 14, 20, 21, 51, 53, 60, 61, 69–71, 81, 91, 103, 137, 139, 140, 143, 166, 169, 175, 180, 197–201, 203–7, 209–10
Mecca, 37, 76, 101, 177, 190
Menteng, 24, 25, 61, 74, 207
Merauke, 159
Molenvliet, 208
Moluccas, 145
Myanmar (Burma), 81

Nanggung (Nanggoeng, map of Buitenzorg, IX), 41, 165
The Netherlands, 9, 30, 31, 100, 101, 121, 141, 142, 160, 164, 169, 171
New York, 74
Noordwijk, 23

Oldemarkt, 136

Pabayuran, 53
Padang, 73, 129
Pajajaran, 24
Palmerah (Paal Merah), 53, 143
Pamanukan, 165

Pamuka, 34
Pasar Baru (Pasar Baroe), 23, 61
Pasar Minggu, 25
Pasar Senen, 25, 140
Pasaruan, 31
Pegu, 81
Pekayon, 164
Pekalongan, 31
Pengumben, 143
Penjaringan, 112, 143
Peru, 150
Pesing, 134
Petodjo, 130
Philippines, 147
Pondok Gedé, 41, 158
Preanger, 83, 96, 158
Pulau Seribu, 116

Rawa Bokor, 116
Rawabelong, 143
Rijnland, 149

Salak, 23, 24
Sawah Lunto, 60–1
Semarang, 83, 121, 169
Serang, 177
Siam (Thailand), 81
Sicily, 6, 65, 147
Singapore, 53, 81, 139, 171
Solo, 81, 127
Sri Lanka (Ceylon), 28, 72
Suez Canal, 4, 9, 186
Sumatra, 60, 81, 129, 163
Sunda, 6
Surabaya (Soerabaja), 31, 169
Surakarta, 11

Tambun (Tamboen, map of Batavia, LXIII), 20, 29, 41, 84
Tanah Abang, 25, 115, 130, 137, 140, 141, 203, 205, 206
Tanah Tinggi, 86
Tangerang, 4, 23, 24, 29, 35, 38, 52, 66, 69, 80, 95, 110, 116–8, 124, 161, 198, 202
Tanjung Priok (Tandjoeng Priok), 23, 35, 140, 142, 200, 211
Telok Betong, 163
Ternate, 129
Thailand (Siam), 81
Tomang, 144

Ukraine, 150

Vorstenlanden, 2, 10, 11

Weltevreden, 19, 23, 141
West Indramayu, 165
West Tanjung (Tandjoeng-west, map of Batavia, XLII), 41
Western Java, 96, 180
Western Europe, 5

Yogyakarta, 11, 81